OPENGL

A Primer

D0537265

OpenGL®
A Primer

SECOND EDITION

EDWARD ANGEL

PEARSON
Addison
Wesley

Boston San Francisco New York
London Toronto Sydney Tokyo Singapore Madrid
Mexico City Munich Paris Cape Town Hong Kong Montreal

Executive Editor	Susan Hartman Sullivan
Acquisitions Editor	Matt Goldstein
Project Editor	Katherine Harutunian
Marketing Manager	Nathan Schultz
Senior Marketing Coordinator	Lesly Hershman
Senior Production Supervisor	Jeffrey Holcomb
Project Management	Techsetters, Inc.
Copyeditor	Cheryl Adam/Adamworks Editorial Service
Proofreader	Carol Sawyer/The Perfect Proof
Composition	WestWords, Inc.
Illustration	Techsetters, Inc.
Cover Designer	Alison R. Paddock
Prepress and Manufacturing	Caroline Fell

Access the latest information about Addison-Wesley titles from our World Wide Web site:
http://www.aw-bc.com/computing

Many of the designations used by manufacturers and sellers to distinguish their products are claimed as trademarks. Where those designations appear in this book, and Addison-Wesley was aware of a trademark claim, the designations have been printed in initial caps or all caps.

The programs and applications presented in this book have been included for their instructional value. They have been tested with care, but are not guaranteed for any particular purpose. The publisher does not offer any warranties or representations, nor does it accept any liabilities with respect to the programs or applications.

If you purchasd this book within the United States or Canada you should be aware that it has been wrongfully imported without the approval of the Publisher or the Author.

ISBN 0-321-26982-9
1 2 3 4 5 6 7 8 9 10-PHT-06 05 04

To Rose Mary

CONTENTS

Preface   xv

CHAPTER 6   Lights and Materials   123

CHAPTER 7   Images   143

PREFACE

When I wrote the first edition of this Primer in 2000, I intended it to be both a companion to my graphics textbook (*Interactive Computer Graphics: A Top-Down Approach Using OpenGL,* Third Edition, Addison-Wesley 2003) and a stand-alone beginners guide to OpenGL for programmers who already knew some computer graphics and wished to get started with OpenGL. For the second group, my intention was—and still is—to not replace the standard references for OpenGL: the *OpenGL Programming Guide*, Fourth Edition (Addison-Wesley), the "red book," or the *OpenGL 1.4 Reference Manual*, Fourth Edition (Addison-Wesley), the "blue book." I wanted a book that would allow application programmers to get started without reference to these other worthy volumes.

I think that the first edition of the *OpenGL Primer* achieved those objectives. In many ways I was surprised that the second group, at least as judged by the feeback I've received, is larger than I thought. I was also surpised to find that the *Primer* has been used as a stand-alone textbook for graphics courses at a variety of levels.

When we considered a second edition, I had to make some hard decisions as to how to change what I considered a fairly successful book. I wanted the book to remain fairly small and inexpensive but I also wanted to respond to user feedback and to advances in graphics and the OpenGL Application Programmers Interface (API). In reponse to these somewhat contradictory desires, the second edition of the *OpenGL Primer* is only about 20% longer than the first edition. I have added some additional examples. I have added an additional chapter that introduces programmable graphics pipelines, a facility that represents a major advance in computer graphics. I have also been more explicit about the additions to OpenGL approved by the OpenGL ARB over the past twelve years. Of course, I also tried to clarify the presentation.

The *Primer* follows the top-down philosophy towards teaching computer graphics that I introduced in *Interactive Computer Graphics*. This approach is based on the idea that students learn modern computer graphics best if they can start programming significant applications as soon as possible. The OpenGL API works well with this approach. Its success is evidenced by the large number of adoptions in universities and colleges around the world.

Students who have used *Interactive Computer Graphics* realize that while it makes heavy use of OpenGL, it does not claim to be an OpenGL programming guide or a user's manual. Consequently, the information on OpenGL in the text is incomplete. Not only are not all OpenGL functions covered, there is no detailed listing of the functions and their parameters. For students, the former usually does not present problems; however, the latter does. Thus, the *Primer* fills that need without requiring students to purchase the excellent but more expensive *OpenGL Programming Guide* and *OpenGL 1.4 Reference Manual*.

Students in university graphics classes make up only a small part of the graphics community and an even smaller part of the programming community, many of whose members have at least a passing interest in computer graphics and how to write graphics programs. For them, OpenGL is an attractive way to get started with graphics. The second motivation for the Primer is to provide an easy method of accessing OpenGL. In my opinion, even for those who will eventually work with Direct X for Windows platforms, it is much easier to get started with OpenGL and use it to master the basic concepts. For those of us who work with scientific applications and in a cross platform environment, OpenGL is the API of choice.

The *Primer* is done almost entirely without the mathematics used in my textbook. So, for example, the chapter on curves and surfaces deals with the details of how to program applications using Bézier curves and surfaces but never derives them. The chapter on transformations shows how to use rotation, translation, and scaling but does not derive the underlying matrices. The order of topics roughly follows that of the textbook but also is a natural progression in learning OpenGL. We start with two-dimensional problems in Chapter 2, move on to interactivity in Chapter 3 and to basic three-dimensional programs in Chapters 4 and 5. Chapter 6 covers lights and materials. Chapters 7 and 8 cover using OpenGL to display discrete entities, first through pixels and bitmaps and then through texture mapping. Chapter 9 introduces curves and surfaces. Chapter 10 presents a longer example than in previous chapters; the example includes most of the topics covered in previous chapters and touches on some advanced OpenGL features. Chapter 11 introduces what is possible with the latest generation of programmable graphics cards.

This *Primer* includes both complete programs and partial code. As you will discover, once you write your first few OpenGL applications, much of the code is repeated in subsequent programs. Consequently, after the first few examples, I have left out much of the repeated code. Readers can find the complete examples either through my Web site, `www.cs.unm.edu/~angel`, or at the FTP site `ftp.cs.unm.edu` under `pub/angel`.

Many people provided significant help in various aspects of the *Primer*. Special thanks go to the following reviewers who provided very useful comments in the initial survey questionnaire: Kai H. Chang, Auburn University; A. Ardeshir Goshtasby, Wright State University; Paul Plassmann, Penn State University; Ha-Wei Shen, The Ohio State University; and Robert R. Snapp, University of Vermont. I also want to thank a group of people who are or were at Silicon Graphics for helping me learn and appreciate OpenGL. In particular, Mark Kilgard and Mason Woo helped me when I first started using OpenGL with my classes at the University of New Mexico. Mason, Kathleen Danielson, Dave Shreiner, and Vicki Shreiner invited me to teach OpenGL tutorials with them at SIGGRAPH over the past seven years, an enterprise that forced me to learn much more about the API and formed many of my ideas about how to teach with OpenGL. Mark, Nate Robins, and Brian Paul have made great contributions to all of us who use and teach OpenGL, through the creation of the GLUT library, the Mesa implementation, and many OpenGL example programs. The first edition of the *Primer* was written very quickly to fill a need that existed in the graphics community. I'm indebted to the many readers who sent me their comments and typos. Of all of them, I owe a special thanks to Karen Collins of Montgomery Blair High School in Silver Spring, MD, who sent me more typos than I'd like to admit I'm responsible for. For the second edition, Mark Kilgard (NVIDIA) and Dave Shreiner (SGI) made extensive reviews of the manuscript. I was already greatly indebted to them for how much I've learned about OpenGL from their work. Now I'm (happily) even further in their debt.

Having done five books with Addison-Wesley, I still marvel at the competence and professionalism of the entire production crew there. My editors at Addison-Wesley, Matt Goldstein, Maite Suarez-Rivas, and Peter Gordon, are as good friends and dinner companions as they are editors. Rose Mary Molnar, my wife and partner in all things, has survived yet another book production cycle with me, something for which she deserves more credit than I can ever express.

Introduction

OpenGL is an interactive computer graphics system that allows programmers to write programs that access graphics hardware. OpenGL has two important benefits for application programmers. It is close enough to the hardware so that programs written with OpenGL run efficiently, and OpenGL is easy to learn and use. In this chapter, we shall give an overview of OpenGL, what it can (and cannot) do, how it is organized, and how we shall present it.

1.1 The OpenGL API

Computer graphics is an important part of almost everything that we do with modern computers. Whether we are accessing a Web page, playing an interactive game, or designing a house using a CAD package, we are using computer graphics. As hardware and software have become faster and more sophisticated, so have the graphical applications that we use. Developers of these applications rely upon standard software interfaces to build their applications. Such interfaces prevent the developer from having to write the code for standard functions that are common to many applications and shield the application from details of the hardware. Thus, we can develop programs faster and these programs become more portable. The application programmer sees the graphics system through a set of functions with a well-defined interface that we call the **Application Programmer's Interface (API)**.

Over the years, there have been many graphics APIs. Some, such as GKS and PHIGS, have risen to the level of international standards. Others have been widely used for specific applications. Most have had short lifetimes. Other APIs, such as Microsoft's Direct X, are for specific platforms. OpenGL came from an interface called GL, short for Graphics Library, originally developed for Silicon Graphics Inc. (SGI) hardware. GL proved to be a simple yet powerful interface. It formed the basis for OpenGL, which could then be used with a variety of graphics hardware. OpenGL contains over 200 functions for building application programs. Programs written using OpenGL are portable to any computer that supports the interface.

Implementations are available for almost all hardware and operating systems. These implementations range from pure software implementations to implementations that use the most sophisticated hardware presently available. A typical OpenGL application program should run on any implementation after recompilation with the OpenGL libraries for that system. In addition, OpenGL provides a high degree of stability so that applications written with OpenGL tend to have a long lifetime, even as the API evolves to incorporate the functionality provided by the latest hardware.

The OpenGL API is concerned primarily with **rendering**, which is taking the specification of geometric objects and their properties and forming a picture of them with a virtual camera and lights. OpenGL programs are meant to be platform independent. Thus, the OpenGL API contains neither input nor windowing functions, both of which tend to be platform specific. However, every graphics program must interact with an operating system and the local windowing system, be it Windows, linux, or the Macintosh. Rather than write platform-dependent code, we shall use a simple toolkit, the OpenGL Utility Toolkit (GLUT), a library that has been implemented for the standard programming environments. Its API includes the standard operations that are common to most windowing systems and will allow us to use the mouse and keyboard in our applications.

1.2 Three Views of OpenGL

Although at one level, OpenGL is simply a library of functions that access the graphics capabilities of computers, we shall find it useful to look at OpenGL in three related ways. Understanding these views should help you to better understand how OpenGL and graphics systems function and enable you to write better code.

1.2.1 The Programmer's View

Generally, most graphics application programs consist of three major elements:

- Specifying a set of objects to render
- Describing properties of these objects
- Defining how these objects should be viewed

Modern graphics systems support two distinct object types: geometric and image. Geometric objects exist in a typically three-dimensional world and include both fundamental primitives such as lines, points, and polygons, and more complex entities such as quadrics and more general curves and surfaces. Historically, computer graphics systems dealt exclusively with geometric objects, and most of this book will deal with them. However, recent advances in hardware allow graphics systems to also work with images, which are rectangular arrays of picture elements, each of which has one or more values representing the element's color, luminance, or other property.

Most APIs separate what an object is—a line, a polygon—from how it is displayed. Thus, a solid green line and a red dashed line are the same object type but have different appearances. Although this separation appears to violate many concepts of object-oriented programming, it is closer to how the hardware works and allows the programmer to separate tedious details of specifying many parameters describing surface properties from the logical flow of the program.

Computer graphics follows modern physics and engineering modeling in that it separates the description and behavior of objects from the viewing of these objects. To form an image or picture, we must describe both the objects and the camera or viewer that forms the picture. In OpenGL, there is a small set of functions devoted to the positioning and description of a virtual camera.

While any program that produces graphical output must have the above three elements, if the program is interactive, it will also have some input functions. Finally, all programs will have some initialization and termination functions that interact with the local operating system and window environment.

The programmer's view gives a way of categorizing the OpenGL functions, which we shall do in the next section. But it does not tell us anything about how OpenGL works. Two other views provide some additional insight.

1.2.2 The OpenGL State Machine

If we take a slightly different perspective, we can think of OpenGL as a **state machine** with inputs and outputs, as shown in Figure 1.1. The inputs are descriptions of geometric objects, such as line segments and polygons, and discrete objects, such as bitmaps, that are specified through OpenGL function calls. The output is the image that we see on our display. Between the inputs and output is a machine that takes the descriptions of objects and converts them to an image. How the machine processes its inputs depends on its state. From this perspective, OpenGL has two types of functions, those that specify inputs to the machine—objects—and those that change the state of the machine. State-changing functions include those that specify colors, viewing conditions, material properties, and many other variables. The state determines how the inputs are processed.

1.2.3 The OpenGL Pipeline

From an implementation perspective, we can view OpenGL program behavior in a different manner. OpenGL is based upon what is called a **pipeline model**. A simple pipeline is shown in Figure 1.2. All real-time systems and commodity graphics

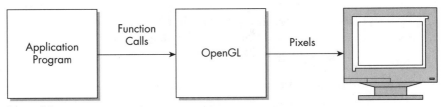

Figure 1.1 OpenGL as a state machine

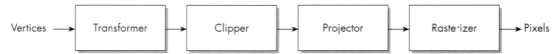

Figure 1.2 Pipeline model for OpenGL

cards incorporate a hardware pipeline. Primitives are generated in the application program and flow through the pipeline. Within the pipeline, there is a sequence of modules, each of which performs one or more functions on the primitives as they stream through. Some modules do transformations that rotate, translate, and scale the object. Another is responsible for positioning the objects relative to OpenGL's camera. Still another determines if an object is within the camera's view. At the end of the pipeline, those primitives that are visible are converted into colored picture elements on the display.

We can look at the pipeline as a particular implementation of the OpenGL state machine. More importantly, the pipeline model is close to the way that most graphics hardware systems are built. The pipeline model also emphasizes that primitives are processed independently; that is, each primitive has its color and potential visibility determined independently of all other primitives. Consequently, there is a tradeoff between the high throughput of a pipeline architecture versus its inability to incorporate global effects such as shadows that depend on the relationships among the primitives.

1.3 What's in OpenGL

OpenGL contains over 200 functions. It is helpful to group them by their functionality.

Primitive functions define the elements that can produce images on the screen. These are of two types: geometric primitives, such as polygons, that can be defined in two, three, or four dimensions; and image primitives, such as bitmaps.

Attribute functions control the appearance of primitives. These functions define colors, line types, material properties, light sources, and textures.

Viewing functions determine the properties of the camera. OpenGL provides a virtual camera that we can position and orient relative to the objects defined by the primitive functions. We can also control the lens of the camera so as to produce wide-angle and telephoto views.

Windowing functions are not part of the core of OpenGL but, due to their importance for interactive applications, are contained in separate libraries such as GLUT. These functions allow us to control the windows on the screen and use the mouse and keyboard.

Control functions allow us to turn on various OpenGL features. They also allow us to find out the capabilities of a particular implementation.

Note that all but the first group are state-changing functions and by themselves cannot generate changes to the display.

1.4 OpenGL Versions and Extensions

OpenGL is controlled by the OpenGL Architectural Review Board (ARB), which has members from companies such as Silicon Graphics, IBM, and NVIDIA. The present version of OpenGL is now 1.5. OpenGL is very stable and most programs using previous specifications have no problem with running on later versions. The capabilities in OpenGL reflect what is available on most graphics systems and even if a particular platform lacks the hardware to implement certain features, they usually can be implemented in software. In this text, we shall need only the functionality of version 1.2. In Chapter 11, we shall summarize the additional features in versions 1.3, 1.4, and 1.5.

Many high-end users have access to equipment with special capabilities or have need for particular functionality that is not very general. However, these application programmers still prefer to program with OpenGL. Implementers handle these situations through **OpenGL extensions**, which pass through the ARB but are not (yet) part of the core OpenGL specification. One example of a popular extension is for image processing. The image-processing extensions are extensions of the pixel operations that we shall discuss in Chapter 7, but often make use of special hardware features available in high-end graphics workstations.

1.5 Languages

We shall use the C language binding for OpenGL, which is the most popular. There is also an official Fortran version. There is not, unfortunately, an official language binding for other popular languages, such as Java. There are some unofficial Java bindings that you can find from the Web sites given below.

1.6 Programming Conventions

The OpenGL functions are contained in two libraries usually called gl and glu (or GL and GLU). The first library, the core OpenGL library, contains all the required OpenGL functions while the second, the OpenGL Utility Library, contains functions that are written using functions in the core library and are helpful to have available to users. Functions in the core library have names that begin with **gl**, for example glVertex3f(), while functions in the utility library have names beginning with **glu**, for example gluOrtho2D().

OpenGL is not object oriented and we shall be using its C language binding. Thus, the API does not make use of features, such as overloading, that are available in object-oriented languages such as C++. Of course, application programmers can use C++ to develop object-oriented applications and link with the OpenGL C implementation. To support the variety of data types that C programmers use, many OpenGL functions have multiple forms. For example, the function glVertex3f() takes floats as arguments while the function glVertex3i()

takes ints as arguments. We shall use the notation glVertex*() to refer to all the forms of the vertex function.

Many OpenGL functions have parameters whose values are chosen from small discrete sets of integers. To avoid the use of "magic numbers," OpenGL defines macros for these values that are specified in the include files gl.h and glu.h. The prefixes **GL_** and **GLU_** define from which include file the macro comes, for example GL_LINES and GL_LIGHT0.

OpenGL uses the basic C data types: floats, doubles, ints, chars. However, to allow an implementation to redefine its basic types, the include file gl.h defines the basic types GLint, GLfloat, GLdouble, and GLubyte. Although these types are generally what you would expect, they are used in the definitions of the OpenGL functions. For example, the function

```
void glVertex3f(GLfloat x, GLfloat y, GLfloat z)
```

defines a vertex in three-dimensional space using three GLfloats. In practice, there is a line in gl.h for each type of the form

```
typedef GLfloat float
```

so that these values are what we would expect. Occasionally, you will also see less familiar types such as GLclampf (for floats in the range from 0.0 and 1.0) and GLsizei (for as large nonnegative integers as are available on the implementation).

OpenGL also provides an alternative function to many functions that require parameters to allow specification through pointers to arrays. These functions have a v before the argument list. Hence, there is a function glVertex3fv() that we might use as

```
GLfloat point[3] = {1.0, -2.5, 0.5};
glVertex3fv(point);
```

In our description of functions, we will use braces and the word TYPE to allow us to specify the many forms of a function. For example, we can list all the forms of glVertex*() as

```
glVertex{234}{sifd}(TYPE coords, ....);
glVertex{234}{sifd}v{TYPE *coords);
```

We have to select a dimension (two, three, or four) and a data type (short [s], integer [i], float [f], or double [d]). TYPE matches the chosen data type. For the direct form, there must be the same number of parameters as dimensions. For the pointer form, we need give only a pointer of the correct type. Thus, the following are all valid invocations of vertex functions:

```
GLint ix, iy;
GLfloat x, y, z, point[3];
/* set values */
glVertex2i(ix, iy);
glVertex2f(x, y);
glVertex3f(x, y, z);
glVertex3fv(point);
```

In the final form, `point` is assumed to be an array of the form

```
float point[3];
```

The details of each function will be in a description box of the form

void glFunctionName(GLboolean param)

This function does not exist, but the value of **param** can be **GL_TRUE** or **GL_FALSE**.

that will appear near where the function is first introduced. There will also be some alerts or warnings that also will be in description boxes, such as:

Read the contents of comments like this one.

1.7 Compiling

Generally, compiling an OpenGL program should not be a problem. For UNIX systems, a typical compile line looks like

```
cc myapp.c -o myapp -lglut -lGLU -lGL -lX11 -lm
```

For linux, you can use almost the same line but you may have to specify where the X libraries are located. Usually adding a flag indicting a directory, such as

```
-L/usr/X11R6/lib
```

works. You can make a simple makefile that usually works for UNIX and linux based on the four lines

```
CC = cc
LDLIBS = -lglut -lGL -lGLU -lX11 -lm -L/usr/X11R6/lib
.c:
   $(CC) $@.c $(LDLIBS) -o $@
```

A makefile with these lines will allow you to compile a single file via the command line

```
make progname
```

which will start with `progname.c` and result in the binary `progname`. Occasionally, you may need to add `-lXmu` for the X miscellaneous utility library to the loader line.

You may have to add in a -L flag if your X libraries are in a nonstandard place or a -I flag if your OpenGL include files are in a nonstandard place.

Under Windows with Visual C++, you want to build a console application. The `OpenGL32.dll` and `glu32.dll` files should already be in the system folders. The corresponding lib files should be `..\VC\lib`. The include files should be in `..\VC\include\GL`. A similar process works with other compilers such as Borland. You will have to get the GLUT files from the Web. You can get the files in a precompiled form or you can build them yourself from Nate Robins's GLUT site for Windows: www.xmission.com/~nate/glut.html. These files (`glut.h`, `glut32.lib`, and `glut32.dll`) go in the same places as the other OpenGL files.

1.8 Sources

There is a wide variety of OpenGL information available. First, there are books on OpenGL. The most important are known as the Redbook and the Bluebook:

OpenGL Architecture Review Board, *OpenGL Programming Guide* (Fourth Edition), Addison-Wesley, 2003.

OpenGL Architecture Review Board, *OpenGL Reference Manual* (Fourth Edition), Addison-Wesley, 2004.

The Redbook uses GLUT for its examples. If you want to develop code for the X Windows system, see

Kilgard, M., *OpenGL Programming for the X Windows System*, Addison-Wesley, 1996.

If you are developing applications exclusively for Windows, see

Fosner, R., *OpenGL Programming for Windows 95 and Windows NT*, Addison-Wesley, 1996.

Wright, R., and M. Sweet, *OpenGL SuperBible* (Second Edition), Waite Group Press, 1999.

This primer assumes that you already know some computer graphics. If you need an introduction to computer graphics that uses OpenGL, then see

Angel, E., *Interactive Computer Graphics, A Top-Down Approach with OpenGL* (Third Edition), Addison-Wesley, 2003.

The standard reference in computer graphics is

Foley, J., A. van Dam, S. Feiner, and J. Hughes, *Computer Graphics, Principles and Practice* (Second Edition), Addison-Wesley, 1990.

There are many Web resources available. The best place to start is with the OpenGL.org site (www.opengl.org), which is filled with pointers to books, code, articles, and documentation. Support for this book can be found from the Addison-Wesley site (www.awl.com) or from the author's site (www.cs.unm.edu/~angel or ftp.cs.unm.edu under pub/angel).

If your system lacks OpenGL, there is an open source version called Mesa that is distributed as both source and as libraries with most linux distributions. Mesa is available through www.mesa3d.org. You can obtain the GLUT library in a variety of places. There are pointers on the OpenGL Web site. It is usually included with the Mesa distribution.

SGI has its own OpenGL Web site: www.sgi.com/software/opengl.

There are also some very helpful OpenGL tutorial programs from Nate Robins that illustrate viewing, transformations, texture mapping, and a few other topics. These tutorials are interactive and will give you the opportunity to experiment with a variety of OpenGL functions and parameters. They are available at www.xmission.com/~nate/tutors.html.

There are many good demo programs available. All the programs in the Redbook are available and are included with Mesa. There are additional demos and test programs included with Mesa and GLUT.

1.9 Who Should Use This Primer

Hopefully you read the preface before you bought this book. But in case you jumped right in, here is a reminder about who should be using this primer (and who should not). This primer is an introduction to the OpenGL API. We do not pretend to have complete coverage (even though there is a lot of material in the next ten chapters). If you need complete coverage and documentation, see the Redbook and the Bluebook. If you want to get started with OpenGL, this book should be right for you.

We assume you know some computer graphics. We pretty much avoid all mathematics in this primer; that's part of learning computer graphics. There are some excellent graphics texts around, including the two mentioned above. If you are a student taking a class in computer graphics that is using OpenGL, this primer should help.

1.10 Outline

In Chapter 2, we start with two-dimensional problems. Although, in OpenGL, two-dimensional graphics are a special case of three-dimensional graphics, it is easier to get started with two-dimensional problems. We will introduce all the basic OpenGL primitives and their attributes.

Chapter 3 is concerned with interactivity. Although input functions are not part of the core of OpenGL, we use OpenGL for interactive applications. We use the GLUT library to develop simple portable interactive applications.

Chapters 4 and 5 present three-dimensional graphics with OpenGL. We divide the material into two parts. In Chapter 4, we introduce three-dimensional objects that can be built from the basic OpenGL primitives. We introduce some additional objects provided by the GLU and GLUT libraries. We discuss how to produce an image of these objects by specifying the parameters for OpenGL's camera and positioning the objects relative to the camera. In Chapter 5, we introduce OpenGL's powerful transformation capabilities. We show how transformations can be used to create instances of basic objects at any desired size, orientation, and locations. We shall also see how transformations can be used to model the relationships between parts of objects.

In Chapter 6, we introduce light-material interactions through the Phong lighting model, which is implemented in OpenGL. We shall also discuss how to work with translucent surfaces in OpenGL.

Chapters 7 and 8 are concerned with OpenGL's capabilities for manipulating bits and pixels. In Chapter 7, we discuss displaying images directly and how to move bits between various buffers in OpenGL. In Chapter 8, we introduce texture mapping, which allows us to combine the geometric and bit-manipulation capabilities of OpenGL.

In Chapter 9, we leave the flat polygon world and learn to use OpenGL's curves and surfaces.

In Chapter 10, we survey a few advanced features of OpenGL. We also present a final nontrivial example that illustrates most of OpenGL's features. Chapter 11 provides a deeper look at the graphics pipeline and introduces the ideas behind the programmable pipelines that are on the latest graphics cards and supported by the latest version of OpenGL.

Throughout this primer, there will be a mixture of code snippets and complete illustrative OpenGL programs. The complete programs are available at the author's Web and FTP sites given above.

Finally, graphics programming is fun. Try to enjoy learning how to do it.

Two-Dimensional Programming in OpenGL

OpenGL is a three-dimensional system. From an application programmer's perspective, OpenGL primitives describe three-dimensional objects that exist in a three-dimensional world. Two-dimensional problems are a special case of three-dimensional problems, namely those whose objects reside in a plane. Nevertheless, this special case is important as many applications are two-dimensional. For these applications, it is easier to work directly in two dimensions, something that is allowed by OpenGL. We start with these simpler problems as they provide a straightforward way of getting started with OpenGL.

In this chapter, we shall start by dissecting a very simple program to understand the basics of an OpenGL program. Then we shall enhance the program, introducing additional OpenGL functions. Finally, we shall introduce the full set of basic OpenGL primitives.

2.1 A Simple Program

Our first program, `simple.c`, draws a white rectangle on a black background. Although it makes heavy use of default values for many parameters, it still illustrates the structure of most OpenGL programs.

The program consists of two functions: `main()` and `display()`. The `main()` function initializes OpenGL, and `display()` defines the graphical entity to be drawn. First, we examine `main()`. Although OpenGL contains no input or window commands, any user program must interact with the window system, and interactive programs have input from devices, such as the mouse and keyboard. However, the user interface to window systems is system dependent. An OpenGL program written for Microsoft Windows that manipulates the window or uses the mouse differs from one with the same functionality written for the X Window System under linux. We can interface with these systems using a minimum amount of "glue" contained in system-specific libraries (GLX for X Windows, wgl for Windows, agl for the Macintosh). The OpenGL libraries and their interface with the application program are shown in Figure 2.1 for a typical linux system that uses

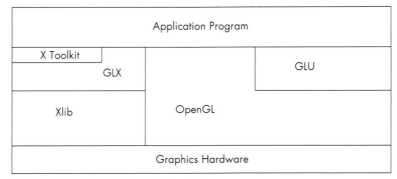

Figure 2.1 Library organization for linux implementaion

the X Window system. A similar figure holds for Windows or the Macintosh. A program can use the functions in the OpenGL, GLU, and GLX libraries. It can also use the X libraries directly or even one of the X toolkits. Of course, any calls to X-specific libraries make the program harder to port to other platforms.

There is an alternate path through the GLUT library that will allow the same program to run across most platforms.

```
/* simple.c */
#include <GL/glut.h>
void display()
{
  glClear(GL_COLOR_BUFFER_BIT);

  glBegin(GL_POLYGON);
    glVertex2f(-0.5, -0.5);
    glVertex2f(-0.5, 0.5);
    glVertex2f(0.5, 0.5);
    glVertex2f(0.5, -0.5);
  glEnd();

  glFlush();

}
int main(int argc, char** argv)
{
  glutInit(&argc, argv);
  glutCreateWindow("simple");
  glutDisplayFunc(display);
  glutMainLoop();

}
```

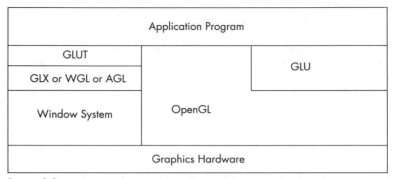

Figure 2.2 Library organization with GLUT

2.2 GLUT

The OpenGL Utility Toolkit (GLUT) is a library of functions that are common to virtually all modern windowing systems. GLUT has been implemented on all the popular systems, so that programs written using the GLUT API for windowing and input can be compiled with the source code unchanged on all these systems. The library organization is as shown in Figure 2.2. The application program uses only the GL, GLU, and GLUT libraries. Depending on the platform, GLUT uses glX, wgl, or agl. We shall use GLUT throughout this volume. There are some toolkits that have been built on top of GLUT that provide additional functionality. However, if you need higher performance or want to use a specific toolkit, then most likely you will have to write platform-dependent code for the interactive parts of your application.

void glutInit(int *argc, char **argv)

initializes GLUT and should be called before other GLUT and OpenGL functions. **glutInit()** takes the arguments from **main()** and the program can use them in an implementation-dependent manner.

Starting with the first function in main(), glutInit(), we see that the name (as it is for all GLUT functions) begins with the letters glut. Although we can pass in command line arguments from main(), their interpretation within GLUT is implementation dependent. We shall not use implementation-dependent arguments in our examples. The function glutCreateWindow() puts a window on the screen in a default position (at the upper-left corner) and at a default size (300 × 300 pixels). The argument allows us to put an optional title on the top border of the window.

> **int glutCreateWindow(char *title)**
>
> creates a window on the screen with the title given by the argument. The function returns an integer that can be used to refer to the window in multiwindow situations.

Later we shall see how to alter the defaults in GLUT.

2.3 Event Loops and Callback Functions

Most interactive programs are based on the program reacting to a variety of discrete **events**. Events include mouse events, such as moving the mouse or clicking a mouse button; keyboard events, such as pressing a key; and window events, such as the resizing of a window by the user or the covering up of a window by another window. The programming paradigm used to work with events is to have events handled by the window system and placed in an **event queue**. Events are processed sequentially from the event queue. The application programmer needs only to write a set of **callback functions** that define how the program should react to specific events. In GLUT, the most common events are recognized. The application program can define its own callback functions, rely on default callbacks for a few events, or do nothing, in which case events without callbacks are ignored.

Our simple program contains only a single callback, the **display callback**, which is invoked whenever OpenGL determines that the window has to be redrawn. One of these times is when the window is first opened. Consequently, if we put our OpenGL rendering commands in the display callback, we can be assured that they will be drawn at least once. Note that the form of the display callback, a function with no arguments, is registered by

> **void glutDisplayFunc(void (*func) (void))**
>
> The function **func()** is called each time the window needs to be redrawn.

GLUT. If we wish to pass values to the display callback function, we can use globals in our programs. After the callbacks have been registered, the program enters the event loop by executing the function `glutMainLoop()`. Once we have entered the loop, we cannot escape except through a callback or some outside intervention such as hitting a "kill" key. Any code after this call will never be executed.

Some compilers insist that because correct C requires the `main` function to return a value, OpenGL `main` programs should end with the code

```
    glutMainLoop();
    return(0);
}
```

We will not use this form. We prefer to not insert code that cannot be reached, even when doing so is technically correct.

> The form of GLUT callback functions is fixed. Consequently, global variables may be necessary to pass values between functions.

void glutMainLoop()

causes the program to enter an event-processing loop. It should be the last statement in the **main()** function.

2.4 Drawing a Rectangle

Now we have to define our display callback, which we have chosen to name `display`. First, note that we include the file `glut.h`, which is usually stored in a directory named **GL** wherever the standard include files are stored. This file contains the prototypes for the GLUT functions and the #defines for a variety of constants that are used in OpenGL programs. This file also contains the lines

```
#include <GL/gl.h>
#include <GL/glu.h>
```

to include similar definitions for the OpenGL and GLU functions and constants.

The fundamental entity for specifying geometric objects is the **vertex**, a location in space. Simple geometric objects such as lines and polygons can be specified through a collection of vertices. OpenGL allows us to work in two, three, or four dimensions through variants of the function `glVertex*()`.

void glVertex{234}{sifd}(TYPE xcoordinate, TYPE ycoordinate, ...)

void glVertex{234}{sifd}v(TYPE *coordinates)

specifies the location of a vertex in two, three, or four dimensions with one of the types short (**s**), int (**i**), float (**f**), or double (**d**). If v is present, **TYPE** is a pointer to the array **coordinates** of the type specified.

We shall use the notation `glVertex*()` to refer to all of these variants. Thus, for example, `glVertex2f(x, y)`defines a vertex in two dimensions at the point (x, y) where x and y are floats, while `glVertex2fv(p)` specifies a vertex at the first two locations of an array of floats, that is $(p[0], p[1])$.

Because vertices can define a variety of objects, we must tell OpenGL what type of object a list of vertices defines and denote the beginning and end of the list. We make these specifications through the functions `glBegin()` and `glEnd()`.

void glBegin(GLenum mode)

specifies the beginning of an object of type **mode**. Modes include **GL_POINTS**, **GL_LINES**, and **GL_POLYGON**.

void glEnd()

specifies the end of a list of vertices.

Don't forget to include the `glEnd()` after a list of vertices.

Using these three functions, we can define our rectangle

```
glBegin(GL_POLYGON);
    glVertex2f(-0.5, -0.5);
    glVertex2f(-0.5, 0.5);
    glVertex2f(0.5, 0.5);
    glVertex2f(0.5, -0.5);
glEnd();
```

OpenGL puts the rendered image in an area of memory called a **color buffer** that usually resides on the graphics card. Color buffers are one of a number of types of buffers that make up the **frame buffer**. We shall see other types of buffers later. Before we draw the rectangle, we clear the color buffer we are using through the function `glClear()`.

void glClear(GLbitfield mask)

clears all buffers whose bits are set in mask. The **mask** is formed by the logical OR of values defined in `gl.h`. **GL_COLOR_BUFFER_BIT** refers to the color buffer.

Figure 2.3 Output from simple.c

Because OpenGL implementations buffer commands for efficiency, we can force the renderer to output the results immediately by issuing a glFlush().

---

void glFlush()

forces previously buffered OpenGL commands to execute.

Figure 2.3 shows the output from our program. Although the program obviously produces an image, there is a variety of questions that we need to address, including:

- What do we do if we want the image to be a different size?
- What do we do if we want the image to appear in a different place on the screen?
- Why does the white rectangle occupy half the area in the window?
- Why is the background black and the rectangle white? How can we use other colors?
- Can we end the program in some manner other than by using the kill box provided by the window system?
- How do we define more complex objects?

2.5 Changing the GLUT Defaults

First, let's add a few GLUT functions that will give us a little finer control over the image that appears on our screen. The functions glutInitDisplayMode(), glutInitWindowSize(), and glutInitWindowPosition() allow us to define what type of window we want, its size, and its position. Generally, an implementation will support a variety of properties that can be associated with a window on the screen. An application program, through the function `glutInitDisplayMode()`, requests the type of window that it requires. The most common window properties to specify are what type of color we wish to use and whether or not we need double buffering (see Section 3.4). The defaults in GLUT are RGB color and single buffering, which can be specified explicitly by the function call

```
glutInitDisplayMode(GLUT_RGB | GLUT_SINGLE);
```

> **void glutInitDisplayMode(unsigned int mode)**
>
> requests a display with the properties in **mode**. The values of **mode** are combined by using the logical OR of options such as color model (**GLUT_RGB**, **GLUT_INDEX**) and buffering of color buffers (**GLUT_SINGLE**, **GLUT_DOUBLE**).

The function `glutInitWindowSize()` specifies the initial size of the window on the screen, and `glutInitWindowPosition()` gives its initial position.

> **void glutInitWindowSize(int width, int height)**
>
> specifies the initial height and width of the window on the screen in pixels.
>
> **void glutInitWindowPosition(int x, int y)**
>
> specifies the top-left corner of the window measured in pixels from the top-left corner of the screen.

2.6 Color in OpenGL

OpenGL supports two basic color models: **RGB** (or **RGBA**) **mode** and **color-index mode**. In RGB mode, each color is a triplet of red, green, and blue values. The eye adds or blends these primary colors (or **color components**), forming the color that we see. This additive model is appropriate for monitors and projective systems. The print industry uses a subtractive model, which is discussed in most graphics texts.

If we use real numbers to specify colors, then 0.0 is none of a component and 1.0 is the maximum amount of that component. Thus, the RGB triplet of (1.0, 0.0, 0.0) is a bright red, (0.5, 0.5, 0.0) is a dark yellow, (1.0, 1.0, 1.0) is white, and (0.0, 0.0, 0.0) is black. In RGBA mode, we use a fourth color component, A or alpha, which is an **opacity**. An opacity of 1.0 means the color is opaque and cannot be "seen through" while a value of 0.0 means that a color is transparent. We will not need opacity until much later. If we use an integer type to specify a color, the range is from 0 to the maximum value of the type. If, for example, we use unsigned bytes, the color values range from 0 to 255. Note that specifying a color to a given precision does not guarantee that the physical display can support the specified precision. There is no reason that we cannot specify each component of a color as a real number even if the display can show only two colors, a foreground color and a background color.

The color precision of the display may be less than that used to specify a color by `glColor*()`.

In color-index mode, colors are specified as indices into a table of red, green, and blue values. In this mode, we form a table of the allowed colors, usually with 256 possible colors. Historically, color-index mode was common on graphics systems. Now with inexpensive memory, this mode is not used often. In addition, color-index mode requires more detailed interaction with the windowing system than does RGB color. Hence, we shall always use RGB or RGBA color.

2.6.1 Setting Colors

In our simple program, we used the default values for our colors. The default color for clearing the screen was black and the default drawing color, the color that was used to fill the polygon, was white. These can be changed by the functions `glColor*()` and `glClearColor()`.

void glColor3{b i f d ub us ui}(TYPE r, TYPE g, TYPE b)

void glColor3{b i f d ub us ui}v(TYPE *color)

void glColor4{b i f d ub us ui}(TYPE r, TYPE g, TYPE b, TYPE a)

void glColor4{b i f d ub us ui}v(TYPE *color)

specify RGB and RGBA colors using the standard types. If the **v** is present, the color is in an array pointed to by **color** in which each component is of type **TYPE**.

void glClearColor(GLclampf r, GLclampf g, GLclampf b, GLclampf a)

specifies the RGBA color used when clearing the color buffer.

The clear color must be specified as an RGBA color.

2.6.2 Color and State

In OpenGL, colors are part of the OpenGL state. We can think of there being a *current drawing color*, which we set by glColor*(), and a *current clear color*, set by glClearColor(). These colors remain the same until we change them in the application program. Thus, colors are not attached to objects but rather to the internal state of OpenGL. The color used to render an object is the current color. Although in the code, it may appear that colors are associated with objects and their vertices, in fact OpenGL uses the current state to find the color at the time the program defines a vertex. Application programmers must be very careful as to where colors are changed in their code. Later, we shall learn how to bind colors more closely to our objects.

With glColor*(), we can set either RGB or RGBA colors using the standard C data types. OpenGL actually has only one internal form for the present color, which is in RGBA form, usually a floating point number for each color component. If we use glColor3*(), it is the same as using RGBA color with the alpha value set to 1.0. The clear color specified by glClearColor() must be specified as an RGBA color using floats of type GLclampf.

Don't lose track of state changes, such as changing colors.

2.7 Coordinate System Differences Between GLUT and OpenGL

OpenGL uses a variety of coordinate systems. Generally, users describe their geometry in **object coordinates**, which are the coordinates of the application. For two-dimensional applications, this coordinate system has the positive x values increasing to the right and the positive y values increasing as we go up. Thus, if we placed the origin at the bottom-left corner of this page, all the locations on the page would have positive x and y values. Most windowing systems use a system in which the values of y increase as we go down. In such a system, if we want all x and y values to be positive, then we would put the origin in the upper-left corner. This orientation is an artifact of the fact that in most CRT display systems, the screen is generated from top to bottom and the counting of rows and columns starts from the top-left corner. Because GLUT interacts with the window system and thus the display, it uses the second form and we should think of the origin of the screen as being in its upper-left corner and the locations of the pixels numbered starting from (0, 0) and increasing down and to the right. For functions such as glut-InitWindowPosition(), there should be little difficulty. Later, when we use input from the mouse, we will have to work with values in both systems and there can be some confusion.

For two-dimensional problems, the directions of positive increments in *x* and *y* in OpenGL are to the right and up. For input functions used in GLUT and windowing systems, positive increments usually are down and to the right.

2.8 Two-Dimensional Viewing

In our first version of the program, we used the default viewing conditions. In OpenGL, two dimensions is a special case of three dimensions. Two-dimensional objects have spatial coordinates of the form (x, y) but from an OpenGL perspective these are three-dimensional (x, y, z) values with z set to zero.[1] Consequently, two-dimensional viewing issues, such as which objects appear on the screen and at what size, are special cases of the same issues in three-dimensional viewing. However, as we are interested in getting started through two-dimensional programs, we can develop simple two-dimensional viewing independently.

The fundamental model that we use in viewing is called the **synthetic camera model**. It makes an analogy between a viewer (observer, photographer) forming a picture of a set of objects and what we do in the computer to produce an image. In Chapter 4, we shall explore this model in detail for three-dimensional viewing. In two dimensions, the model is as in Figure 2.4.

In two dimensions, we can define our objects by specifying or calculating a set of vertices, using some combination of `glVertex*()`, `glBegin()`, and `glEnd()` in our program. We can think of our code as describing objects on an infinite sheet

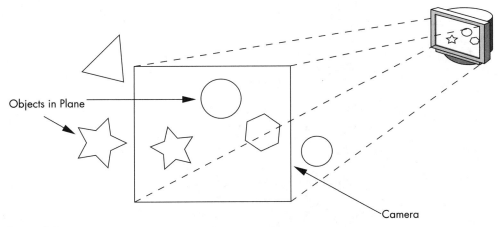

Figure 2.4 Two-dimensional viewing

---

1. Actually, OpenGL uses four dimensions. Three-dimensional space is a special case of four-dimensional space, but we do not have to worry about that yet.

of paper. The viewing step is specifying what part of that virtual sheet of paper is seen by our synthetic camera and thus appears on the screen. If we assume that the camera is aligned with the *x* and *y* axes, we need only specify a rectangular region through maximum and minimum values of *x* and *y*. We make this specification through the function gluOrtho2D().

---

void gluOrtho2D(GLdouble left, GLdouble right, GLdouble bottom,
   GLdouble top)

specifies a rectangular clipping region in two dimensions whose lower-left corner is at (**left, bottom**) and whose upper-right corner is at (**right, top**).

The prefix **glu** indicates that the function is the GLU library (because it is a special case of the three-dimensional function glOrtho()). The rectangle defined by gluOrtho2D() is called the **clipping window**. Objects that lie within this window can be visible while objects outside are not and are said to be clipped out.

2.9 The Viewport

So far we have used the entire window for our graphics. We can also restrict OpenGL to draw to any part of the window through the use of a **viewport**. A viewport is a rectangular area of the window on the screen. Its size is measured in pixels. We set the viewport by the function glViewport().

---

void glViewport(GLint x, GLint y, GLsizei w, GLsizei h)

sets the viewport of width **w** and height **h** pixels in the window with its lower-left corner at (**x, y**). The default viewport is the entire initial window.

One use of viewports is to divide the window so that different types of information can be rendered to different parts of the window. For example, in a CAD application we might use some viewports for menus and instructions and another for constructing the design. Each of these parts can have its own viewing conditions specified by its own use of gluOrtho2D(). By using viewports that do not overlap, we can produce a complex image in a single window with a minimum complexity in the code.

In Chapter 3, we will use viewports to control the appearance of our images when the user changes the shape of the window.

2.10 Coordinate Systems and Transformations

At this point we have seen two coordinate systems in our functions. The first is called **object coordinates** (or **world coordinates**[2]). It is the application coordinate system that programmers use to write their programs. Each application programmer can decide what units she prefers, then specify values in these units in OpenGL functions such as glVertex*(). Thus, she might use microns for problems in VLSI design or light years for astronomical problems. The second coordinate system is called **window coordinates** (or **screen coordinates**) and uses units measured in pixels. The allowable range of window coordinates is determined by properties of the physical display and what part of that display is selected by the application program.

OpenGL automatically makes a coordinate transformation from object to window coordinates as part of the rendering process.[3] The only information required is the size of the display window on the screen and how much of the object space the user wishes to display. The former is determined by glutInitWindow-Size() (and possibly modified by later interactions), while the latter is set by gluOrtho2D().

The required coordinate system transformations in OpenGL are determined by two matrices, the **model-view matrix** and the **projection matrix**, that are part of OpenGL's state. We shall study these matrices in detail in Chapter 5. However, we need to use a simple projection matrix in even the most basic programs. The function gluOrtho2D() is used to specify a projection matrix for two-dimensional applications. The typical sequence to set either of the matrices requires that we perform three steps:

1. Identify which matrix we wish to alter.
2. Set the matrix to an identity matrix.
3. Alter the matrix to form the desired matrix.

The second step is not required if we want to alter an existing matrix incrementally. Thus, if we want to set up a two-dimensional clipping window whose lower-left corner is at $(-1.0, -1.0)$ and whose upper-right corner is at $(1.0, 1.0)$, which are the default values we used in OpenGL, we execute the functions

```
glMatrixMode(GL_PROJECTION);
glLoadIdentity();
gluOrtho2D(-1.0, 1.0, -1.0, 1.0);
```

---

2. Technically, in OpenGL objects are specified in object coordinates and can be transformed by OpenGL transformations into world coordinates.

3. OpenGL uses a series of other coordinate systems internally as part of the rendering pipeline. Some of these are not visible to the application program, while others, such as camera coordinates, will be needed when we discuss three-dimensional applications in Chapter 5.

> **void glMatrixMode(GLenum mode)**
>
> specifies which matrix will be affected by subsequent transformation functions. The mode is usually **GL_MODELVIEW** or **GL_PROJECTION**.

> **void glLoadIdentity()**
>
> initializes the current matrix to an identity matrix.

Because these matrices are part of the OpenGL state, OpenGL will use their current values whenever a primitive is specified. These matrices can be changed virtually anywhere in an application program. For our simple example, where there is no user interaction, we can set the matrices once as part of the initialization phase of the program. In Chapter 3, we will change transformation matrices in response to user events, such as the resizing of the screen window.

2.11 Simple.c, Second Version

We can now incorporate all these changes into our program. The resulting program will behave the same as the first program, but its structure is more general and characterizes more complex two-dimensional applications.

```c
/* simple.c second version */
/* This program draws a white rectangle on a black background.*/

#include <GL/glut.h>          /* glut.h includes gl.h and glu.h*/

void display()
{
/* clear window */

   glClear(GL_COLOR_BUFFER_BIT);

/* draw unit square polygon */

  glBegin(GL_POLYGON);
    glVertex2f(-0.5, -0.5);
    glVertex2f(-0.5, 0.5);
    glVertex2f(0.5, 0.5);
    glVertex2f(0.5, -0.5);
  glEnd();

/* flush GL buffers */

  glFlush();
}
```

```
void init()
{

/* set clear color to black */

  glClearColor (0.0, 0.0, 0.0, 0.0);

/* set fill color to white */

  glColor3f(1.0, 1.0, 1.0);

/* set up standard orthogonal view with clipping */
/* box as cube of side 2 centered at origin */
/* This is default view and these statements could be removed.*/

  glMatrixMode(GL_PROJECTION);
  glLoadIdentity ();
  gluOrtho2D(-1.0, 1.0, -1.0, 1.0);
}

int main(int argc, char** argv)
{

/* initialize mode and open a window in upper-left corner of
screen */
/* window title is name of program (arg[0]) */

  glutInit(&argc, argv);
  glutInitDisplayMode(GLUT_SINGLE | GLUT_RGB);
  glutInitWindowSize(500, 500);
  glutInitWindowPosition(0, 0);
  glutCreateWindow("simple");
  glutDisplayFunc(display);
  init();
  glutMainLoop();
}
```

Program 2 illustrates the organization that we shall use for almost all our programs. Our programs will consist of four major parts:

1. A main() function that initializes GLUT, puts a window on the screen, identifies the callback functions, and enters the main loop
2. An init() function that sets state variables to their initial values
3. A display callback, display(), that contains the code describing our objects
4. Other callbacks that deal with input and window events

Although other structures are possible, this organization has some advantages. The main() function is almost the same from program to program. Differences are usually due to which callbacks and menus are used in a particular application. Using init() allows us to place a lot of detailed state information and desired parameters in one place, separate from the geometry (which is in the display callback) and from the dynamics of animated and interactive programs (which usually are in the callbacks).

2.12 Primitives and Attributes

Primitives are the fundamental entities that we work with in our graphics system. We have seen that the one primitive we have seen so far, a polygon, is defined by a set of vertices. The polygon is a geometric primitive. That is, it exists in a space, usually a two- or three-dimensional user-defined space, and can be rendered by our graphics system. Later, we shall see that OpenGL allows us to apply transformations to geometric primitives so that we can move them, resize them, and reorient them. There are also nongeometric primitives in OpenGL, such as bitmaps and pixel rectangles, that are dealt with in quite a different manner. We shall not introduce these primitives until Chapter 7.

In OpenGL, there are three basic types of geometric primitives: points, line segments, and polygons. More sophisticated objects can be built out of these primitives or we can use OpenGL curves and surfaces (see Chapter 9). The basic geometric primitives are all determined by vertices. Thus, they are specified as was the polygon in `simple.c`, but the type parameter in `glBegin()` varies.

Each primitive has properties called **attributes** that determine how it is displayed by OpenGL. For example, the polygon in our simple program was drawn in white. A line segment might be drawn in green and be thick or thin. In Chapter 6, we shall introduce more sophisticated attributes called material properties that determine how light interacts with the primitive.

It is important to remember that although we conceptualize attributes as being associated with objects—a red line, a blue point—in fact, OpenGL regards attributes as part of its state. Thus, when we produced a white polygon in `simple.c`, the whiteness of the polygon was due to the current color, which was part of the state, being white. In Chapter 3, we shall learn how the programmer can more easily bind attributes to objects.

2.12.1 Points

Points are the most basic primitive. The type in `glBegin()` is `GL_POINTS`. Each vertex specifies a point, and points that are within the clipping window are displayed using the current point size attribute that is set by `glPointSize()` and the current color.

---

void glPointSize(GLfloat size)

sets the point size state variable. Size is measured in pixels on the screen, and the default is 1.0.

We can thus use the same four vertices we used for our polygons but display them as points in four different colors with the code

```
glPointSize(2.0);
glBegin(GL_POINTS);
   glColor3f(1.0, 1.0, 1.0);
   glVertex2f(-0.5, -0.5);
   glColor3f(1.0, 0.0, 0.0);
   glVertex2f(-0.5, 0.5);
   glColor3f(0.0, 0.0, 1.0);
   glVertex2f(0.5, 0.5);
   glColor3f(0.0, 1.0, 0.0);
   glVertex2f(0.5, -0.5);
glEnd();
```

Note that `glPointSize()` is one of the functions that cannot go between a `glBegin()` and a `glEnd()`.

2.12.2 Lines

There are three choices (see Figure 2.5) for `type` that we can use to define one or more line segments between a `glBegin()` and a `glEnd()`:

GL_LINES: Each successive pair of vertices between `glBegin()` and `glEnd()` defines a line segment. Thus, the code

```
glBegin(GL_LINES);
   glVertex2f(-0.5, -0.5);
   glVertex2f(-0.5, 0.5);
   glVertex2f(0.5, 0.5);
   glVertex2f(0.5, -0.5);
glEnd();
```

defines two line segments, the first from $(-0.5, -0.5)$ to $(-0.5, 0.5)$ and the second from $(0.5, 0.5)$ to $(0.5, -0.5)$.

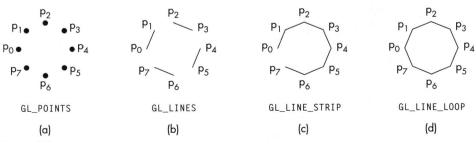

Figure 2.5 Point and line types

GL_LINE_STRIP: The vertices define a sequence of line segments with the end point of one segment starting the next line segment. Thus the code

```
glBegin(GL_LINE_STRIP);
   glVertex2f(-0.5, -0.5);
   glVertex2f(-0.5, 0.5);
   glVertex2f(0.5, 0.5);
   glVertex2f(0.5, -0.5);
glEnd();
```

defines three line segments, the first from $(-0.5, -0.5)$ to $(-0.5, 0.5)$, the second from $(-0.5, 0.5)$ to $(0.5, 0.5)$, and the third from $(0.5, 0.5)$ to $(0.5, -0.5)$.

GL_LINE_LOOP: Connects the line segments as in GL_LINE_STRIP but, in addition, the last vertex is connected to the first. Thus the code

```
glBegin(GL_LINE_LOOP);
   glVertex2f(-0.5, -0.5);
   glVertex2f(-0.5, 0.5);
   glVertex2f(0.5, 0.5);
   glVertex2f(0.5, -0.5);
glEnd();
```

defines a square.

The attributes for line segments are the color, the line thickness, and a pattern, called the **stipple pattern**, that allows us to create dashed and dotted lines.

void glLineWidth(GLfloat width)

sets the width in pixels for the display of lines. The default is 1.0.

void glLineStipple(GLint factor, GLushort pattern)

defines a 16-bit pattern for drawing lines. If a bit in a pattern is 1, a pixel on the line is drawn. If it is zero, the pixel is not drawn. Succesive groups of ones and zeros in **pattern** are repeated **factor** times for values of factor between 1 and 256. The stipple pattern is repeated as necessary to draw the line. The bits are used starting with the lowest-order bits.

For example, the commands

```
glColor3f(1.0, 1.0, 0.0);
glLineWidth(2.0);
glLineStipple(3, 0xcccc);
```

set the drawing color to yellow, define lines as two pixels wide, and define a dashed stipple pattern in which groups of six pixels are not colored and the following six pixels are rendered in yellow.

2.12.3 Enabling OpenGL Features

Stippling is one of many OpenGL features that have to be enabled specifically. The renderer has many capabilities such as lighting, hidden-surface removal , and texture mapping it can perform, although generally each feature will slow down the rendering processing. A program can turn on—enable—or turn off—disable—each of these features individually with the application program. Some features such as lighting may be required in one part of a program but not in others, so an OpenGL program may be more efficient if that feature is disabled when it is no longer needed.

> **void glEnable(GLenum feature)**
>
> **void glDisable(GLenum feature)**
>
> turns on or off the OpenGL option **feature**.

Line stippling is enabled by

```
glEnable(GL_LINE_STIPPLE);
```

Don't forget to enable features you want to use. Setting the parameters is not sufficient if the feature has not yet been enabled.

One of the characteristics of high performance graphics hardware is that many features such as lighting and texture mapping are carried out in hardware rather than software. Consequently, enabling these features may not incur a significant performance penalty.

2.12.4 Filled Primitives

The polygon primitive with which we started is one example of a filled primitive: a primitive with an interior that can be filled with a color or a pattern when it is displayed. There are six filled primitives with the type parameters, as shown in Figure 2.6:

GL_POLYGON: Defines a polygon by a sequence of `glVertex*()` calls between a `glBegin()` and `glEnd()`.

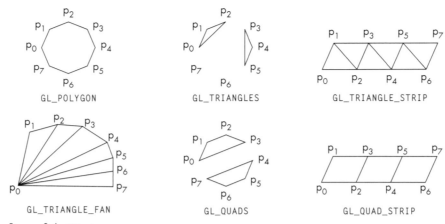

Figure 2.6 Filled types

GL_TRIANGLES: Treats each successive group of three vertices between a `glBegin()` and `glEnd()` as a triangular polygon. Extra vertices are ignored.
GL_TRIANGLE_STRIP: The first three vertices after a `glBegin()` define the first triangle. Each subsequent vertex is used with the previous two to define the next triangle. Thus, after the first polygon is defined, the others require only a single `glVertex*()` call.
GL_TRIANGLE_FAN: The first three vertices define the first triangle. Each subsequent vertex is used with the first vertex and the previous vertex to define the next triangle.
GL_QUADS: Successive groups of four vertices define quadrilaterals.
GL_QUAD_STRIP: The first four vertices define a quadrilateral. Each subsequent pair of vertices is used with the previous pair of vertices to define the next quadrilateral.

These multiple-polygon types have two advantages. First, a particular OpenGL implementation may have special software and hardware to render triangles or quadrilaterals faster than general polygons. Second, many CAD applications generate triangles or quadrilaterals with shared edges. Strip primitives allow us to define these primitives with far fewer OpenGL function calls than if we had to treat each as a separate polygon. In Chapter 4, we shall introduce vertex arrays as another way that we can reduce the number of function calls required to define complex objects that share vertices.

2.12.5 Rectangles

OpenGL provides a function, `glRect*()`, for drawing two-dimensional filled rectangles aligned with the axes.

> **void glRect{sifd}(TYPE x1, TYPE y1, TYPE x2, TYPE y2)**
>
> **void glRect{sifd}v(TYPE *v1, TYPE *v2)**
>
> specifies a two-dimensional rectangle using the standard data types by the x and y values of the corners or by pointers to arrays with these values.

2.12.6 Polygon Stipple

All the filled types are treated as polygons by the rendering process and thus have the same attributes. The simplest way to display a polygon is to fill it with a solid color. As we saw in `simple.c`, we can obtain a solidly colored polygon by using `glColor*()`. We can also fill the polygon with a stipple pattern by enabling polygon stipple by

```
glEnable(GL_POLYGON_STIPPLE);
```

and by setting the pattern by `glPolygonStipple()`.

> **void glPolygonStipple(const Glubyte *mask)**
>
> sets the stipple pattern for polygons. The **mask** is a 32×32 pattern of bits.

The pattern is used as in line stipple but is two dimensional and is aligned with the window. Thus, if we rotate the polygon by changing its vertices and redrawing it, the stipple pattern will not be rotated.

2.13 Polygon Types

The nonfilled primitives, such as lines and line loops, pose no difficulties whether the vertices are defined in two or three dimensions. Such is not the case for filled primitives. Consider a polygon whose edges cross as in Figure 2.7. It is somewhat arbitrary which points we consider to be inside the polygon and which outside. Unless polygons are **simple polygons**—polygons whose edges do not cross—two different OpenGL implementations may render them differently. OpenGL does not check if a polygon is simple; that is left to the application program.

Two-dimensional polygons have an additional feature: all the vertices lie in the same plane and thus, for nonsimple polygons, an interior is well defined. In three dimensions, a list of more than three vertices needs not lie in the same plane. Mathematically, if the vertices do not all lie in the same plane, an interior is not

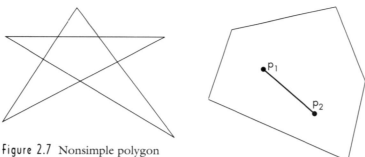

Figure 2.7 Nonsimple polygon

Figure 2.8 Convex polygon

even defined. Once more, different OpenGL implementations might render such lists of vertices differently, and if this situation is a potential problem, it must be dealt with within the application program.

A third issue is that even when all vertices lie in the same plane, rendering a complex polygon with many vertices can present problems for the implementation. **Convex objects** are ones for which if we connect any two points in the object, the entire line segment connecting these points lies inside the object (Figure 2.8). Convex polygons are much easier to render. Because triangles are always convex and every triangle is planar, graphics systems usually work best with triangles.

In OpenGL, a polygon can be displayed in three different ways: filled, by its edges, or just as a set of points corresponding to the vertices. In addition, because our two-dimensional polygons are really three-dimensional polygons that are restricted to the plane $z = 0$, they have two faces, a front face and a back face. OpenGL can render either or both faces.

By default, a **front face** is one in which the order of the vertices is counter-clockwise when we view the polygon. A **back face** is one in which the vertices are specified in a clockwise order. These definitions make sense for convex polygons. There can be difficulties in defining front and back for nonconvex polygons, but OpenGL does not promise anything for such polygons anyway.

The function `glPolygonMode()` lets us tell OpenGL how to render the faces.

---

void glPolygonMode(GLenum face, GLenum mode)

specifies how the faces (**GL_FRONT, GL_BACK,** or **GL_FRONT_AND_BACK**) are to be rendered (**GL_POINT, GL_LINE,** or **GL_FILL**). The default is to fill both faces.

We can also not render either or both faces by culling front or back facing polygon using `glCullFace()`.

void glCullFace(GLenum mode)

causes the faces specified by **mode** (**GL_FRONT**,   **GL_BACK**,   or **GL_FRONT_AND_BACK**) to be ignored during rendering.

Culling must be enabled by

```
glEnable(GL_CULL_FACE);
```

OpenGL allows us to change the definition of front and back facing through the function `glFrontFace()`.

void glFrontFace(GLenum mode)

allows the specification of either the counterclockwise (**GL_CCW**) or clockwise (**GL_CW**) directions for defining a front face.

Suppose that we want to display a polygon *both* by filling it and by displaying its edges. For example, we might want to display a polygon with yellow edges and filled in red. In OpenGL, the edges of a polygon are part of the inside of the polygon, so we cannot show both the edges and the inside with a single rendering. Instead we can render the polygon twice, once with the polygon mode set to GL_FILL and the color set to red and a second time with the mode set to GL_LINE and the color set to yellow as in the code

```
glPolygonMode(GL_FRONT_AND_BACK, GL_FILL);
glColor3f(1.0, 0.0, 0.0);
square();
glPolygonMode(GL_FRONT_AND_BACK, GL_LINE);
glColor3f(1.0, 1.0, 0.0);
square();
```

In this code, the polygon is defined in the function `square()`. There is a potential problem here. The two renderings of the polygon are on top of each other and even though the edge is drawn after the fill, small numerical errors in the renderer can cause parts of the yellow edge to be hidden by the red fill. We can ask OpenGL to move the lines slightly forward by the function `glPolygonOffset()`. The offset is a linear combination of two parameters weighted by two internal constants, hence, it is not simple to set these parameters in terms of units of the application. Nevertheless, if you cannot get the desired effects without using the offset, some trial and error with the parameters may give a better image.[4]

---

void glPolygonOffset(GLfloat factor, GL float units)

sets the offset for polygons. The offset can be positive or negative and can be enabled for any of the polygon modes.

Polygon offset can be enabled separately for any of the three polygon modes. For example

```
glPolygonOffset(1.0, 1.0);
glEnable(GL_POLYGON_OFFSET_LINE);
```

with a positive offset should work for our example.

2.14 Color Interpolation

The color used to render a polygon is the current color state. When we change colors between calls to glVertex*(), we change the state but conceptually we are associating the new color with the next vertex. In OpenGL, we often refer to **vertex colors** when we use them in this manner. Suppose that we have a line segment defined by

```
glBegin(GL_LINES);
  glColor3f(1.0, 0.0, 0.0);
  glVertex2f(1.0, 0.0);
  glColor3f(0.0, 0.0, 1.0);
  glVertex2f(0.0, 1.0);
glEnd();
```

The vertices are defined as red and blue, but in what color will OpenGL render the points in between the vertices? The default is to use **smooth shading** where OpenGL will interpolate the colors at the vertices to obtain the colors of intermediate pixels. Thus as we go along the line, we see the color starting as red and then passing through various shades of magenta before becoming blue.

For polygons, the same is true except that the interpolation formula must interpolate the vertex colors across the interior of the polygons. Usually OpenGL ren-

---

4. Polygon offset is only needed if we are doing hidden-surface removal (Chapter 4).

ders polygons as a set of triangles and uses a simple two-dimensional interpolation formula called **bilinear interpolation**. Interpolating vertex properties will arise in other contexts later, such as in texture mapping and using material properties.

OpenGL also allows us to use the color at the last vertex to determine the properties of the entire primitive. Thus, we could have a solid blue line or we could obtain a green polygon, even if there were color changes between vertex definitions. This style is called **flat shading** and is set by setting the shading model by the function `glShadeModel()`.

---

void glShadeModel(GLenum mode)

sets the shading model to smooth (**GL_SMOOTH**) or flat (**GL_FLAT**). Smooth shading is the default.

2.14.1 Tessellation and Edge Flags

Suppose that you have an application that generates nonconvex, nonplanar polygons. What can you do? You could hope for the best, as generally OpenGL will produce something. Or you could break up (or **tessellate**) your polygons into triangles within your application. There is a problem, however, if we wish to display only the edges. Consider the polygon in Figure 2.9. When we break it up for display into five triangles, there will be no problem if we fill the five polygons. However, if the polygon mode is set to display edges, we only want the edges corresponding to the original polygon to be displayed and not the new edge created by the tessellation. We can decide which edges to display by using the function `glEdgeFlag*()`. If the flag is set to `GL_TRUE`, each vertex is considered the

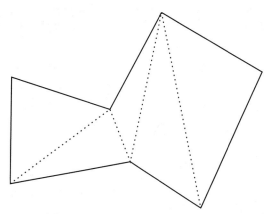

Figure 2.9 Tessellating a polygon

beginning of a line segment to be displayed. If it is set to GL_FALSE, the vertices do not start edges that are to be displayed.

> **void glEdgeFlag(GLboolean flag)**
>
> **void glEdgeFlagv(GLboolean *flag)**
>
> sets the edge flag (**GL_TRUE, GL_FALSE**) that determines if subsequent vertices are the start of edges that should be displayed if the polygon mode is GL_LINE.

There is a third option. The GLU library provides a tessellator. The tessellator makes the decisions as to how to break up a general polygon and takes cares of issues such as creating faces that have a consistent facing and setting the edge flags. Use of the tessellator requires a large number of additional functions, however, so we will not discuss it further here.

2.14.2 Tessellation and Subdivision

In Chapter 4 we shall introduce some quadrics (disks, cones), and in Chapter 9 we shall discuss more general curves and surfaces that are supported by OpenGL. Ultimately, most curves are rendered as a set of approximating line segments while surfaces are approximated by sets of polygons. We can use what we have done thus far to tessellate a simple polygon and produce a curved two-dimensional object.

Consider the triangle in Figure 2.10a. We can bisect the sides of the triangle and connect the bisectors to subdivide the triangle into four triangles as in Figure 2.10b. If we repeat the process on each of the smaller triangles, we create four times as many triangles each time, resulting in a finer tessellation of the original triangle. The code for this **subdivision** process is remarkably simple if we use recursion.

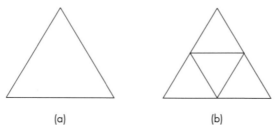

(a)   (b)

Figure 2.10 (a) Triangle, (b) triangle subdivided into four triangles

Consider the function `triangle()` that takes three two-dimensional vertices and draws the resulting polygon

```
void triangle(GLfloat *a, GLfloat *b, GLfloat *c)
{
  glBegin(GL_TRIANGLES);
    glVertex2fv(a);
    glVertex2fv(b);
    glVertex2fv(c);
  glEnd();
}
```

We can start with a single triangle and recursively subdivide it m times and finally draw all the resulting smaller triangles by the code

```
void divide_triangle(GLfloat a, GLfloat b, GLfloat c, int m)
{
  GLfloat v[3][2];
  int j;
  if(m>0)
  {
    for(j = 0; j < 2; j++) v[0][j] = (a[j] + b[j])/2;
    for(j = 0; j < 2; j++) v[1][j] = (a[j] + c[j])/2;
    for(j = 0; j < 2; j++) v[2][j] = (b[j] + c[j])/2;
    divide_triangle(a, v[0], v[1], m-1);
    divide_triangle(v[0], b, v[2], m-1);
    divide_triangle(v[1], v[2], c, m-1);
    divide_triangle(v[0], v[1], v[2], m-1);
  }
  else (triangle(a, b, c));
}
```

We can generate 4n triangles with the display callback

```
GLfloat v[3][2] = {.............};
void display(void)
{
  glClear(GL_COLOR_BUFFER_BIT);
  divide_triangle(v[0], v[1], v[2], n);
  glFlush();
}
```

Figure 2.11 shows the triangles after four subdivisions, assuming that we have set the polygon mode by

```
glPolygonMode(GL_FRONT, GL_LINE);
```

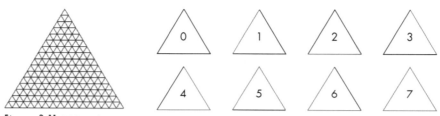

Figure 2.11 Triangle after four subdivisions

Figure 2.12 Possible edge flags for a triangle

Now suppose that we want to show only the outer perimeter of the whole collection. We would like to use the glEdgeFlag() function. We can do so if we recognize that we can generate the eight different edge colorings of a triangle as in Figure 2.12. Here a black edge denotes that the edge flag should be true, while a gray edge indicates that the edge flag should be false.

We can now rewrite the triangle functions to include a type parameter that indicates which type of triangle is created

```
void triangle(GLfloat *a, GLfloat *b, GLfloat *c, int type)
{
  glBegin(GL_POLYGON);
    switch(type)
    {
    case(2):
    case(4):
    case(6):
    case(7):
      glEdgeFlag(GL_FALSE);
      break;
    default:
      glEdgeFlag(GL_TRUE);
    }
    glVertex2fv(a);
    switch(type)
    {
    case(3):
    case(4):
    case(5):
    case(7):
      glEdgeFlag(GL_FALSE);
      break;
    default:
      glEdgeFlag(GL_TRUE);
    }
    glVertex2fv(b);
    switch(type)
    {
```

```
       case(1):
       case(5):
       case(6):
       case(7):
         glEdgeFlag(GL_FALSE);
         break;
       default:
       glEdgeFlag(GL_TRUE);
       }
       glVertex2fv(c);
   glEnd();
}
void divide_triangle(GLfloat *a, GLfloat *b, GLfloat *c, int m,
int k)
{

/* triangle subdivision using vertex numbers */

   GLfloat v[3][2];
   int j, flag[4];
   if(m > 0)
   {
   for(j = 0; j < 2; j++)
   {
     v[0][j] = (a[j] + b[j])/2;
     v[1][j] = (b[j] + c[j])/2;
     v[2][j] = (a[j] + c[j])/2;
   }
     switch(k)
     {
     case(0):
       flag[0] = 3;
       flag[1] = 1;
       flag[2] = 2;
       break;
     case(1):
       flag[0] = 5;
       flag[1] = 1;
       flag[2] = 6;
       break;
     case(2):
       flag[0] = 4;
       flag[1] = 6;
       flag[2] = 2;
       break;
     case(3):
       flag[0] = 3;
       flag[1] = 5;
       flag[2] = 4;
       break;
```

```
      case(4):
        flag[0] = 4;
        flag[1] = 7;
        flag[2] = 4;
        break;
      case(5):
        flag[0] = 5;
        flag[1] = 5;
        flag[2] = 7;
        break;
      case(6):
        flag[0] = 7;
        flag[1] = 6;
        flag[2] = 6;
        break;
      case(7):
        flag[0] = 7;
        flag[1] = 7;
        flag[2] = 7;
        break;
      }
        flag[3] = 7;
      divide_triangle(a, v[0], v[2], m - 1, flag[0]);
      divide_triangle(v[0], b, v[1], m - 1, flag[1]);
      divide_triangle(v[2], v[1], c, m - 1, flag[2]);
      divide_triangle(v[0], v[1], v[2], m - 1, flag[3]);
    }
    else(triangle(a, b, c, k));
}

void display(void)
{
  glClear(GL_COLOR_BUFFER_BIT);
  divide_triangle(v[0], v[1], v[2], n, 0);
  glFlush();
}
```

If you complete the program and run it, you will indeed see only the outer edge of the original triangle, and the tessellation will be invisible. So you might be wondering what is the point of our tessellation. Let's consider a two-dimensional twist. If we rotate a point (x, y) about the origin by θ degrees, its new location is at

$$x' = x \cos \theta - y \sin \theta,$$
$$y' = x \sin \theta + y \cos \theta$$

(see Figure 2.13).

If we make the amount of rotation depend on how far the point is from the origin, then we are said to be twisting the object rather than simply rotating it. The required changes to our tessellation program are only in the triangle display

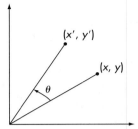

Figure 2.13 Rotating a
point about the origin

```
#include <math.h>

float twist;

void triangle(GLfloat *a, GLfloat *b, GLfloat *c, int type)
/* display one triangle */
{
  GLfloat v[2];
  double d;
  glBegin(GL_POLYGON);
    switch(type)
    {
    case(2):
    case(4):
    case(6):
    case(7):
      glEdgeFlag(GL_FALSE);
      break;
    default:
      glEdgeFlag(GL_TRUE);
    }
    d = sqrt(a[0]*a[0] + a[1]*a[1]);
    v[0] = cos(twist*d)*a[0] - sin(twist*d)*a[1];
    v[1] = sin(twist*d)*a[0] + cos(twist*d)*a[1];
    glVertex2fv(v);
    switch(type)
    {
    case(3):
    case(4):
    case(5):
    case(7):
      glEdgeFlag(GL_FALSE);
      break;
    default:
      glEdgeFlag(GL_TRUE);
    }
```

```
    d = sqrt(b[0]*b[0] + b[1]*b[1]);
    v[0] = cos(twist*d)*b[0] - sin(twist*d)*b[1];
    v[1] = sin(twist*d)*b[0] + cos(twist*d)*b[1];
    glVertex2fv(v);
    switch(type)
    {
    case(1):
    case(5):
    case(6):
    case(7):
       glEdgeFlag(GL_FALSE);
       break;
    default:
       glEdgeFlag(GL_TRUE);
    }
    d = sqrt(c[0]*c[0] + c[1]*c[1]);
    v[0] = cos(twist*d)*c[0] - sin(twist*d)*c[1];
    v[1] = sin(twist*d)*c[0] + cos(twist*d)*c[1];
    glVertex2fv(v);
  glEnd();
}
```

The results now are dramatically different. Figure 2.14 shows the results with
two different levels of tessellation. In effect, we have used our tessellation to create
a curved object. The higher the number of triangles in the tessellation, the
smoother the resulting outline appears. Note that if we simply wanted to create
the images in Figure 2.13, we could have subdivided the three line segments that
form the sides of the initial triangle and not have to worry about the edge flag.
However, the tessellation approach is far more general and extends directly to
working with surfaces in three dimensions.

2.15 Text

Text is not one of the OpenGL primitives. This fact may seem a bit strange given
the importance of text in applications such as labeling graphs. However, it is
important to remember that OpenGL provides a minimal set of primitives that

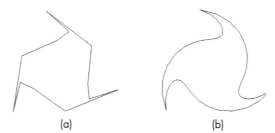

(a)   (b)

Figure 2.14 Tessellated triangle after twisting
(a) two subdivisions and (b) four subdivisions

provide building blocks for the application programmer. We could attempt to build a set of characters from the primitives that we have seen, but that might not be a very appealing task.

In general, text generation presents a few problems that must be confronted. Suppose that we want to create a **font**, a set of characters in a given size and style, such a 10-point Times-Roman bold font. There are two principal forms for generating such characters: **bitmap characters** and **stroke characters**. Bitmap characters are stored as rectangular patterns of bits in which if a bit is one, that bit is displayed; otherwise it is not displayed. We shall study how OpenGL allows the user to define and output bitmaps in Chapter 7. Such characters are very fast to render, because each can be requested by a single OpenGL call. However, bitmap characters cannot be modified by operations such as scaling. In addition, bitmap characters will remain the same size even when a window resize scales the geometric primitives. Stroke characters are generated using the standard OpenGL primitives, such as lines, polygons, and curves. They can be modified by the transformations that we will discuss in Chapter 5. However, stroke characters require more storage and are slower to render. You can generate either type of characters. OpenGL supports both.

A simpler approach might be to use the fonts that are provided by most windowing systems. Programs that do so might not be portable to a different environment, but often switching to another font in another system does not present major problems. We can obtain such a font through system-specific functions.

GLUT offers a third possibility by providing a few of its own bitmap and stroke fonts. We can obtain a bitmap character through the function `glutBitmapCharacter()`, which uses the patterns from certain fonts in the X Window System.

> **void glutBitmapCharacter(void *font, int char)**
>
> renders the character **char**, given by an ASCII code, in the font given by **font**.

Thus, we can get a bitmapped Times-Roman 10-point character "a" by

```
glutBitmapCharacter(GLUT_BITMAP_TIMES_ROMAN_10, 'a');
```

and an 8×13 bit character for "a" by

```
glutBitmapCharacter(GLUT_BITMAP_8_BY_13, 'a');
```

But where does the character appear on the screen? In OpenGL, bitmaps are handled differently from our geometric primitives. Bitmaps appear at a location determined by the **raster position**, which is part of the OpenGL state. This position determines where the lower-left corner of the next bitmap will appear on the display. We can set it with the function `glRasterPos*()`.

> **void glRasterPos{234}{sifd}(TYPE x, TYPE y, TYPE z, TYPE w)**
>
> **void glRasterPos{234}{sifd}v(TYPE *array)**
>
> specifies the raster position. The position is transformed to window coordinates using the current model-view and projection matrices.

Thus, we can set the raster position in object coordinates. The current raster position is offset automatically so that the next character will not be rendered on top of the previous one. GLUT provides the helper function `glutBitmapWidth()`, which allows the application program to determine the width of a character so that it can determine how to change the raster position if it is needed.

> **int glutBitmapWidth(void *font, int char)**
>
> returns the width in pixels of **char** in the GLUT font named by **font**.

The corresponding functions for stroke fonts are `glutStrokeCharacter()` and `glutStrokeWidth()`.

> **void glutStrokeCharacter(void *font, int char)**
>
> renders the character **char**, given by an ASCII code, in the stroke font given by **font**.
>
> **int glutStrokeWidth(void *font, int char)**
>
> returns the width in bits of **char** in the GLUT font named by **font**.

The fonts `GLUT_STROKE_MONO_ROMAN` and `GLUT_STROKE_ROMAN` are mono-spaced and proportionally spaced stroke fonts, respectively. However, their sizes are not in pixels. Their sizes are approximately 100×100 units in world coordinates. Because they are defined as other geometric primitives, they pass through the geometric pipeline. Consequently, the usual way to position stroke characters is through the OpenGL transformations, such as scaling and translation, that we shall discuss in Chapter 5.

2.16 Queries and Errors

Thus far, we have assumed that everything works perfectly; our programs compile and run just as we imagined. Now let's consider reality. We make errors, programs may run but not give the results we expect, or they may run and display nothing.

OpenGL provides some error-checking facilities. OpenGL also allows us to obtain the values of any part of the state.

The OpenGL state can be queried through the six functions `glGetBooleanv()`, `glGetIntegerv()`, `glGetFloatv()`, `glGetDoublev()`, `glGetPointerv()`, and `glIsEnabled()`. The first five write the results in the array to which a pointer is supplied. The application program needs to know the parameter it is seeking. We can obtain both present values that are part of the state and system parameters. For example

```
GLFloat color_array[4];
glGetFloatv(GL_CURRENT_COLOR, color_array);
```

returns the current RGBA values to the array that should have been allocated with four values. The call

```
GLint bits;
glGetIntegerv(GL_RED_BITS, &bits);
```

returns the number of red bits used for color in the implementation. There are a few other get functions in OpenGL that we will introduce later.

---

void glGetBooleanv(GLenum name, GLboolean *value)

void glGetIntegerv(GLenum name, GLint *value)

void glGetFloatv(GLenum name, GLfloat *value)

void glGetDoublev(GLenum name, GLdouble *value)

void glGetPointerv(GLenum name, GLvoid **value)

writes the present values of parameters in the state or system parameters named by **name** to user variables.

The function `glIsEnabled()` allows a program to check if a particular feature has been enabled by a `glEnable()`.

GLboolean glIsEnabled(GLenum feature)

returns **GL_TRUE** or **GL_FALSE** depending on whether or not **feature** is enabled.

Error checking can be done in two parts. We can check if an error has been made by `glGetError()`, which returns an error type or GL_NO_ERROR if no error has been made. Errors are measured from initialization until this function is called. When the function is called, the error flag is reset to GL_NO_ERROR. A string for the particular error can be obtained by `gluGetErrorString()`.

> **GLenum glGetError()**
>
> returns the type of the last error since initialization or the last call to **glGetError()**. If no error has occurred, then **GL_NO_ERROR** is returned.
>
> **GLubyte* gluErrorString(GLenum error)**
>
> returns a string corresponding to the error returned by **glGetError()**.

The error-reporting mechanism in GLUT is implementation dependent. Generally, if you request a facility that is unsupported, the program will terminate with an error message. GLUT provides a function `glutGet()` that lets the application obtain information about the state of GLUT.

> **int glutGet(GLenum state)**
>
> returns the state of the specified GLUT **state** variable.

We can obtain information ranging from depth of the color buffer (`GLUT_WINDOW_BUFFER_SIZE`) to whether the current display mode is supported (`GLUT_DISPLAY_MODE_POSSIBLE`).

2.17 Saving the State

The OpenGL state determines how primitives are rendered. Virtually all changes we make to attributes and to other state variables, such as the model-view and projection matrices, change the state. Programs that alter these variables can spend most of their time making state changes, many of which require recalculation of variables. For example, we often have to compute our camera parameters or the colors we wish to use. Rather than recalculate values that we have used previously, OpenGL provides two types of stacks on which we can store values for later use.

The **matrix stacks** store projection and model-view matrices, with a separate stack for each type. We push and pop matrices with `glPushMatrix()` and `glPopMatrix()`. The stack used is the one corresponding to the present matrix mode (`GL_MODELVIEW` or `GL_PROJECTION`).

> **void glPushMatrix( )**
>
> **void glPopMatrix( )**
>
> pushes and pops matrices to a stack corresponding to the present matrix mode.

There are two major uses of matrix stacks. When we build hierarchical models in Chapter 5, we shall use stacks to traverse the tree data structures that we will use to describe these models. This application involves the model-view matrix. The second use involves the projection matrix. We often have to do a fair amount of calculation or user input to determine the required projection matrix. Suppose that we then want to zoom in on the scene temporarily. We can do this by altering the present projection matrix in a fairly simple manner. The problem is that when we want to return to the unzoomed view, we do not want to (or may be unable to) recalculate the original projection matrix. Saving it on the stack before we zoom solves the problem. Thus, we often see code such as

```
glMatrixMode(GL_PROJECTION);
/* set projection matrix */
/* draw scene */
glPushMatrix();
/* change the projection matrix */
/* draw scene */
glPopMatrix();
```

Note the pairing of the push and pop operations; one pop for each push. In hierarchical systems, not having the correct pairing can leave the stack in an undesired state.

Pushes and pops must be paired in a program to be able to return to the desired state.

OpenGL breaks its attributes into 20 groups corresponding to sets of related attributes. For example, all the polygon attributes are in the group `GL_POLYGON_BIT`. All the line attributes are in the group `GL_LINE_BIT`. We can push any groups of attributes or all attributes (`GL_ALL_ATTRIBUTE_BITS`) onto the attribute stack through the function `glPushAttrib()` and recover them through `glPopAttrib()`.

> **void glPushAttrib(GLbitfield mask)**
>
> **void glPopAttrib( )**
>
> pushes and pops groups of attributes to the attribute stack. The identifiers for the groups are combined with logical OR to form **mask**.

2.18 Programming Exercises

1. Write a program to draw approximations to circles using either lines or polygons. One simple method is to use simple trigonometry to calculate the locations of points on a circle. Another is to subdivide a simple regular polygon such as an equilateral triangle into finer and finer polygons.

2. Rewrite the triangle subdivision program that we used to demonstrate tessellation so that each time it does a subdivision step, the middle triangle is omitted. You can display the resulting object either as a filled polygon or by the edges of the triangles. The resulting object is a simple fractal known as the Sierpinski gasket.

3. Start with a triangle formed by three line segments in which the bottom side is parallel to the x axis. Divide the other two sides recursively, each time moving the new vertex a small but random amount. The resulting shape should look like the outline of a mountain.

4. Obtain some two-dimensional data. Write a program that will plot these data as a polyline (line segments connecting successive data points). Your program should scale the data so that they fit nicely in the window. Add axes and a title.

5. Use the results of Exercise 1 to draw pie charts from some data.

Interaction and Animation

CHAPTER

3

Our next step will be to add dynamics to our simple graphics. To do so, we must be able to create or change objects in a manner that leads to a smooth display process. We also want to be able to interact with our graphics by using menus, pointing to objects, and using the mouse for specifying locations. Although the required functionality is not provided by OpenGL directly, the extra functions that we need are in the OpenGL Utility Toolkit (GLUT).

3.1 The Reshape Callback

We saw in Chapter 2 that a typical OpenGL main function ends in an infinite event loop. Within the loop, the program responds to discrete events involving the keyboard and the mouse through callback functions that the application programmer writes.

One of the most common interactive operations is resizing the screen. Usually, this operation is initiated when the user uses the mouse to move a corner or edge of the window. This action generates a window event that is handled by the **reshape callback**. The information returned to the callback function is the new height and width, in pixels, of the window. Hence, the programmer defines a callback function and then registers it in `main()` by `glutReshapeFunc()`.

---

void glutReshapeFunc(void (*f) (int width, int height))

is invoked whenever the user changes the size of the window using the mouse. The **height** and **width** of the new window are returned to the function **f()**. A display callback is invoked automatically after executing **f()**.

The reshape callback is invoked when a window is first created and thus becomes a handy place to put viewing functions. As the height and width of the window are returned to the callback, we can have the viewing conditions change as the user alters the size and shape of the window. There is a default reshape callback in GLUT but, because there are many different effects that can be created by the reshape callback, it is common not to rely on the default.

Suppose that our initial window size, as specified by `glutInitWindowSize()`, is square and the user resizes the window so that it is smaller and no longer is square. When a window becomes smaller, the programmer must decide whether the same objects should be displayed at a smaller size or a smaller region of object space should be shown. The programmer must also decide if the shape of the objects should be unchanged, even though the window no longer is square. Obviously, these decisions depend on the particular application. Let's consider the case where we want to see the same objects but ensure that their shapes are not changed. Thus, a circle will still appear as a circle, but at a smaller size. We can accomplish both these tasks by altering both the window and the viewport. Consider the typical reshape callback defined by

```
glutReshapeFunc(myreshape);
```

where `myreshape()` is given by

```
GLsizei ww, hh;

void myreshape(GLsizei w, GLsizei h)
{
/* adjust clipping box */
  glMatrixMode(GL_PROJECTION);
  glLoadIdentity();
  if (w <= h)
    gluOrtho2D(-2.0, 2.0, -2.0 * (GLfloat) h /
    (GLfloat) w, 2.0 * (GLfloat) h / (GLfloat) w);
  else
    gluOrtho2D(-2.0 * (GLfloat) w / (GLfloat) h,
               2.0 * (GLfloat) w / (GLfloat) h, -2.0, 2.0);
  glMatrixMode(GL_MODELVIEW);
/* adjust viewport */
  glViewport(0, 0, w, h);
/* set global size for use by drawing routine */
  ww = w;
  wh = h;
}
```

The first part of the function alters the projection matrix. We start, as usual, by loading an identity matrix. The **aspect ratio**, the width-to-height ratio of the window, is used to determine a clipping window. If the screen window is square, the clipping window is a 4.0×4.0 window centered at the origin of the object coordinate system. If the screen window is not square, we set a window whose shortest side is 4.0 units. We also set the viewport so that we will use the entire new screen window. We reset the matrix mode back to modelview mode. This step is not necessary but often is a convenience as programs tend to alter the model-view matrix more than the projection matrix. Note that ww and wh are defined outside the callback as global variables so that the size of the window can be used by other functions.

Consider what happens if our display callback draws a single square of side length 2.0 units, as in our simple example from the previous chapter. If our initial window is square, we will see a square in the middle of the window whose sides are half the length of the window. Now suppose that we resize the screen window so that it is five times longer than it is wide. The reshape callback will change the clipping window so that its height is still 4.0 units but its width is now 20.0 units. Our 2.0×2.0 cube will still appear in the middle of the window and will still appear as a square. The change to the viewport is necessary so that the full clipping window set by gluOrtho2D() will be visible regardless of how the screen window is resized. A display callback is generated automatically so that resizing the screen window not only changes the size of the window but also causes all the geometry defined in the display callback to be redrawn.

3.2 The Idle Callback

Suppose that we want to animate our square from the previous chapter. One simple method is to use the **idle callback** function from GLUT. The idle callback function is identified by glutIdleFunc(), which should be located in the main() function. The idle callback identifies a function, which should be executed whenever there are no other events to be handled, that is, whenever the event queue is empty.

---

void glutIdleFunc(void (*f) (void))

The function **f**() is executed whenever there are no other events to be handled.

Here is a trivial example. Suppose that we modify our simple.c program from the previous chapter by adding the line

```
glutIdleFunc(myidle);
```

to the main() function and define myidle() as

```
void myidle()
{
   glutPostRedisplay();
}
```

The new function `glutPostRedisplay()` performs a function similar to that of directly invoking the display callback (the function `display()` from the `simple.c` program) but allows the implementation to be smarter in deciding when to actually carry out the display callback. As GLUT goes through the event loop, there can be more than one event that requires that the window be redrawn. If each were to call the display function directly, we would have the window redrawn multiple times. Use of `glutPostRedisplay()` ensures the window gets drawn at most once each time that GLUT goes through the event loop. In general, it is a good idea to never call the display callback directly but rather to use the `glutPostRedisplay()` whenever the display needs to be redrawn.

> **void glutPostRedisplay()**
>
> requests that the display callback be executed after the current callback returns.

If we make these changes to our `simple.c` program, we will probably see little change on the screen of our display, although you might notice that our computer is doing more work and the screen may appear to flicker. What we have done is ask our computer to redraw the display whenever it has nothing else to do. But as we have not changed what is in the display callback, the computer is drawing the same object over and over. Thus, we first clear the screen, which accounts for any flashes that we may see, and then we draw our square. More computer resources are being consumed than in our first program, where we drew the square only once. A more realistic use of the idle callback is to alter some of the data that are used in drawing the square.

3.3 A Rotating Square

Suppose that we define the four vertices of the square to lie at four equally spaced points on a circle, as in Figure 3.1. In terms of an angle θ, the four points $(\sin\theta, \cos\theta)$, $(-\sin\theta, \cos\theta)$, $(-\sin\theta, -\cos\theta)$, and $(\sin\theta, -\cos\theta)$ form the vertices of a cube, regardless of the value of θ.

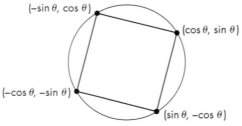

Figure 3.1 Square inside of a unit circle

If we change this angle as part of our idle callback and then redisplay, we should see the cube in a new position each time that the cube is redrawn. Thus, consider the idle callback

```
void myidle()
{
  theta += 2.0;
  if(theta > 360.0) theta -= 360.0;
  glutPostRedisplay();
}
```

Each time that `myidle()` is called, the value of theta is increased 2 degrees. Now, all we need to do is rewrite the display callback such that it uses θ for the vertices. We also have to be careful as to where we define the vertices. Because the form of the callbacks is fixed by GLUT, we must define θ as a global in order to use it both in the display callback and the idle callback.

```
#include <math.h>
#define DEG_TO_RAD 0.017453 /* degrees to radians */
GLfloat theta = 0.0;
void mydisplay()
{
  glClear(GL_COLOR_BUFFER_BIT);
  glBegin(GL_POLYGON):
    glVertex2f(sin(DEG_TO_RAD*theta)),
        cos(DEG_TO_RAD*theta);
    glVertex2f(-sin(DEG_TO_RAD*theta)),
        cos(DEG_TO_RAD*theta);
    glVertex2f(-sin(DEG_TO_RAD*theta)),
        -cos(DEG_TO_RAD*theta);
    glVertex2f(sin(DEG_TO_RAD*theta)),
        -cos(DEG_TO_RAD*theta);
  glEnd();
  glFlush();
}
```

These modifications leave us with a program that, although inefficient, works. Later we shall replace the use of trigonometric functions with rotation operations in OpenGL. You may, however, be annoyed with the appearance of the screen. It probably is flashing and does not appear to display a square. This problem is due to the interaction between the application program and the display process. Fortunately, we can handle this problem simply by requesting double buffering.

3.4 Double Buffering

Most graphics displays are built so that the screen that you see is redrawn or **refreshed** at a fixed rate. This process requires that the display hardware take the contents of the color buffer and use these values to determine the colors in the graphics window on the screen. This refresh process is not controllable from the user program and in fact is uncoordinated (or asynchronous) with it. Consequently, the user program is creating new values in the color buffer at the same time that the display process is taking these values out for display. The values used for display are not those of a single square drawn for a particular value of θ but rather some combination of values from more than one execution of the display callback.

Although we cannot couple the two processes, we can ensure that we will display only a single fully drawn square through a technique called **double buffering**. The main idea is to use two color buffers, called the **front buffer** and the **back buffer**, rather than just one. The front buffer is the one that is displayed by the display hardware, while the back buffer is the one into which the application draws. All we need to do is swap the two buffers after we have finished constructing an entire square. We can do this swap by replacing the `glFlush()` by `glutSwapBuffers()` in our display callback.

> **void glutSwapBuffers()**
>
> swaps the front and back buffers.

Note that `glutSwapBuffers()` is a GLUT function rather than an OpenGL function because the swap involves an interaction with the windowing system. We must request double buffering in our initialization because single buffering is the default. We do so through the initialization statement, assuming we also want RGB color:

```
glutInitDisplayMode(GLUT_DOUBLE | GLUT_RGB);
```

3.5 Using the Keyboard

We now turn to using the two most important interactive devices, the mouse and the keyboard. For the keyboard, events are generated every time that we press or release a key. GLUT has a keyboard callback identified through the function `glutKeyboardFunc()`. This callback is invoked whenever a key is pressed. GLUT ignores releasing of the key, although many window systems allow the application program to respond to key-release events.

> **void glutKeyboardFunc(void *f(unsigned char key, int x, int y))**
>
> identifies the function **f**() that is called when any key is pressed on the keyboard. The key pressed is returned to **f**(), as is the position of the mouse in the window. Note that the position is given in pixels measured from the upper-left corner of the window.

The key pressed is returned as an `unsigned char` to the callback function. Generally, the keyboard callback uses a simple control structure such as `if` or `switch` to determine if the key pressed is one that the callback should handle and, if it is, then how to handle it. For example, suppose that we want to end the program if the user hits either a Q or a q or the escape key (\27 or x1b). In the `main()` function, we register a keyboard callback

```
glutKeyboardFunc(mykey);
```

and then define the function

```
void mykey(unsigned char key, int x, int y))
{
   if(key == 'q' || key == 'Q' || key == '\27') exit(0);
}
```

All GLUT callbacks that return a mouse position give the position in screen coordinates with the origin in the top-left corner.

`glutKeyboardFunc()` only responds to the pressing of a key and not to its release.

The keyboard callback also returns the position of the mouse at the time that a key was depressed. We can use these values to cause keys to have different effects that depend on where the mouse is located. For example, in a drawing program, we might use the keyboard to exit the program except if the mouse is located in the drawing area. Here the keyboard callback might be used to enter text onto the screen. Note that because the mouse position is given as a position on the screen, the values returned are in pixels measured from the top-left corner of the screen.

3.5.1 Special Keys

GLUT has provisions for using the various special keys, such as the function and arrow keys, that are on most keyboards. These keys are handled through the `glutSpecialFunction()` callback.

---

void glutSpecialFunc (void (*f) (int key, int x, int y))

specifies the special key callback. The function **f()** is executed when **key** is pushed. The mouse position (**x, y**) is also returned.

Each special key is designated by a string defined in glut.h. Thus, within the callback, we might see code such as

```
if(key == GLUT_KEY_F1) ...... /* function key 1 */
if(key == GLUT_KEY_UP) ... .   /* up arrow key */
```

We can also make use of the **modifier keys**—control, alt, and shift—through the glutGetModifiers() function that can be called from within the mouse or keyboard callbacks.

> **int glutGetModifiers()**
>
> returns the logical AND of **GLUT_ACTIVE_SHIFT**, **GLUT_ACTIVE_CTRL**, or **GLUT_ACTIVE_ALT** if that key is depressed at the time a mouse or keyboard event is generated.

Thus, to have control-c or control-C terminate a program, we could have the following within the keyboard callback:

```
if((glutGetModifiers() GLUT_ACTIVE_CTRL) &&
    ((key == 'c') || (key == 'C'))) exit(0);
```

The modifiers can be helpful in situations where we have either a one-button or two-button mouse and would like to use some of the options that are available with a three-button mouse. For example, with a one-button mouse, we could use a mouse click, control-mouse click, and shift-mouse click to get the functionality of a three-button mouse.

3.6 Using the Mouse Callback

For the mouse, we use glutMouseFunc() to register the mouse callback function.

> **void glutMouseFunc(void (*f)(int button, int state, int x, int y))**
>
> identifies the mouse callback function f() that returns the position of the mouse in the window, its state (**GLUT_UP** or **GLUT_DOWN**) after the event, and which button caused the event (**GLUT_LEFT_BUTTON**, **GLUT_MIDDLE_BUTTON**, or **GLUT_RIGHT_BUTTON**).

The simplest and most common way that a mouse is used is to return a position on the screen to the application program. A **mouse event** occurs when a button on a mouse is pushed or released. The callback returns the position of the mouse in units of pixels measured, as usual, from the upper-left corner of the window. It also returns which button caused the event and the state of that button after the event. In our examples, we shall consider only events generated by pushing a button, so the state that we shall check for is GLUT_DOWN. Thus, if we want to use the left mouse button to end our program, we can register a mouse callback in the main() function

```
glutMouseFunc(mymouse);
```

and then use the callback function

```
void mymouse(int button, int state, int x, int y)
{
   if(state == GLUT_DOWN&&button == GLUT_LEFT_BUTTON)
     exit(0);
}
```

The mouse callback can also be used interactively to control what is drawn. Suppose that we want to draw a box whose corners are given by two successive mouse clicks with the right mouse button and whose sides are aligned with the screen. The left mouse button will still be used to exit the program.

The first problem we must confront is locating where in the program we actually do the drawing; that is, where do we place the OpenGL functions that draw the box? There are two simple strategies. In the first, we do everything within the mouse callback. Thus, the first time that the user pushes the right button, we save the position; the second time we push this button, we draw a rectangle. Thus, the mouse callback looks something like

```
int hh; /* global for viewport height */

void mymouse(int button, int state, int x, int y)
{
   static bool first = true;
   static int xx, yy;
   if(state == GLUT_DOWN&&button == GLUT_LEFT_BUTTON)
     exit(0);
   if(state == GLUT_DOWN&&button == GLUT_RIGHT_BUTTON)
   {
     if(first)
     {
       xx = x;
       yy = hh - y;
       first = !first;
     }
```

```
    else
    {
      first = !first;
      glClear(GL_COLOR_BUFFER_BIT);
      glBegin(GL_POLYGON);
        glVertex2i(xx, yy);
        glVertex2i(xx, hh - y);
        glVertex2i(x, hh - y);
        glVertex2i(x, yy);
      glEnd();
    }
  }
}
```

There are a few subtleties in this code. The most important is the necessity of inverting the y value returned by the mouse callback. This inversion is required because the values returned to the mouse callback are given in screen coordinates whose origin is at the upper-left corner. The values used for the clipping window and specification of the geometry are in world coordinates where the origin is at the lower-right corner. However, to carry out the inversion, we need the height of the screen window, a value that can change during the execution of the program if the user resizes the window. We handle this problem using the global value of the window height (hh), which is updated automatically by the reshape callback.

Keep the window size as globals so that you can convert the mouse position to world coordinates correctly.

The vertices specified in our example use the integer form of glVertex2i(). The values used for the locations of the vertices are those obtained from the mouse callback and thus are integers. A little thought will show that the clipping window that we defined in the reshape callback is too small. A better choice for this example would be to use the reshape callback to have the clipping window match the screen window, as in the code

```
int ww, hh; /* globals for viewport height and width */

void myReshape(GLsizei w, GLsizei h)
{
  glMatrixMode(GL_PROJECTION);
  glLoadIdentity();
  gluOrtho2D(0.0, (GLfloat) w, 0.0, (GLfloat) h);
  glMatrixMode(GL_MODELVIEW);
  glViewport(0, 0, w, h);
  ww = w;
  hh = h;
}
```

As we have developed the code, there is no display callback; all the work is done in the mouse callback. As a practical matter, GLUT insists that every program have a display callback. We could just put in the dummy display callback

```
void mydisplay() {}
```

but, although this display callback will work, many application programmers would object to this style.

A more general strategy is to place drawing functions in the display callback and use the other callbacks for state changes. Although in many situations we may not always be able to do this, we can do it easily for this example through the two callbacks

```
GLint x1, y1, x2, y2;
int hh;

void mymouse(int x, int y, int button, int state)
{
   static bool first = true;
   int x1, yy;
   if(state == GLUT_DOWN&&button == GLUT_LEFT_BUTTON)
     exit();
   if(state == GLUT_DOWN&&button == GLUT_RIGHT_BUTTON)
   {
      if(first)
      {
        x1 = x;
        y1 = hh - y;
        first = !first;
      }
      else
      {
        first = !first;
        x2 = x;
        y2 = hh-y;
      }
      glutPostRedisplay();
   }
}

void mydisplay()
{
  glClear(GL_COLOR_BUFFER_BIT);
  glBegin(GL_POLYGON);
    glVertex2i(x1, y1);
    glVertex2i(x1, hh - y2);
    glVertex2i(x2, hh - y2);
    glVertex2i(x2, y1);
  glEnd();
}
```

3.7 Mouse Motion

We also generate events when the mouse moves, whether or not any of the mouse buttons are held down. If the mouse moves with a button held down, then we call this event a **move event**. If the mouse is moved without a button held down, a **passive motion event** is generated. We also generate an event called an **entry event** whenever the mouse enters or leaves the window. The motion callback function is specified by glutMotionFunc() and the passive motion callback by glutPassiveMotionFunc(). Both return the position of the mouse.

> **void glutMotionFunc(void (*f) (int x, int y))**
>
> **void glutPassiveMotionFunc(void (*f) (int x, int y))**
>
> specify the motion and passive motion callback functions. The position of the mouse (x, y) is returned to the callback.

Events occur whenever the mouse moves a small system-dependent amount. One use of the motion callback is in programs that draw curves while the mouse is moved with a button held down. As long as a button is held down, we can extend a polyline through a line in the callback of the form

```
int points [2][100];
int i = 0
void mymotion(int x, int y)
{
.
.
  points [0][i] = x;
  points [j][i] = h - 4;
  itt;
.
.
.
}
```

In this code, the vertical mouse position is inverted to be in OpenGL's coordinate system and the values saved. After the mouse is released, the array can be used to draw a polyline.

The mouse generates an entry event whenever it enters or leaves the OpenGL window.

> **void glutEntryFunc(void (*f) (int state))**
>
> specifies the entry callback function. The returned state is either **GLUT_ENTERED** or **GLUT_LEFT**.

3.8 Menus

Interactive programs are characterized by far more elaborate types of interactions than the simple uses of the mouse and keyboard that we have discussed so far. All modern windowing systems support a set of **widgets**, which are special types of windows with which the user can interact. Typical widget sets include menus, buttons, slide-bars, and dialog boxes. Most widgets are provided by system-specific toolkits that exploit all the capabilities of the window system. Because GLUT is simple and portable, it provides only a limited set of widgets. Of course, because widgets, such as buttons and dials, can be viewed as graphical objects, we could use OpenGL and GLUT to create any particular type of widget.

GLUT does provide one important widget: menus. Usually these menus are implemented as "pop-up" menus that appear when a particular mouse button is depressed. There are three steps in defining a menu. We must decide what entries are in the menu; that is, what strings will be displayed in each row of a menu. Second, we must tie specific actions to the rows; and third, we must tie each menu to a mouse button. The menu mechanism works just as other callbacks. When a user releases the mouse button that popped up the menu, an identifier for the row on which the mouse was located is passed to the menu callback function.

Menus are usually created either in main() or in an initialization function called from main(). GLUT allows for hierarchical menus by allowing a menu entry to refer to a submenu. Top-level menus are created by glutCreateMenu(), which is given the name of the callback function for the menu and returns an integer identifier for the menu.

int glutCreateMenu(void (* f) (int value))

creates a top-level menu that uses the callback **f**(), which is passed an integer **value** for the menu entry. A unique identifier is returned for the menu created.

The menu created becomes the current menu. The current menu can be changed by glutSetMenu().

void glutSetMenu(int id)

sets the current menu to the menu with identifier **id**.

Entries are added into the current menu by glutAddMenuEntry(). Each entry consists of two parts: a string that is displayed for the entry and a value that is returned when that entry is selected.

> **void glutAddMenuEntry(char *name, int value)**
>
> adds an entry with **name** displayed to the current menu; **value** is returned to the menu callback.

Finally, we can attach the menu to a mouse button by glutAttachMenu().

> **void glutAttachMenu(int button)**
>
> attaches the current menu to the specified mouse button (**GLUT_RIGHT_BUTTON**, **GLUT_MIDDLE_BUTTON**, or **GLUT_LEFT_BUTTON**).

Suppose that we want to use the right mouse button to pull down a menu that will have two entries: one will clear the screen and the other will end the program. We set up our menu in init() or in main() by

```
glutCreateMenu(mymenu);
glutAddMenuEntry("Clear Screen", 1);
glutAddMenuEntry("Exit", 2);
glutAttachMenu(GLUT_RIGHT_BUTTON);
```

Note that with only one menu, we do not need its identifier. Now we write the menu callback function mymenu().

```
void mymenu(int value)
{
  if(value == 1)
  {
    glClear(GL_COLOR_BUFFER_BIT);
    glutSwapBuffers(); /* or glFlush() */
  }
  if(value == 2) exit(0);
}
```

3.8.1 SubMenus

We can also add submenus to a menu. A submenu will have a name that appears as an entry in its parent menu. When the user moves the mouse to this entry, the submenu pops up. We add an entry for a submenu by glutAddSubMenu().

> **void glutAddSubMenu(char *name, int menu)**
>
> adds a submenu entry **name** as the next entry in the current menu. The value of **menu** is the id of the submenu returned when the submenu was created.

We create the submenu just as we do the main menu, but we must create the submenu first so that we can pass its identifier to `glutAddSubMenu()` when we create the main menu.

3.9 The NULL Callback

Callback functions can be redefined during execution by simply naming a new callback function in the appropriate function. At times, we want to simply eliminate a callback. For example, suppose at some point in a program, we no longer want an idle callback defined. We can accomplish this by passing NULL as the name of the new callback function

```
glutIdleFunc(NULL);
```

3.10 SubWindows and Multiple Windows

In many applications, both interactive and noninteractive, we want to use multiple windows. For example, in a CAD application we might want one window for creating objects, another for instructions, and perhaps a third for warning messages. We might want windows to be created and destroyed during the execution of our program. The function `glutCreateWindow()`, which we introduced in the previous chapter, returns an integer identifier for each window that we create. The function `glutDestroyWindow()` allows us to get rid of windows.

> **int glutCreateWindow(char *name)**
>
> creates a top-level window **name** and returns an identifier for it.
>
> **void glutDestroyWindow(int id)**
>
> destroys top-level window **id**.

When a window is created, it becomes the current window. Normally, primitives are rendered to the current window. We can change the current window by `glutSetWindow()`.

> **void glutSetWindow(int id)**
>
> sets the current window to the window with identifier **id**.

Each window can have its own properties, referred to as its **context**. Thus, if we precede the creation of a window by a `glutInitDisplayMode(properties)`, the window that we create will have the specified properties. We can also use the set functions such as `glutInitWindowSize()` to affect the current window. Thus, we can have multiple windows, each with the specific properties needed by the application.

We can also create subwindows of any window, including both top-level windows and subwindows. Subwindows can have their own context. Each is defined to be a subrectangle of its parent through the function `glutCreateSubWindow()`.

> **int glutCreateSubWindow(int parent, int x, int y, int width, int height)**
>
> creates a subwindow of **parent** and returns its id. The subwindow has its origin at **(x, y)** and has size **width** by **height** in pixels.

The subwindow becomes the current window when it is created. The function `glutPostWindowDisplay()` posts a redisplay for a particular window.

> **void glutPostWindowRedisplay(int winid)**
>
> posts a redisplay for window **winid**.

3.11 Example: single__double.c

Our next example will illustrate many of the concepts that we have just introduced. It will demonstrate single and double buffering using a rotating square. We will also be able to stop the rotation at will. Let's start with the `main()` function.

```
int singleb, doubleb; /* window ids */

int main(int argc, char** argv)
{
    glutInit(&argc, argv);
```

```
    /* create a single buffered window */

glutInitDisplayMode(GLUT_SINGLE | GLUT_RGB);
singleb = glutCreateWindow("single buffered");
myinit();
glutDisplayFunc(displays);
glutReshapeFunc(myReshape);
glutIdleFunc(spinDisplay);
glutMouseFunc(mouse);
glutKeyboardFunc(mykey);

    /* create a double buffered window to right*/

glutInitDisplayMode(GLUT_DOUBLE | GLUT_RGB);
glutInitWindowPosition(310, 0);
doubleb = glutCreateWindow("double buffered");
myinit();
glutDisplayFunc(displayd);
glutReshapeFunc(myReshape);
glutIdleFunc(spinDisplay);
glutMouseFunc(mouse);
glutCreateMenu(quit_menu);
glutAddMenuEntry("quit", 1);
glutAttachMenu(GLUT_RIGHT_BUTTON);

    /* enter event loop */

glutMainLoop();

}
```

Note that each window has some callbacks defined for it. Although the two windows share some of the callbacks, callbacks for either can be changed later independently of the other. The spinning square can be defined as before using the idle callback SpinDisplay() to spin it.

```
void displays()
{
  glClear(GL_COLOR_BUFFER_BIT);
  glBegin(GL_POLYGON):
        glVertex2f(sin(DEG_TO_RAD*theta),
            cos(DEG_TO_RAD*theta));
        glVertex2f(-sin(DEG_TO_RAD*theta),
            cos(DEG_TO_RAD*theta));
        glVertex2f(-sin(DEG_TO_RAD*theta),
            -cos(DEG_TO_RAD*theta));
        glVertex2f(sin(DEG_TO_RAD*theta),
            -cos(DEG_TO_RAD*theta));
  glEnd();
  glFlush();
}
```

```
void displayd()
{
  glClear(GL_COLOR_BUFFER_BIT);
  glBegin(GL_POLYGON):
        glVertex2f(sin(DEG_TO_RAD*theta),
            cos(DEG_TO_RAD*theta));
        glVertex2f(-sin(DEG_TO_RAD*theta),
            cos(DEG_TO_RAD*theta));
        glVertex2f(-sin(DEG_TO_RAD*theta),
            -cos(DEG_TO_RAD*theta));
        glVertex2f(sin(DEG_TO_RAD*theta),
            -cos(DEG_TO_RAD*theta));
  glEnd();
  glutSwapBuffers();
}

void spinDisplay (void)
{
    /* increment angle */

  theta += 2.0;
  if (theta > 360.0) theta -= 360.0;

    /* draw single buffer window */

  glutSetWindow(singleb);
  glutPostWindowRedisplay(singleb);

    /* draw double buffer window */

  glutSetWindow(doubleb);
  glutPostWindowRedisplay(doubleb);
}
```

The two windows share the mouse callback function. This function allows the user to stop the rotation in both windows by setting the idle function to NULL (and to restore the spinning later). Although the two windows use the same callback, each maintains its own state. Thus, if we stop rotation in one window, we do not alter the state of the other window. To change the callback for the other window, we first must click the mouse in the other window.

```
void mouse(int btn, int state, int x, int y)
{
  if(btn == GLUT_LEFT_BUTTON && state == GLUT_DOWN)
    glutIdleFunc(spinDisplay);
  if(btn == GLUT_MIDDLE_BUTTON && state == GLUT_DOWN)
    glutIdleFunc(NULL);
}
```

The reshape callback is standard and sets up the clipping window.

```
void myReshape(int w, int h)
{
    glViewport(0, 0, w, h);
    glMatrixMode(GL_PROJECTION);
    glLoadIdentity();
    gluOrtho2D(-2.0, 2.0, -2.0, 2.0);
    glMatrixMode(GL_MODELVIEW);
    glLoadIdentity();
}
```

To illustrate two of the other callbacks, we use both a keyboard callback and a menu to end the program. However, each was assigned to only one of the two windows, so each can use a different method to exit.

```
void mykey(int key)
{
    if(key == 'Q' || key == 'q') exit(0);
}

void quit_menu(int id)
{
    if(id == 1) exit (0);
}
```

3.12 Display Lists

The standard rendering mode in OpenGL is known as **immediate mode**. Primitives are passed through the OpenGL pipeline as soon as they are defined in the program. They are then no longer in the system; only their image is on the screen. When something changes and the screen needs to be redrawn, we have to regenerate the primitives, typically in the display callback, and pass them through the pipeline again. Depending on the complexity of the scene, this redisplay process can be very time-consuming. It can be especially slow when the application program (the **client**) is on one side of a network and the renderer and display (the **graphics server**) is on the other. In this situation, all the primitives, whether or not they appear on the screen, must be sent over a potentially slow connection before passing through the pipeline.

In **retained mode** graphics, collections of primitives and other information can be stored as objects on the server, thus avoiding costly transfers and regeneration problems. OpenGL's mechanism for defining such objects is through **display lists**. Display lists can be thought of as a type of graphics file in which we can place OpenGL rendering and state update commands. We open a display list, give it a name, place commands in it, and close it. Display lists store their contents in an internal format that makes for fast redisplay. When we form a display list, we are said to be **compiling** it. Display lists reside on the server and are executed by simple OpenGL calls.

Suppose that we want to create a display list with a red square in it. We create it by calling glNewList(). We then define the square as usual and end the list with a glEndList().

```
#define RED_SQUARE 1
glNewList(RED_SQUARE, GL_COMPILE);
  glPushAttrib(GL_CURRENT_BIT);
  glColor3f(1.0, 0.0, 0.0);
  glRectf(-1.0, -1.0, 1.0, 1.0);
  glPopAttrib();
glEndList();
```

The flag GL_COMPILE causes OpenGL to place the display list on the server but the display list is not displayed. If we also want it displayed when it is created, we use the flag GL_COMPILE_AND_EXECUTE. Note that we push and pop the current attributes, which include the present color. We must do this action to prevent the state change due to setting a new color from affecting anything that we do subsequently. Often we can prevent unforeseen side effects of state changes by starting a display list by pushing the matrices and the state at the beginning of the display last and popping them at the end.

> **void glNewList(GLuint name, GLenum mode)**
>
> creates a new display list with an unsigned integer id **name**. The value of **mode** (**GL_COMPILE, GL_COMPILE_AND_EXECUTE**) determines if the list is placed on the server with or without being executed.
>
> **void glEndList()**
>
> ends the definition of a display list.

We execute a display list through the function glCallList().

> **void glCallList(GLuint name)**
>
> executes display list **name**.

Most OpenGL functions can be put into display lists. Of the ones that we have seen so far, only functions that return state variables, such as glGet*(), cannot be inside a display list. Display lists can be called from within other display lists, which is one method of creating hierarchical objects.

Display lists cannot be changed once they are created. If we wish to change the contents of a display list, then we have to create a new one with the desired contents and delete the present one by `glDeleteLists()`.

> **void glDeleteLists(GLuint first, GLsizei number)**
>
> deletes number display **lists** starting with **first**.

3.12.1 Multiple Display Lists

Usually we work with more than a single list. We can execute multiple lists with the function `glCallLists()`. The identifiers of the display lists are counted relative to a list base, which is set by `glListBase()` and stored in an array.

> **void glListBase(GLuint offset)**
>
> sets the **offset** used by `glCallLists()`. The default is **0**.
>
> **void glCallLists(GLsizei num, GLenum type, GLvoid *lists)**
>
> executes **num** display lists from the integers stored in the array **lists** of **type**. The present **offset** is added to each integer in **lists** to obtain the id of the display list to be executed.

Often when working with multiple display lists, we need some unused ids for new lists. The function `glGenLists()` lets us obtain a set of consecutive unused integers for defining new display lists.

> **GLuint glGenLists(GLsizei n)**
>
> returns the first of **n** consecutive integer ids available for new display lists.

3.12.2 Display Lists and Text

Text can be rendered more efficiently by using a display list for each character. Regardless of whether we are using a stroke or bitmap font, the descriptions of the characters are on the server. To generate a character string on the display, we do one function call per character.

Suppose that we decide to use the GLUT bitmap proportional 10-point Times-Roman font. We need 256 display lists (assuming that we generate display lists even for the nonprinting characters). We can get the required ids by

```
base = glGenLists(256);
```

We can now set up the display lists.

```
for(i = 0; i < 256; i++)
{
  glNewList(base + i, GL_COMPILE);
  glutBitMapCharacter(GLUT_BITMAP_TIMES_ROMAN_10, i);
  glEndList();
}
```

Because we are using a GLUT bitmap font, the raster position is automatically moved to the right by the width of the character.

We next set the list base

```
glListBase(base);
```

so that we can refer to each display list by its ASCII code. Now suppose that we have a character string

```
char *text;
```

We can draw it with the single function call

```
glCallLists((GLint) strlen(text), GL_UNSIGNED_BYTE, text);
```

Here we have used the standard function `strlen()` to determine the length of the string that is the number of display lists we must execute. The character string can then be regarded as an array of unsigned bytes, each of which is the number (its ASCII code) that has to be added to `base` to obtain the id of the call list to be executed.

The example would have been essentially the same if we had used a stroke font, except that we would have then had to deal with the problem of moving to the right each time we drew a character. This problem can be dealt with best by using OpenGL transformations that we will introduce in Chapter 5.

3.12.3 Display Lists and Objects

Although in many situations, our graphics cards are so fast that it may not be clear that display lists provide a speed advantage over immediate-mode graphics, display lists can give the user a way of building more object-oriented programs than in immediate mode. The ability to include the attributes of the object, such as the red color of the square, binds the color to the geometry even though OpenGL itself considers color part of the state. Even more powerful is the ability to have a given display list execute other display lists, thus creating a method of building hierarchical objects. Consider, for example, constructing a cartoonlike face object. Each face has two eyes, two ears, a mouth, and a nose. The code for the face might look like

```
glNewList(FACE, GL_COMPILE);
/* position first eye */
```

```
  glCallList(EYE);
/*position second eye */
  glCallList(EYE);
/* position first ear */
  glCallList(EAR);
/* position second ear */
  glCallList(EAR);
/* position nose */
  glCallList(NOSE);
/* position mouth */
  glCallList(MOUTH);
glEndList();
```

Note that we can change the face by changing any of the display lists that define the parts. By positioning the face before we call the display list, we position all its parts.

3.13 Picking and Selection Mode

There is one operation that is fundamental to many interactive programs that we have yet to discuss. **Picking** is the operation of locating an object on the screen. This operation presents a few difficulties for OpenGL. First we must define what we mean by an object. One way we have seen is through display lists. But we can think of others. We could create some sort of tag system that would give labels to parts of our programs. Next we have to decide exactly what we mean by picking an object. This issue is somewhat tricky. Do we have to click the mouse on a primitive that belongs to the object? Or just close to it? What do we do if objects overlap? We can come up with a number of perhaps system-dependent ways of handing such issues.

An even more difficult issue is how to implement picking within the OpenGL pipeline. The problem for a pipeline system is that we cannot go backwards directly from the position of the mouse to primitives that were rendered close to that point on the screen. Users have found a variety of ways to get around this problem. Some use table lookups based on the position of the mouse to locate objects. Others involve multiple renderings and reading the contents of the frame buffer, a topic that we shall discuss in Chapter 7.

OpenGL provides a somewhat complex process called **selection mode** to do picking at the cost of an extra rendering each time we pick. The basic idea of selection mode is that the objects in a scene can be rendered but not to the color buffer. As we render objects, OpenGL can keep track of which objects render to any chosen area by determining if they are in a specified clipping volume that does not have to be the same as the clipping volume used to render into the color buffer.

There are a number of steps and functions that are required to do picking. We shall examine each step and then put them together in a simple program. The function `glRenderMode()` lets us select one of three modes: normal rendering to the color buffer (GL_RENDER), selection mode (GL_SELECT), or feedback mode (GL_FEEDBACK). Feedback mode can be used to obtain a list of which primitives were rendered. Because it is used in limited applications, we will not discuss this mode.

GLint glRenderMode(GLenum mode)

Choose between normal (**GL_RENDER**), selection (**GL_SELECTION**), and feedback (**GL_FEEDBACK**) render modes. The return value can be used to determine the number of hits in selection mode or of primitives in feedback mode.

When we enter selection mode and render a scene, each primitive that renders within the clipping volume generates a message called a **hit**, which is stored in a buffer called the **name stack**. We use the function glSelectBuffer() to identify an array for the selection data. There are four functions for initializing the name stack, for pushing and popping information on it, and for manipulating the top entry on the stack. The information that we produce is called the **hit list** and can be examined after the rendering to obtain the information needed for picking.

---

void glSelectBuffer(GLsizei n, GLunint *buff)

specifies the array **buff** of **size** n in which to place selection data.

void glInitNames( )

initializes the name stack.

void glPushName(GLuint name)

pushes **name** on the name stack.

void glPopName( )

pops the top name from the name stack.

void glLoadName(GLuint name)

replaces the top of the name stack with **name**.

In general, each object that we wish to identify is a set of primitives to which we assign the same integer name. Before we render the object, we load its name on the name stack. We cannot load a name onto an empty stack, so we usually enter an unused name onto the stack when we initialize it.

```
glInitNames();
glPushName(0);
```

| When using selection mode, make sure the name stack is initialized with an unused name. |

We usually use the mouse callback to enter selection mode and leave selection mode before the end of the mouse callback. When we return to render mode, `glRenderMode()` returns the number of hits that have been processed. We then examine the hit list. We also can change the clipping volume within the mouse callback so that we obtain hits in the desired region, usually an area that is close to the location of the mouse.

We can set the clipping volume in two ways. We could simply set the view volume through `gluOrtho2D()` (or use other viewing functions). We would probably first want to save the present clipping volume with a `glPushMatrix()`. Then any primitive that fell within this new clipping volume would generate a hit regardless of where the mouse is located. This option works for selection, but when we pick we want only those objects that render near the cursor.

Suppose that we want all the objects that render into a small, user-defined rectangle centered at the cursor. The size of the rectangle is a measure of how sensitive we want our picking to be. This rectangle is a small part of the viewport. Given the viewport, the location of the cursor, the size of the rectangle, and the viewing parameters, we can find a new viewing parameters such that all the objects in the new clipping window render into the full viewport. Thus, if we choose the new clipping window so that only the objects near the cursor are in it, we will generate hits for only a subset of the objects that can be picked. Mathematically, the calculation of the new window and viewport is an exercise in proportions and involves the inverse of the projection matrix. We can let OpenGL do this calculation for us through the GLU function `gluPickMatrix()`, that should be is applied before `gluOrtho2D()` when we are in selection mode.

void gluPickMatrix(GLdouble x, GLdouble y, GLdouble w,
    GLdouble h, GLint *vp)

creates a projection matrix for picking that restricts drawing to a **w** × **h** area centered at (**x, y**) in window coordinates within the viewport **vp**.

Assuming that we have set up the viewing conditions for normal rendering during initialization or in the reshape callback, the mouse callback is of the form

```
#define size 500
#define N 3
void mouse(int button, int state, int x, int y)
```

```
{
  GLuint nameBuffer[SIZE];
  GLint hits;
  GLint viewport[4];
  If(button == GLUT_LEFT_BUTTON && state == GLUT_DOWN)
  {
                  /* initialize the name stack */
    glInitNames();
    glPushName(0);
    glSelectBuffer(SIZE, nameBuffer);

                  /* set up viewing for selection mode */
    glGetIntegerv(GL_VIEWPORT, viewport);
    glMatrixMode(GL_PROJECTION);

                  /* save original viewing matrix */
    glPushMatrix();
    glLoadIdentity();

                  /* N X N pick area around cursor */
                  /* must invert mouse y to get in world coordinates */
    gluPickMatrix((GLdouble) x, (GLdouble)
      (viewport[3] - y), N, N, viewport);

                  /* same clipping window as in reshape callback */
    gluOrtho2D(xmin, xmax, ymin, ymax);

    glRenderMode(GL_SELECT);
    draw_objects(GL_SELECT);
    glMatrixMode(GL_PROJECTION);

                  /* restore viewing matrix */
    glPopMatrix();

                  /* return to normal render mode */
    hits = glRendrerMode(GL_RENDER);

                  /* process hits from selection mode rendering */
    processHits(hits, nameBuff);

                  /* normal render */
  }
}
void display()
{
  glClear(GL_COLOR_BUFFER_BIT);
  draw_objects(GL_RENDER);
  glFlush();
}
```

Note that we have to call the function that draws the objects directly rather than use glutPostRedisplay() in the mouse callback because GLUT will only carry out one execution of the display callback each time through the event loop. Here is a simple function that draws two partially overlapping rectangles:

```
void drawObjects(GLenum mode)
{
   if(mode == GL_SELECT) glLoadName(1);
   glColor3f(1.0, 0.0, 0.0);
   glRectf(-0.5, -0.5, 1.0, 1.0);
   if(mode == GL_SELECT) glLoadName(2);
   glColor3f(0.0, 0.0, 1.0);
   glRectf(-1.0, -1.0, 0.5, 0.5);
}
```

Note that for this example we need change only the top element on the name stack. If we had a hierarchical object in which multiple parts of the object could all be located near the cursor, we could use glPushName() so that we could have multiple names on the stack for a given hit. For an object with multiple parts, all the parts that were close to the cursor would have their names placed in the same stack.

The final piece we need to write is the function that examines the name stack. For our simple example, we will have our program print out how many hits were placed in the stack for each left mouse click and the names of any objects that were picked.

The hit buffer contains one record for each hit. Thus, every object that is rendered near the mouse cursor will generate a record. If there are no names on the hit list—no primitives were rendered near the mouse cursor—then there is a zero for the hit record from our initialization of the stack. Otherwise, we find three types of information, all stored as integers. First, there is the number of names on the name stack when there was a hit. For our example, this number can only be one. It is followed by two integers that give scaled minimum and maximum depths for the hit primitive. Because we are working in two dimensions, these values will not provide us with useful information and we skip over them. For three-dimensional applications, we can use these values to determine the front object that was picked. These three integers are followed by entries in the name stack. For our example, we will find the identifier of either the red or the blue rectangle here (a 1 or a 2). The following function will print out this information.

```
void processHits(GLint hits, GLuint buffer[])
{
   unsigned int i, j;
   GLuint names, *ptr;

   printf ("hits = %d\n", hits);
```

```
ptr = (GLuint *) buffer;
  /* loop over number of hits */
for (i = 0; i < hits; i++)
{
  names = *ptr;
      /*skip over number of names and depths */
      ptr += 3;
      /* check each name in record */
  for (j = 0; j < names; j++)
  {
      if(*ptr == 1) printf ("red rectangle\n");
      else printf("blue rectangle\n");

      /* go to next hit record */

      ptr++;
  }
 }
}
```

3.14 Programming Exercises

1. Create a simple drawing program that uses the mouse to create simple shapes such as line segments, rectangles, and triangles. You can use menus to select modes and to allow the user to change the drawing color.
2. Add a freeform drawing capability to the drawing program by using the motion callback. A user should be able to use this capability to draw polylines that approximate curves.
3. Using display lists, write an interactive program that allows the user to construct faces as seen in Section 3.12. The menus might include different parts that the user can place on the face, for example a menu of noses and a menu of eyes.
4. Take one of the programs from Chapter 2 and modify it so it works interactively. For example, for any of the programs that use a triangle, allow the user to enter the vertices with the mouse.

Basic Three-Dimensional Programming

CHAPTER

4

We shall now introduce three-dimensional OpenGL programs in a simple way. We shall start with an orthogonal camera to view objects that are defined in a similar manner to our two-dimensional programs. We shall use the same primitives that we used in two dimensions and introduce some predefined objects contained in the GLU and GLUT libraries. Finally, we shall discuss perspective views.

4.1 Cameras and Objects

The basic paradigm used to conceptualize image formation by three-dimensional graphics systems is known as the **synthetic camera model**. With this model, we emulate what is done by most real-world imaging systems, such as cameras and the human visual system. The synthetic camera model recognizes that to form an image we need two independent entities: a set of geometric objects and a viewer of these objects. Each can be specified independently of the other.

The image that is produced from a set of geometric objects and a camera, which is itself a three-dimensional object, is two-dimensional. The process of combining the specifications of objects and camera is called **projection** and is carried out by OpenGL within its pipeline. Application programs need only specify the camera and objects. Figure 4.1 shows the model. Lines called **projectors** are drawn from each point on an image and pass through the center of the lens on the camera (the **center of projection**). The place where a projector from a point on an object passes through the film plane is where the image of that point is located. Figure 4.2 shows a slightly reorganized view of the information in Figure 4.1. In this view the film plane has been moved in front of the camera and thus avoids the inversion of the image that is caused by the lens.

In computer graphics, the image on the "film plane" or **projection plane** of the synthetic camera is what we see on the screen. Equivalently, we can think of the film plane in Figure 4.2 as being ruled into pixel-sized pieces, each pixel corresponding to one or more projectors. The projection process can be described mathematically but we need not do so to write an OpenGL program in three dimensions. We need only specify the objects and camera. OpenGL will carry out the projection within its implementation.

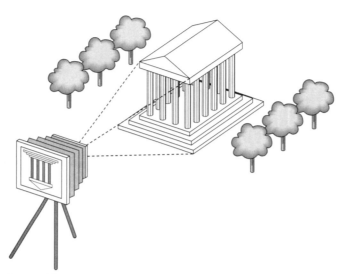

figure 4.1 Projection

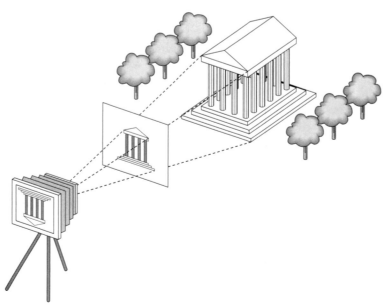

figure 4.2 Projection with projection plane moved in front of the camera

Three-dimensional objects can be specified in OpenGL through three-dimensional versions of `glVertex*()` such as `glVertex3f(x, y, z)` and `glVertex3fv(array)`. In this chapter, we shall specify the vertices directly. In the next chapter, we shall use OpenGL's transformations to create more complex objects. Thus, a triangle in three dimensions can be defined by

```
glBegin(GL_POLYGON)
    glVertex3f(0.0, 1.0, 0.0);
    glVertex3f(0.0, 0.0, 1.0);
    glVertex3f(1.0, 0.0, 0.0);
glEnd();
```

As long as the three vertices are not collinear, they define a plane and thus the interior of the triangle is well defined. If we add another vertex as in the code

```
glBegin(GL_POLYGON)
    glVertex3f(0.0, 1.0, 0.0);
    glVertex3f(0.0, 0.0, 1.0);
    glVertex3f(1.0, 0.0, 0.0);
    glVertex3f(1.0, 1.0, 2.0);
glEnd();
```

the four vertices may not lie in the same plane and in a mathematical sense the four vertices do not define a polygon. OpenGL does not check the vertices and will usually tessellate polygons as part of the rendering process. Consequently if the color does not change between the specification of the vertices, the resulting polygon will appear in a solid color. However, if a new color is assigned to each vertex, OpenGL will interpolate colors based on how it tessellates the quadrilateral. If we use light and the material properties of the surface (Chapter 6) to determine the colors of the interior, the effects of the tessellation may be noticeable.

Polygons defined by more than three vertices might not be planar.

Specifying a camera is not as straightforward as specifying objects. If we think of a real camera, we can set its position and then rotate it in three independent directions. Thus, we need six parameters (or **degrees of freedom**) for the camera position alone. We also have to specify a lens—normal, wide angle, or telephoto—and different cameras use different film sizes. OpenGL allows us to specify all these parameters for our virtual camera. We shall start, however, with a very simple camera, the one for which our two-dimensional camera is a special case. This simple camera will produce **orthographic projections**, which are the simplest type of projection.

Actually, there are two parts to the projection process. The first is deciding which objects might be visible. OpenGL's viewing functions define a **viewing** (or **clipping**) **volume** that is analogous to the volume that a real camera would see

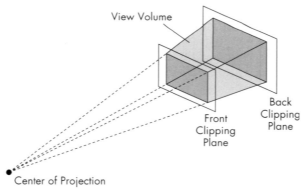

Figure 4.3 Viewing frustum

through its lens. Objects that lie outside this volume cannot appear in the image and are said to be **clipped** out of the scene. In the real world, we see only objects that are in front of the camera and even those that can be infinitely far away, as long as they are in front. In computer graphics, we add both a near and far clipping plane as in Figure 4.3 so that we see only the objects in a finite volume. Thus the clipping volume is a truncated pyramid called a **frustum**.

The second part of projection is determining where the image of a particular location on the object within the clipping volume lies on the film.

4.2 Orthographic Projections in OpenGL

We can think of an orthographic projection as constructing the type of image that we would see with a long telephoto lens. It would look somewhat flat but would preserve distances and shapes. In terms of the synthetic camera of Figure 4.2, we obtain an orthographic projection when we move the camera an infinite distance from the objects but leave the projection plane near the objects. Moving the camera to infinity makes all the projectors parallel, and the center of projection can be replaced by a **direction of projection**. The viewing frustum becomes a right parallelepiped—a rectangular box—as shown in Figure 4.4.

The fundamental orthographic viewing function is glOrtho(), which we can use to set up the proper viewing matrix.

void glOrtho(GLdouble left, GLdouble right, GLdouble bottom,
**   GLdouble top, GLdouble near, GLdouble far)**

sets up an orthographic projection matrix and defines a viewing volume, which is a right parallelepiped. The distances are measured *from the camera*, so we should have **right > left, top > bottom, far > near.**

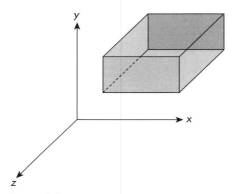

Figure 4.4 Orthographic viewing volume

The viewing volume is shown in Figure 4.4. Note that gluOrtho2D() is derived from glOrtho() by setting near and far to −1 and +1 respectively.

Viewing with an orthographic camera is particularly simple. Suppose that we want to alter the projection matrix. The glOrtho() function changes the present matrix incrementally, so we usually start by loading an identity matrix. Hence, the code for a cubic clipping volume of side length 2, centered at the origin, is

```
glMatrixMode(GL_PROJECTION):
glLoadIdentity();
glOrtho(-1.0, 1.0, -1.0, 1.0, -1.0, 1.0);
```

4.3 Viewing a Cube

We can write a simple three-dimensional program analogous to our first two-dimensional program by defining an object within a display callback. We shall discuss modeling objects a bit later. For now, we can use an object supplied by GLUT, a wire-frame cube. The wire-frame cube is composed of line segments. The solid cube is built from polygons. GLUT also has functions to define spheres, cones, tori, regular polyhedra (dodectahedra, octahedra, tetrahedra, icosahedra), and a famous graphics object known as the Utah teapot. We shall examine these objects at the end of this chapter.

void glutWireCube(GLdouble size)

void glutSolidCube(GLdouble size)

generates wire frame and solid cubes centered at the origin with sides of length **size** aligned with the coordinate axes.

Thus, we can display the cube using the display callback (for a double buffered display)

```
void display()
{
  glClear(GL_COLOR_BUFFER_BIT);
  glutWireCube(0.5);
  glutSwapBuffers();
}
```

and the basic `init()` and `main()`

```
void init
{
  glClearColor(0.0, 0.0, 0.0, 0.0);
  glColor3f(1.0, 1.0, 1.0);
  glMatrixMode(GL_PROJECTION);
  glLoadIdentity();
  glOrtho(-1.0, 1.0, -1.0, 1.0, -1.0, 1.0);
}

int main(int argc, char** argv)
{
  glutInit(&argc,argv);
  glutInitDisplayMode(GLUT_SINGLE | GLUT_RGB);
  glutInitWindowSize(500,500);
  glutInitWindowPosition(0,0);
  glutCreateWindow("simple");
  glutDisplayFunc(display);
  init();
  glutMainLoop();
}
```

4.4 Locating the Camera

One problem with our example is that the camera is pointed at one face of the cube and we will see only one face of the cube. If we want to see the other faces of the cube so as to see more of its three-dimensional structure, we have to either move the camera or the object. It turns out that in OpenGL, these operations are the same. Moving an object relative to a fixed camera and moving a camera relative to a fixed object produce the same image. In computer graphics, the difference between these views is less real than in the real world, where there is an obvious difference between walking around the side of a building to see the other side and asking someone to rotate the building. The mathematical equivalence of these two approaches is implemented through the model-view matrix, whose name expresses this equivalence.

Given this point of view, it would seem to make sense to rotate the cube and perhaps move it away from the origin. There are two ways we could do this. We could compute new locations for the vertices of the cube. However, because we are using the cube from GLUT, we do not have direct access to these vertices. The second approach would be to use transformations. We could then rotate the cube and then translate it to the desired new location. However, we have yet to discuss transformations, and computing the parameters for a desired view can be tricky. OpenGL provides a helpful function, `gluLookAt()`, within the GLU library that provides a simple user interface for many viewing situations.

Suppose that we have some objects whose locations we know. To obtain a desired view, we can position and orient the camera within the world coordinate system. We can decide on a position for the camera (called the **eye point**) and decide where to aim it to by specifying a point at which it is pointing (the **at point**). This situation is shown in Figure 4.5. Note that the two points do not fully fix the camera as we can still rotate the camera about the line between the eye and at points and not violate the specifications. We need a third input, the direction we want to consider as up in the image (the **up vector**). Technically, OpenGL will project this vector onto the back of the virtual camera to obtain the up direction. As long as the vector between the eye and at points is not parallel to the up vector, there is not a problem. A simple choice of the up vector is often $(0, 1, 0)$ or the y direction in world coordinates.

---

void gluLookAt(GLdouble eyex, GLdouble eyey, GLdouble eyez, GLdouble atx, GLdouble aty, GLdouble atz, GLdouble upx, GLdouble upy, GLdouble upz)

determines a matrix that can be used to position and orient the camera using a camera location (the **eye** point), a point (the **at** point) to aim it, and the desired **up** direction.

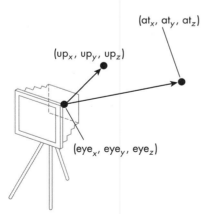

(at_x, at_y, at_z)

(up_x, up_y, up_z)

(eye_x, eye_y, eye_z)

Figure 4.5 Specifying the camera with the at vector

Figure 4.6
Isometric image of a cube

The matrix determined by gluLookAt() is applied to the existing matrix. Hence, we must first make sure we are in the desired matrix mode, usually the model-view mode, and have initialized this matrix.

Suppose that we want an isometric view of the cube, which is centered at the origin and aligned with the axes in world coordinates. An isometric view (Figure 4.6) is symmetric with respect to the vertices of the cube. A simple way to obtain such a view is to place the camera on a line passing through the origin and the point $(1, 1, 1)$. Thus, we can set up our viewing by the OpenGL code

```
glMatrixMode(GL_MODELVIEW);
glLoadIdentity();
gluLookAt(1.0, 1.0, 1.0, 0.0, 0.0, 0.0, 0.0, 1.0, 0.0);
```

The implementation of the function gluLookat() consists of the required translations and rotations to set up the view.

4.4.1 A Cube Display Program

Putting everything together, we get a minimal three-dimensional program.

```
#include <GL/glut.h>

void display()
{
  glClear(GL_COLOR_BUFFER_BIT);
  glMatrixMode(GL_MODELVIEW);
  glLoadIdentity();
  gluLookAt(1.0, 1.0, 1.0, 0.0, 0.0, 0.0, 0.0, 1.0, 0.0);
  glutWireCube(0.5);
  glutSwapBuffers();
}

void reshape(int w, int h)
```

```
{
  glViewport(0, 0, w, h);
  glMatrixMode(GL_PROJECTION);
  glLoadIdentity();
  glOrtho(-4.0, 4.0, -4.0, 4.0, -4.0, 4.0);
}

void init()
{
  glClearColor(1.0, 1.0, 1.0, 1.0);
  glColor3f(0.0, 0.0, 0.0);
}

int main(int argc, char** argv)
{
  glutInit(&argc,argv);
  glutInitDisplayMode(GLUT_DOUBLE | GLUT_RGB);
  glutInitWindowSize(500, 500);
  glutInitWindowPosition(0, 0);
  glutCreateWindow("cube");
  glutReshapeFunc(reshape);
  glutDisplayFunc(display);
  init();
  glutMainLoop();
}
```

Note that we are using the default colors so we could have left out the color functions in `init()`. The program is not interactive, so double buffering is not required and we could have located the camera in `init()`. However, our choices are probably better as we want to expand this structure to interactive three-dimensional applications.

Although we could have obtained the same isometric view of the cube by placing the eye point anywhere along the line from the origin through the point $(1, 1, 1)$, if we changed the eye point we would have also had to change the near and far distances in `glOrtho()` because these distances are measured *from the origin in eye space*.

 The clipping volume set in `glOrtho()` is measured from the origin in eye space. Thus, the near distance should be less than the far distance.

4.5 Building Objects

Let's redo the example, building our own cube. This time, we shall use polygons and give a different color to each face. We will center the cube at the origin and let it have sides of length 2. We could start with code something like

```
void cube()
{
  glColor3f(1.0, 0.0, 0.0);
  glBegin(GL_POLYGON);
    glVertex3f(-1.0, -1.0, -1.0);
    glVertex3f(-1.0, 1.0, -1.0);
    glVertex3f(-1.0, 1.0, 1.0);
    glVertex3f(-1.0, -1.0, 1.0);
  glEnd();

/* the other faces */
.
.
.
}

void display()
{
  glClear(COLOR_BUFFER_BIT);
  cube();
}
```

Note that we will be filling the polygons, we should be sure that we specify the vertices in a counterclockwise manner when each face is viewed from the outside so that we will have the correct interpretation of its orientation (front or back facing).

This code requires 42 function calls within cube() to define the cube. We could do slightly better if we use the type GL_QUADS rather than GL_POLYGON in the first glBegin(). We could then eliminate all subsequent uses of glBegin() and omit all the calls to glEnd() except the last because each consecutive group of four vertices would determine a quad.

4.5.1 Using Arrays

We can obtain a better structure for the code by putting the colors and the vertices in arrays. This structure will not only make the code clearer but will also prove more flexible for interactive applications.

We number the vertices as in Figure 4.7. The necessary arrays are then

```
GLfloat vertices[][3] = {{-1.0, -1.0, 1.0}, {-1.0, 1.0, 1.0},
  {1.0, 1.0, 1.0}, {1.0, -1.0, 1.0}, {-1.0, -1.0, -1.0},
  {-1.0, 1.0, -1.0}, {1.0, 1.0, -1.0}, {1.0, -1.0, -1.0}};

GLfloat colors[][3] = {1.0, 0.0, 0.0}, {0.0, 1.0, 1.0},
  {1.0, 1.0, 0.0}, {0.0, 1.0, 0.0}, {0.0, 0.0, 1.0},
  {1.0, 0.0, 1.0}};
```

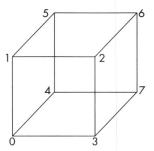

figure 4.7 Numbering of
cube vertices

We could use the previous code simply by substituting glColor3fv() for glColor3f() and glVertex3fv() for glVertex3f(), but that would not be much of a gain. Instead we add a simple function that draws a single polygon in terms of the indices of the vertices.

```
void polygon(int a, int b, int c, int d)
{
  glColor3fv(colors[a]);
  glBegin(GL_POLYGON);
    glVertex3fv(vertices[a]);
    glVertex3fv(vertices[b]);
    glVertex3fv(vertices[c]);
    glVertex3fv(vertices[d]);
  glEnd();
}
```

This function assigns a color to the polygon from the first index, but we could change this choice easily. We can now replace the cube function by

```
void cube()
{
  polygon(0, 3, 2, 1);
  polygon(2, 3, 7, 6);
  polygon(3, 0, 4, 7);
  polygon(1, 2, 6, 5);
  polygon(4, 5, 6, 7);
  polygon(5, 4, 0, 1);
}
```

Although the execution of this code does not save us any function calls, it is a lot cleaner than our previous example. One of its advantages is that the location of each vertex appears only once. In an interactive program, where vertices might be changed by the user during program execution, making changes to vertices is particularly simple.

4.5.2 Vertex Arrays

OpenGL provides a facility called **vertex arrays** that extends the use of arrays in a way that avoids most of the function calls to draw the cube. The main idea is that information stored in arrays can be stored on the clients (the application programs) and accessed by a single function call. We can store the information in a way that retains the structuring that we defined above, such as the order in which vertices are called to draw the cube.

OpenGL provides support for six types of arrays: vertex, color, color index, normal, texture coordinate, and edge flag. We shall see some of the other types later. There are three steps in using vertex arrays. First, like other OpenGL features, we must enable their functionality. Second, we must specify the format of the arrays. These two steps are usually part of the initialization phase of our programs. Finally, we use the arrays to render the scene.

In our example, we need only color and vertex arrays. We enable them by

```
glEnableClientState(GL_COLOR_ARRAY);
glEnableClientState(GL_VERTEX_ARRAY);
```

The form of the arrays is given by

```
glVertexPointer(3, GL_FLOAT, 0, vertices);
glColorPointer(3, GL_FLOAT, 0, colors);
```

> **void glEnableClientState(GLenum array)**
>
> **void glDisableClientState(GLenum array)**
>
> enables and disables arrays of types **GL_VERTEX_ARRAY**, **GL_COLOR_ARRAY**, **GL_INDEX_ARRAY**, **GL_NORMAL_ARRAY**, **GL_TEXTURE_COORD_ARRAY**, or **GL_EDGE_FLAG_ARRAY**.
>
> **void glVertexPointer(GLint dim, GLenum type, GLsizei stride, GLvoid *array)**
>
> **void glColorPointer(GLint dim, GLenum type, GLsizei stride, GLvoid *array)**
>
> provides the information on arrays. The data are in **array**, **dim** is the dimension of the data (two, three, or four), **type** denotes how the data are stored (**GL_SHORT**, **GL_INT**, **GL_FLOAT**, or **GL_DOUBLE**), and **stride** is the number of bytes between consecutive data values (0 means the data are packed in the array).

The first value (3) denotes that the data are three-dimensional. The second and third parameters indicate that the data are floats packed in the arrays given by the fourth paramater.

We need a new array that stores the indices in the order in which we want to use them. The following array contains the necessary information

```
GLubyte cubeIndices[] = {0, 3, 2, 1, 2, 3, 7, 6, 0, 4, 7, 3,
     1, 2, 6, 5, 4, 5, 6, 7, 0, 1, 5, 4};
```

Now we can draw the cube through the function glDrawElements().

void glDrawElements(GLenum mode, GLsizei n, GLenum type,
    void *indices)

draws elements of type **mode** using **n** indices from the array **indices** for each. The array is of **type** (**GL_UNSIGNED_BYTE**, **GL_UNSIGNED_SHORT**, or **GL_UNSIGNED_INT**).

If we render each face individually, we can use the loop

```
for(i = 0; i < 6; i++) glDrawElements(GL_POLYGON, 4,
     GL_UNSIGNED_BYTE, cubeIndices);
```

However, there is a simpler way if we recall that when we use the type GL_QUADS, each successive group of four vertices determines a new quad. Thus, a single function call suffices:

```
glDrawElements(GL_QUADS, 24, GL_UNSIGNED_BYTE, cubeIndices);
```

There is a subtle problem here. When we execute glDrawElements(), all the enabled arrays are rendered. Thus, the rendering is equivalent to what we would see from code of the form

```
glColor3fv(color(cubeIndices[0]));
glVertex3fv(vertex(cubeIndices[0]));
glColor3fv(color(cubeIndices[1]));
glVertex3fv(vertex(cubeIndices[1]));
/* etc */
```

Thus, the code is as if there is a color change before each vertex. We avoided one potential problem by making sure we had the same number of colors as vertices. But we saw in Chapter 2 that the default shading model is smooth. If we assign a different color before each vertex, OpenGL by default will interpolate these vertex colors across the face of each polygon. We can avoid this problem by requesting flat shading:

```
glShadeModel(GL_FLAT);
```

Now, although the color array will be used at each vertex, only the last color for each polygon will be used in the rendering. Thus each time that we render the cube using vertex arrays, we need make but a single function call, which is a dramatic improvement from our original 42 function calls.

We could have also used display lists to reduce the overhead of drawing the cube. If we put the entire cube in one display list, we could have done a single glCallList(). Which form we use will depend on the particular requirements of the application.

4.6 Hidden-Surface Removal

The next problem that we must confront is how to make sure that surfaces that a viewer would not see are not visible in the rendered image. In Chapter 2, we saw a solution for a special case of this **hidden-surface removal** problem, namely that we could cull the back-facing polygons by enabling culling and saying we want the backfaces culled

```
glEnable(GL_CULL_FACE);
glCullFace(GL_BACK);
```

However, this tactic works only for convex objects. Although the cube is convex, we need a more general approach.

Thus far, we are working with polygons that are rendered as opaque or solid. In the real world, a viewer of a scene composed of such objects would not see the parts of any polygons that are behind some other polygons. In some situations, such as with convex objects, we can simply not render back-facing polygons. We can also think about strategies based upon the painter's algorithm, which says that if we can sort the polygons in terms of the distance from the camera, we can render them back to front, with the front polygons hiding the ones further back. Aside from issues of efficiency and establishing under what circumstance such an approach will always work, the problem is that this type of approach cannot work with a pipeline renderer. Polygons (and other primitives) can be generated in an arbitrary order by an application program. With immediate-mode rendering, the default in OpenGL, each polygon is sent down the rendering pipeline as soon as it is defined and thus our method for doing hidden-surface removal must be independent of this order.

The method used by OpenGL for hidden-surface removal is called the **z-buffer algorithm**. It is based on using some extra storage to store depth information about the polygons the renderer has seen during the rendering process. This extra storage is called the **z** or **depth buffer**. Although the user need not know the details of the algorithm, she must enable it and clear the depth buffer before the beginning of the display process. In most programs, the depth buffer should be cleared whenever the color buffer is cleared. Because these operations have to be within the user program, this is the only case where a user needs to know which algorithm is used in the rendering process. In contrast, for other operations, such as drawing lines or filling polygons, the user does not need know anything about the particular algorithms employed by the implementation.

In the initialization, we have to request a depth buffer, so a typical `glutInitDisplayMode()` now looks like

```
glutInitDisplayMode(GLUT_RGB | GLUT_DOUBLE | GLUT_DEPTH);
```

We have to enable depth buffering by

```
glEnable(GL_DEPTH_TEST);
```

and finally, we usually clear the depth buffer when we clear the color buffer in the display callback

```
glClear(GL_COLOR_BUFFER_BIT | GL_DEPTH_BUFFER_BIT);
```

For most programs, that's all we need to do. For more complex situations, such as when we use translucent materials, we will need a few more functions to give us finer control over the depth buffer, but we need not worry about these issues here.

The depth buffer must be enabled and cleared for hidden surface removal.

4.7 GLU and GLUT Objects

We can construct our own objects from the simple set of primitives. Later in Chapter 9 we will introduce curves and surfaces so we can escape from the flat world of lines and polygons. However, in many situations we want a slightly more sophisticated set of objects without introducing the heavy machinery required to deal with curves and surfaces. Of particular importance in many applications are **quadrics**: ellipsoids (including spheres), cones, and cylinders. Both GLUT and GLU provide functions to render some of these objects. What they both really do is provide polygonal approximations to these objects and let the user determine how many polygons should be used. However, the user can access each object with a single function call, thus avoiding the need to build the objects within the application program.

GLU quadrics and GLUT objects are constructed from polygons and may not look smooth if they are not defined with a sufficient number of polygons.

4.7.1 GLU Quadrics

GLU provides three types of quadrics: spheres, cylinders, and disks. These primitives are stored in a more complex way than the simple primitives that we have seen thus far. In particular, we can create these objects with a desired drawing style, with different styles of normals (which we will use in Chapter 6 for lighting calculations), and with texture coordinates (which we will discuss in Chapter 8). Because these objects require more complex data structures than do the simple primitives, they require a little more effort to define. All can be created and deleted through `gluNewQuadric()` and `gluDeleteQuadric()`. Creation returns a pointer to the object that we can use to enter information into its data structure.

> **GLUquadricObj* gluNewQuadric()**
>
> creates a new quadric object and returns a pointer to it.
>
> **void gluDeleteQuadric(GLUquadricObj *obj)**
>
> deletes quadric **obj**.

We can render a quadric object in four ways: displaying points for the vertices of the polygons used to approximate the quadric, displaying the edges of the polygons, filling the polygons, or in a mode (**silhouette mode**) that draws lines between vertices except those between coplanar polygons. These styles are set by `gluQuadricDrawStyle()`.

> **void gluQuadricDrawStyle(GLUquadricObj *obj, GLenum style)**
>
> sets the drawing style (**GLU_POINT, GLU_LINE, GLU_FILL, GLU_SILHOUETTE**) for quadric object **obj**.

We can have OpenGL generate the normals for shading by `gluQuadricNormals()` and the texture coordinates by `gluQuadricTexture()`.

> **void gluQuadricNormals(GLUquadricObj *obj, GLenum mode)**
>
> specifies the normal **mode** for quadric object obj: no normals (**GLU_NONE**), which is the default; one normal per polygon (**GLU_FLAT**); or one normal per vertex (**GLU_SMOOTH**).

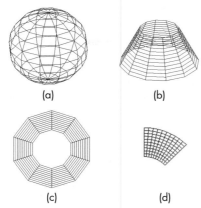

Figure 4.8 GLU quadrics (a) sphere (b) cylinder
(c) disk and (d) partial disk

void gluQuadricTexture(GLUquadricObj *obj, GLboolean mode)

specifies if quadric object **obj** should have texture coordinates generated. The default is
GL_FALSE for no texture coordinates.

Now we can set which object we would like the quadric to be through one
of the functions **gluSphere()**, **gluCylinder()**, **gluDisk()**, or **gluPartialDisk()**.
These objects are shown in Figure 4.8, rendered with lines.

Spheres are approximated using lines of longitude and latitude to create the
approximating polygons. We can use OpenGL transformations to move the
sphere, rotate it, or to scale it into an ellipsoid.

void gluSphere(GLUquadricObj *obj, GLdouble radius, GLint slices,
    GLint stacks)

renders quadric object **obj** as a sphere centered at the origin with the given **radius**. The
sphere is approximated with polygons using **slices** lines of longitude and **stacks** lines of
latitude.

The cylinder is aligned with the z axis. Its base is always in the plane $z = 0$, and
its height, top radius, and bottom radius are set by gluCylinder(). The approximating polygons are determined by the number of stacks we want in z and how
many slices we want going around it. Just as with the sphere we can move, orient,
or scale it with OpenGL transformations.

> **void gluCylinder(GLUquadricObj *obj, GLdouble base, GLdouble top, GLdouble height, GLdouble slices, GLdouble stacks)**
>
> renders quadric object **obj** as a centered cylinder of **height** aligned with the z axis whose base is in the plane $z = 0$. The cylinder has the specified **base** and **top** radii. The polygons are determined by using **stacks** lines in the z direction and **slices** lines around the cylinder.

Disks are flat and have a hole in the center. They are created in the plane $z = 0$. Disks are defined by the radii of the inner and outer circles. They are displayed as concentric rings that are sliced radially like a pie. Partial disks are disks with a wedge removed. The wedge is specified by at what angle it starts and how many degrees are in the wedge. Angles are measured from the positive y axis.

> **void gluDisk(GLUquadricObj* obj, GLdouble inner, GLdouble outer, GLint slices, GLint rings)**
>
> defines a disk in the plane $z = 0$ by its **inner** and **outer** radii. The polygons are formed from concentric **rings** and **slices** around the center.
>
> **void gluPartialDisk(GLUquadricObj* obj, GLdouble inner, GLdouble outer, GLint slices, GLint rings, GLdouble start, GLdouble angle)**
>
> defines a disk with a wedge of **angle** degrees removed starting at **start**.

A typical sequence to create a sphere might look like

```
GLUquadricObj *mySphere;
mySphere = gluNewQuadric();
gluQuadricDrawStyle(mySphere, GLU_LINE);
```

We could create the sphere in `init()` or `main()`. Now we could draw the sphere of radius 1.0 with 12 divisions for both longitude and latitude in the display callback by

```
gluSphere(mySphere, 1.0, 12, 12);
```

4.7.2 GLUT Objects

GLUT adds a few more objects. These functions generate normals automatically and all but the teapot do not generate texture coordinates. Rather than attach the rendering style to the object, each type of object has a function that generates it as a wireframe and a second that generates it with filled polygons. In addition to the cube we have already seen, there is a sphere, a cone, a torus, some regular polyhedra, and the Utah teapot. The wire cone and wire torus are shown in Figure 4.9, the regular wire polyhedra in Figure 4.10, and the wire teapot in Figure 4.11.

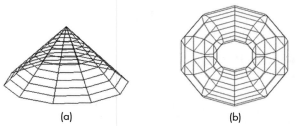

(a)   (b)

Figure 4.9 GLUT (a) cone and (b) torus

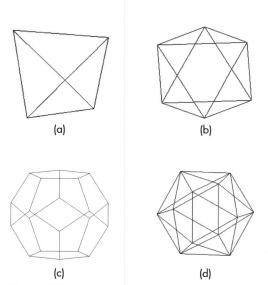

(a)   (b)

(c)   (d)

Figure 4.10 GLUT platonic solids (a) tetrahedron (b) octahedron (c) dodecahedron and (d) icosahedron

Figure 4.11 GLUT teapot

void glutWireSphere(GLdouble radius, GLint slices, GLint stacks)

void glutSolidSphere(GLdouble radius, GLint slices, GLint stacks)

generates polygonal approximations to a sphere centered at the origin with the specified **radius**, through **stacks** lines of latitude and **slices** lines of longitude.

void glutWireCone(GLdouble base, GLdouble height, GLint slices,
    GLint stacks)

void glutSolidCone(GLdouble base, GLdouble height, GLint slices,
    GLint stacks)

generates a polygonal approximation to a cone with its **base** in the plane $z = 0$ and the given **height**. Polygons are formed by **stacks** lines of latitude and **slices** lines of longitude.

void glutWireTorus(GLdouble inner, GLdouble outer, GLint sides,
    GLint slices)

void glutSolidTorus(GLdouble inner, GLdouble outer, GLint sides,
    GLint slices)

defines a torus aligned with the z axis by its **inner** and **outer** radii, **sides** divisions for radial sections, and **slices** around the torus.

The regular polyhedral objects, know as the Platonic solids, are all defined with their vertices on a sphere of radius one.

void glutWireTetrahedron()

void glutSolidTetrahedron()

void glutWireOctahedron()

void glutSolidOctahedron()

void glutWireDodecahedron()

void glutSolidDodecahedron()

void glutWireIcosahedron()

void glutSolidIcosahedron()

generate the regular polyhedra (Platonic solids) with all vertices on the unit sphere.

The Utah teapot is generated using OpenGL surfaces. The teapot has been used for many years for testing rendering algorithms. It is constructed from 192 vertices. The teapot is generated with both normals and texture coordinates.

void glutWireTeapot(GLdouble size)

void glutSolidTeapot(GLdouble size)

generates the Utah teapot of a given **size**.

4.8 Perspective Projections

Now that we have the basics down, we can look at more general viewing. Perspective viewing implements the synthetic camera model in Figure 4.1. The viewing volume is limited on the sides by four planes that meet at the center of projection forming an infinite viewing pyramid. However, just as with orthogonal viewing, we have near and far clipping planes. The resulting clipping frustum is shown in Figure 4.12. Note that the projection plane can be anywhere in front of the camera.

OpenGL provides the function `glFrustum()` to create the required matrix for perspective viewing. Its parameters are the same as for `glOrtho()`.

void glFrustum(GLdouble left, GLdouble right, GLdouble bottom, GLdouble top, GLdouble near, GLdouble far)

defines a matrix for perspective projection. The front and back clipping planes are determined by **near** and **far**, which are measured from the center of projection and must be positive with **far > near**. The bottom-left and top-right corners of the front clipping plane are (**left**, **bottom**, **near**) and (**right**, **top**, **near**) in camera coordinates.

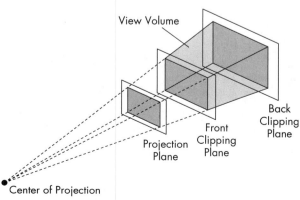

Figure 4.12 Viewing frustum for perspective projections

Unlike the orthographic projection where the camera can lie inside the clipping volume, in perspective viewing the viewing frustum must be in front of the camera. All the parameters are in camera coordinates, so both the near and far distances must be positive with the far distance greater than the near distance.

> Remember that the parameters for viewing are in camera or viewing coordinates. The near and far parameters are measured from the camera to the clipping planes. For perspective views, you should have **far > near > 0**.

The matrix calculated by `glFrustum()` is applied to the current matrix. We must make sure that we are in the proper matrix mode first, and usually we start with an identity matrix so the following sequence is standard

```
glMatrixMode(GL_PROJECTION);
glLoadIdentity();
glFrustum(left, right, bottom, top, near, far);
```

Just as with orthographic views, the projection matrix defines the clipping volume and the type of projection, but not the position and orientation of the camera. The camera in OpenGL is at the origin pointed in the negative z direction. Changes to the viewing via `glFrustum()` are equivalent to changing the lens on a camera but not its position. To change position or orientation, we must move the objects relative to the camera through the model-view matrix, either through OpenGL transformations or with `gluLookAt()`.

Although the viewing volumes formed by `glFrustum()` are fairly general, the interface provided by `glFrustum()` can make it difficult to obtain a desired view. The problem is that as we change the distance between the near and far planes, the angles that the sides of the frustum make with respect to its center can change dramatically. As a user changes these distances to get the desired objects into the scene, object on the sides can be lost as these angles change. A more natural interface is closer to what we do with a real camera. When we want to see more objects with a camera in a fixed location, we change the lens and get one with a wider angle of view. The function `gluPerspective()` provides such an interface.

void gluPerspective(GLdouble fov, GLdouble aspect, GLdouble near, GLdouble far)

specifies a projection matrix by the angle of view (**fov**) in the y direction, the **aspect** ratio of the **near** and **far** clipping planes, and the distances to the **near** and **far** planes.

The near and far clipping planes have the same **aspect** (width to height) ratio. However, if the aspect ratio is not one, then the top and side angles of the frustum are different. The function gluPerspective() uses the angle between the top and bottom of the frustum. Because this clipping volume can be constructed with the correct choice of parameters in glFrustum(), gluPerspective() is in the GLU library. For a user, it is often easiest to set up viewing by positioning the camera, determining the near and far distances, and then using gluPerspective() with a wide angle. Once we are happy with the other parameters, it easy then to narrow the viewing angle.

One potential problem with perspective views is loss of accuracy in depth, which can be noticeable in the display. The problem is due to the limited number of bits in the depth buffer and a nonlinear scaling that is part of the implementation of perspective projections. The problem is worst when the near plane is very close to the center of projection, something we might otherwise want to do so that we can see objects very close to the camera.

Placing the front clipping plane too close to the camera can lead to numerical errors in depth calculations for perspective views.

4.9 Programming Exercises

1. Construct a polygonal approximation to a sphere based on the idea of constructing polygons whose sides are determined by lines of constant longitude and constant latitude. Use quad strips except for triangle fans at the poles.
2. Write a program that moves the camera interactively. Display one or more objects and insure that the camera is always looking at the same spot as it moves.
3. A height field is a two-dimensional array of data in which each value in the array is the height above sea level of the corresponding point. Write a program to display such data in three dimensions as a polygonal mesh.
4. Write an interactive program that will allow the user to enter the vertices of a polygon in the plane $y = 0$. Your program should then allow the user to extrude this polygon into a three-dimensional object by extending lines straight up from each vertex, thus defining the sides of the object. The top will be the same as the original polygon raised to the same height as the sides.

Transformations

Transformations are the key to manipulating geometric objects, to animating scenes, and to obtaining the desired views. We present the fundamentals of transformations in OpenGL. Rather than deriving the various common transformations, such as rotation, translation, and scaling, we shall concentrate on using the transformation functions in OpenGL. We shall show how to use transformations to model a variety of phenomena.

5.1 Line-Preserving Transformations

In computer graphics we work with two fundamental geometric entities: points (or vertices), which are positions in space, and directions or **vectors**. Although each type can be specified in a similar manner, each describes something different from the other. For example, in three dimensions we can talk about the point $(1, 0, 0)$ and the direction $(1, 0, 0)$. The point is fixed in space in its coordinate system. The vector points in the positive x direction but has no position. Both can be transformed. We can move from one indicate another or we can rotate a vector to indicate another direction.

Transformations map vertices and vectors to other vertices and vectors. There are infinite ways that we can transform points to points or directions to directions, but in computer graphics we are interested in one important property for all our transformations: they must preserve lines and line segments. The reasons are both practical and physical.

In the physical world, many of the operations that we perform on objects preserve lines. Consider, for example, translations and rotations. If we start with a cube and rotate it about one of its edges, we still have a cube. Likewise, if we pick up the cube and move it somewhere else, we still have a cube. If we carry out any sequence of rotations and translations of this cube, none of its fundamental geometric properties, such as its size or its angles, are changed. For this reason, rotations and translations are known as **rigid-body transformations**.

All the primitives that we have used so far are defined by vertices. Most use vertices to define line segments that are primitives themselves or form the edges of polygons. Vertices and vectors flow down the OpenGL pipeline. They are assembled into primitives at the end of the pipeline after OpenGL has determined those that are visible. Consider what would happen if we had to implement a general transformation that could transform, for example, a line segment into a curve. We would have to compute all the intermediate points on the curve from points on the line segment, an operation that would not fit with our pipeline. If we restrict ourselves to transformations that preserve line segments, then we need only transform the endpoints—two vertices—of each line segment. We can then let the hardware and software construct the interior points of the transformed line segment at the end of the pipeline.

There are two classes of transformations of importance to computer graphics that preserve lines: **affine transformations** and **projective transformations**. Affine transformations include operations such as translation, rotation, and scaling. Such transformations preserve parallel lines and are reversible. Projective transformations include the perspective projections that we have discussed. Because these transformations project three-dimensional entities into two dimensions, they cannot be inverted. Both affine and projective transformations can be implemented by matrix operations involving vertices and vectors.

5.2 Homogeneous Coordinates

We have seen that many OpenGL functions are the same in two and three dimensions. In fact, there is only a single representation of two- and three-dimensional entities in OpenGL. Two dimensions is a special case of three dimensions with all two dimensional primitives lying in the plane $z = 0$. Thus the two-dimensional point (x, y) is the same as the three-dimensional point $(x, y, 0)$.

In fact, OpenGL works in four dimensions, and three dimensions is a special case. Although you need not know all the mathematics of this system, called **homogeneous coordinates**, some knowledge of this system will make some of OpenGL's functionality a little clearer. Normally, a three-dimensional point is represented internally as $(x, y, z, 1)$ and a two-dimensional point as $(x, y, 0, 1)$. It is possible to create a more general point in four dimensions, either directly or by transformations, in the form (x, y, z, w). Such a point is eventually displayed as the three-dimensional point $(x/w, y/w, z/w)$ as long as w is not zero.

Directions, such as are used for normals, are represented as $(x, y, z, 0)$ and are equivalent to points at infinity.

With this representation, all the transformations that we use for modeling, viewing, and projection are represented by 4×4 matrices that act on the homogeneous coordinate representations of points and directions. When we set up an OpenGL transformation, such as rotation or translation, we are actually setting up 4×4 matrices within OpenGL. We can also set matrices directly by specifying the necessary 16 elements.

5.3 The Model-View and Projection Transformations

A simplified view of the beginning of the OpenGL pipeline in shown in Figure 5.1. Each vertex passes through two transformations that are defined by the current model-view and projection matrices, which are part of the OpenGL state. Initially, both are set to 4 × 4 identity matrices.

Although both these matrices can be set by the same OpenGL functions, they are used for different purposes. The model-view matrix is used to position objects relative to camera. The projection matrix forms the image through projection and also helps with clipping by mapping vertices to a normalized coordinate system.

5.4 Translation

In Figure 5.2, we see a camera and an object. Suppose that in world coordinates, the object is at the origin. Because the camera in OpenGL is also at the origin, we want to move the object away from the camera, or equivalently move the camera away from the object. A simple solution would be to move one or the other along the z axis. The operation of translation adds a **displacement** to every vertex on the object. Thus, if $(x, y, z, 1)$ is the homogeneous coordinate representation of the vertex at (x, y, z), a translation moves this vertex to $(x + d_x, y + d_y, z + d_z, 1)$. We

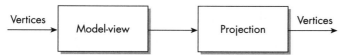

Figure 5.1 Transformation matrices in the OpenGL pipeline

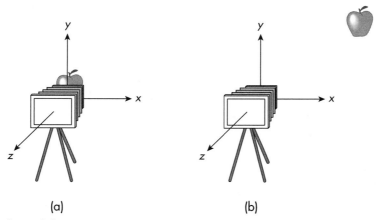

Figure 5.2 Camera and object (a) with camera and object centered at origin and (b) with object moved away from the camera

can apply the translation to all the vertices by making the model-view matrix a translation matrix using glTranslate*().

---

void glTranslate{fd}(TYPE dx, TYPE dy, TYPE dz)

alters the present matrix by multiplying it on the right by a translation matrix with parameters **dx, dy, dz. TYPE** is either GLfloat or GLdouble.

Translation is applied to the current matrix, that is the matrix determined by the current matrix mode (GL_PROJECTION or GL_MODELVIEW). Thus, if we want a pure translation matrix, we first must set the matrix mode, then initialize the matrix to an identity matrix, and finally execute glTranslate(). Thus, if we want to move all the vertices one unit down the negative z axis, we use the sequence

```
glMatrixMode(GL_MODELVIEW);
glLoadIdentity();
glTranslatef(0.0, 0.0, -1.0);
```

Note that one interpretation of parameters in glTranslate*() is that they represent the distances from a fixed camera at the origin that we want to move the objects. Thus, a positive d_x is a translation to the right of the camera, a positive d_y is a translation above the camera, and a positive d_z is a distance *behind* the camera. These distances are correct in the right-handed coordinate system in Figure 5.3.

Note also that the distances are the same as the ones used for drawing the objects; that is, they are in world coordinates.

Distances in translation are in a right-handed coordinate system. A positive displacement in z can move objects from in front of the camera to behind the camera.

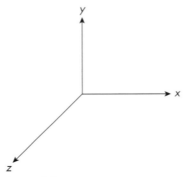

Figure 5.3 Right-handed coordinate system

5.4.1 Concatenating Translations

Now suppose that we want to create a scene with two objects in it, both in front of the camera. We could use the code

```
glMatrixMode(GL_MODELVIEW);
glLoadIdentity();
glTranslatef(0.0, 0.0, -2.0);
glutWireTetrahedron();
glLoadIdentity();
glTranslatef(0.0, 0.0, -3.0);
glutWireCube();
```

or the code

```
glMatrixMode(GL_MODELVIEW);
glLoadIdentity();
glTranslatef(0.0, 0.0, -2.0);
glutWireTetrahedron();
glTranslatef(0.0, 0.0, -3.0);
glutWireCube();
```

These two fragments produce the same output. Why? In the first case we draw a cube and a tetrahedron, each centered at the origin. The first is moved two units from the camera, and the second is moved three units from the origin. As we set the model-view matrix back to the identity matrix before we draw the second cube, the positioning of the cube and tetrahedron is completely independent of each other. In the second case, we do not reset the model-view matrix back to an identity matrix. The function glTranslate*() forms a translation matrix that is applied to the *current* matrix. Thus, the two translations are combined or **concatenated** together to form a compound transformation. In this case, we know that if we do two translations, the result is a translation by the sum of the displacements. The tetrahedron has only the result of the first translation applied to it, while the cube experiences the sum of two translations.

5.5 Rotation

Rotation is more difficult to define because there are more parameters to specify for a general rotation than for a general translation. If you take an object and rotate it, you might note that you can rotate about any axis and that there is a point, not necessarily on the object, that is unaffected by the rotation. We call this point the **fixed point** of the rotation. We also have to specify how many degrees we want to rotate about the chosen axis. Figure 5.4 shows the parameters for a general rotation. Two points, p_1 and p_2, determine a line segment that gives the direction about which we want to rotate. The point p_0 is the fixed point for the rotation and often is the center of the object that is being rotated.

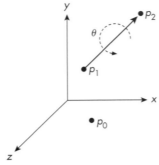

Figure 5.4 Defining a
general rotation

The rotation function in OpenGL, `glRotate*()`, assumes that the fixed point is at the origin. We will see how to deal with a general fixed point later. It forms a rotation matrix about a given axis, which is determined by a vector in three dimensions. The desired amount of rotation about this axis is measured in a counterclockwise direction looking from the positive direction along the given direction back toward the origin. Thus, in a right-handed coordinate system, a 90-degree rotation about the z axis rotates the positive x axis into the positive y axis.

 A positive direction of rotation about a vector is counterclockwise when looking from the head of the vector to its tail.

Just as with translation, rotations can be specified using floats or doubles.

void glRotate{fd}(TYPE angle, TYPE dx, TYPE dy, TYPE dz)

forms a rotation matrix about the axis given by (**dx**, **dy**, **dz**) with a fixed point of the origin. **TYPE** can be `GLfloat` or `GLdouble`.

5.5.1 Concatenation: Rotation with an Arbitrary Fixed Point

We can use both rotation and translation to obtain a rotation about a fixed point other than the origin. The idea is that we can use translation to move the fixed point to the origin. Then we can use `glRotate*()` to do the desired rotation. At the end, we have to do another translation to move the fixed point back. Thus, if we want to rotate about the direction (d_x, d_y, d_z) with the fixed point (x_f, y_f, z_f), we use the sequence

```
glMatrixMode(GL_MODELVIEW);
glLoadIdentity();
glTranslatef(xf, yf, zf);
glRotatef(angle, dx, dy, dz);
glTranslatef(-xf, -yf, -zf);
```

Note the order of the transformations. In OpenGL, the order in which the transformations are applied is the opposite of the order in which they appear in the program. In other words, *the last transformation specified is the first applied*. This unintuitive result is a consequence of the fact that each transformation defined in OpenGL is applied to the current matrix by postmultiplication. So for our example, we start with an identity matrix, then apply a translation that moves the fixed point to the origin. Then we apply the rotation to this matrix. The last translation is by the inverse of the first translation and moves the fixed point back to its original location. Because the vertices postmultiply the model-view matrix, it is this last matrix that is applied first mathematically. Of course, there is only one model-view transformation carried out on the vertices; it is the composite of the transformations that we specified.

Do not forget that the last transformation specified before drawing any geometry is the first applied.

It is important to remember that the model-view matrix is part of the state. Thus, unless we change it, all primitives that appear later in the program will also be rotated about the same fixed point. Any primitives that are in display lists that do not change the current matrices are affected by the same model-view matrix. Conversely, if any matrices are changed in a display list, these changes are in effect after the execution of the display list. We can isolate state changes in the display list by starting a display list by pushing the matrices onto the matrix stack and ending the display list by popping the matrices.

Because transformations affect the OpenGL state, be careful of changes made to matrices within display lists.

5.6 Scaling

The third standard transformation provided by OpenGL is scaling. When we scale an object, we make it bigger or smaller. However, we can scale in multiple ways. Consider the scaling of a cube in Figure 5.5. It has been made longer in one direction and shorter in the other. In the first case, the scaling factor is greater than one; in the second, it is less than one. We also note that scaling has a fixed point that is unchanged by the scaling. In Figure 5.5, the fixed point is the origin. The

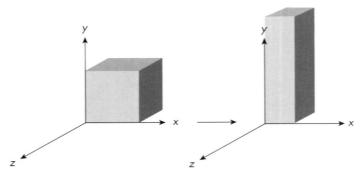

Figure 5.5 Scaling with nonuniform scale factors

function glScale*() allows us to specify different scale factors along the three axes. The fixed point is at the origin, but we can use the same technique as with rotations to obtain any desired fixed point.

> **void glScale{fd}(TYPE sx, TYPE sy, TYPE sz)**
>
> sets up a scaling matrix with scale factors **sx**, **sy**, **sz**, and a fixed point of the origin. **TYPE** is either GLfloat or GLdouble.

Scale factors less than zero are allowed and give us reflection about the axes in addition to scaling. For example, glScalef(1.0, -2.0, 0.5) will leave the *x* values unchanged, reflect about the *y* axis, elongate the object along the *y* direction, and shrink the object in the *z* direction.

5.7 A Rotating Cube

Let's put together our modeling of the cube from Chapter 4 with the idea of the rotating square from Chapter 2. This time, besides working with a three- rather than two-dimensional object, we will use transformations to do the rotation. In addition, we'll make everything interactive.

First, we pick some colors for the faces of the cube:

```
GLfloat colors[][3] = {{1.0, 0.0, 0.0}, {0.0, 1.0, 0.0},
{0.0, 0.0, 1.0}, {1.0, 1.0, 0.0}, {0.0, 1.0, 1.0},
{1.0, 0.0, 1.0}}
```

We can then modify our cube drawing function to

```
void colorcube()
{
  glColor3fv(colors[0]);
  polygon(0, 3, 2, 1);
  glColor3fv(colors[1]);
  polygon(2, 3, 7, 6);
  glColor3fv(colors[2]);
  polygon(3, 0, 4, 6);
  glColor3fv(colors[3]);
  polygon(1, 2, 6, 5);
  glColor3fv(colors[4]);
  polygon(4, 5, 6, 7);
  glColor3fv(colors[5]);
  polygon(5, 4, 0, 1);
}
```

Note that we must also remove the color functions from polygon ( ).

We will use the idle callback to add a fixed number of degrees to one of the three axes of rotation. We use the mouse callback to choose which axis about which to rotate. The display callback rotates the cube about the selected axis. In main( ) we define the callbacks

```
glutDisplayFunc(display);
glutIdleFunc(spinCube);
glutMouseFunc(mouse);
```

The mouse function is straightforward. Note that the array for the angles about each axis and the axis indicator variable are globals.

```
int axis;
float theta[3];
void mouse(int btn, int state, int x, int y)
{
  if(btn == GLUT_LEFT_BUTTON && state == GLUT_DOWN)
    axis = 0;
  if(btn == GLUT_MIDDLE_BUTTON && state == GLUT_DOWN)
    axis = 1;
  if(btn == GLUT_RIGHT_BUTTON && state == GLUT_DOWN)
    axis = 2;
}
```

The idle function increases the selected angle 2 degrees each time and stores the value modulo 360.

```
void spinCube()
{
  theta[axis] += 2.0;
  if(theta[axis] > 360.0)theta[axis] -= 360.0;
  glutPostRedisplay();
}
```

Finally, the display callback does individual rotations in the *x*, *y*, and *z* directions before drawing the cube

```
void display()
{
  glClear(GL_COLOR_BUFFER_BIT | GL_DEPTH_BUFFER_BIT);
  glLoadIdentity();
  glRotatef(theta[0], 1.0, 0.0, 0.0);
  glRotatef(theta[1], 0.0, 1.0, 0.0);
  glRotatef(theta[2], 0.0, 0.0, 1.0);
  colorcube();
  glutSwapBuffers();
}
```

5.8 Setting Matrices Directly

We can construct any affine transformation from a properly chosen sequence of rotations, translations, and scalings. Generally, we do this construction within the user program. However, there are circumstances when we want to construct a model-view or projection matrix directly or use a matrix that we form in our own program to alter an existing projection or model-view matrix.

In OpenGL, the matrices are stored in 16-element, one-dimensional arrays in column order rather than in 4×4 two-dimensional arrays. There are two functions that we can use to manipulate our own matrices: glLoadMatrix*() and glMultMatrix*(). The first function loads a user-defined array as the present matrix. The second postmultiplies the current matrix by a user-defined array.

void glLoadMatrix{fd}(TYPE *m)

loads the array **m**, of **TYPE GLfloat** or **GLdouble**, as the current matrix.

void glMultMatrix{fd}(TYPE *m)

postmultiplies the current matrix by **m**, which is of **TYPE GLfloat** or **GLdouble**.

One of the important uses of setting our own matrices is to add shear to our fundamental operations. Figure 5.6 illustrates shear applied to a two-dimensional square in the *x* direction. It is as if we had pulled the top and bottom faces in

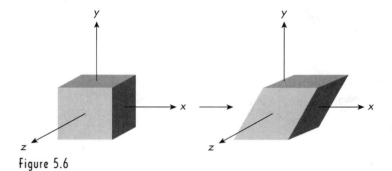

Figure 5.6

opposite directions. This operation is affine as it preserves lines and we can see that there is a fixed point for this transformation, the origin in our figure.

The required matrix is

$$M = \begin{bmatrix} 1 & \cot\theta & 0 & 0 \\ 0 & 1 & 0 & 0 \\ 0 & 0 & 1 & 0 \\ 0 & 0 & 0 & 1 \end{bmatrix}$$

Its derivation is not needed here. We can form it in our code as follows:

```
GLfloat m[16];
for(i = 0; i<16; i++)m[i] = 0.0;
m[0] = m[5] = m[10] = m[15] = 1.0;
m[4] = 1.0tan(DEG_TO_RAD*theta);

glLoadMatrixf(m);
```

We can apply shear in any of the three directions by adding or substituting cotangent terms above the diagonal in our matrix. Shear not only gives us more flexibility in creating objects but also is important in giving us more flexible viewing. For example, the projection of the cube in Figure 5.7 is known as a **oblique projection**. It is a parallel projection but cannot be obtained directly because the only parallel projection matrix we have in OpenGL is the one formed from glOrtho(). We can, however, alter the matrix formed by glOrtho() by a shear matrix similar to M to create a view as in Figure 5.7.

```
glMatrixMode(GL_PROJECTION);
glLoadIdentity();
glOrtho(left, right, bottom, top, near, far);
glMultMatrixf(m);
```

More generally, when we use glMultmatrix*(), the matrix that we form is concatenated with other matrices. The following example generates the shadow of a cube from a point light source at (x_l, y_l, z_l) by projecting it onto the plane $z = 0$.

Figure 5.7 Oblique projection of a cube

The matrix can be formed in three steps. First, we move the light source to the origin, then we do the projection. Finally, we move the light source back. The required projection matrix is given by[1]

$$M = \begin{bmatrix} 1 & 0 & 0 & 0 \\ 0 & 1 & 0 & 0 \\ 0 & 0 & 1 & 0 \\ 0 & -\dfrac{1}{y_l} & 0 & 0 \end{bmatrix}$$

The required code to set up the matrix is

```
GLfloat m[16];
for(i = 0; i < 15; i++)m[i] = 0.0;
m[0] = m[5] = m[10] = 1.0;
m[7] = -1.0/yl;
```

This time we want to render the cube twice. First we render the cube with whatever model-view matrix we have set up. We then change the color to the color assigned for the shadow and alter the model-view matrix by the two translations and the shadow projection matrix. We apply these transformations to the existing matrix because whatever transformations we applied to locate and orient the cube also apply to the shadow polygons.

```
glMatrixMode(GL_MODELVIEW);

/* set up modelview matrix and attributes for cube */

cube();

/* save matrix and color */

glPushMatrix();
glPushAttrib(GL_CURRENT_BIT);

glTranslate(xl, yl, zl);
glMultMatrix(m);
glTranslate(-xl, -yl, -zl);
```

---

1. The details of how we obtain this matrix and those in the next two examples can be found in Angel, *Interactive Computer Graphics* (Addison-Wesley, 2002). These details are not necessary to follow the code.

Figure 5.8 Cube and its projected shadow

```
/* draw shadow in black */

glColor3f(0.0, 0.0, 0.0);
cube();

/* restore matrix and color */

glPopMatrix();
glPopAttrib();
```

Note the necessity of saving (pushing) both the current color and the current model-view matrix so we can proceed with drawing other objects or redrawing the cube if it is moving. An image generated by this procedure is shown in Figure 5.8.

5.9 Transformations and Coordinate Systems

We have seen that OpenGL uses a variety of coordinate systems. Every change of coordinate systems is equivalent to a transformation. Thus, we can take two equivalent views of what the model-view transformation does. We can look at it as a transformation that moves objects relative to the camera. Or we can think of it as an operation that takes specifications of objects in world coordinates and gives their representation in camera coordinates. Both points of view are correct. From the application programmer's perspective, the first view is probably more useful. The second point of view is best suited to understanding what happens internally.

The two points of view help explain why the parameters in the viewing functions, `glOrtho()`, `glFrustum()`, and `gluPerspective()`, are measured from the camera. These transformations are almost always used to form the projection matrix. The vertices that this matrix is applied to have already been transformed by the model-view matrix and thus are already in camera coordinates. Hence, the parameters of any functions that are applied at this stage should also be in camera or eye coordinates.

If we apply the same reasoning to the projection transformation, we see that it transforms the representation of objects in camera coordinates to a representation in **clip coordinates**. Clip coordinates retain the information in homogeneous form and map vertices to a normalized volume. Once the division is done, in case the w term is not unity, vertices are in a three-dimensional coordinate system called **normalized device coordinates**. Although the mathematical process of projection maps vertices in a three-dimensional world to locations on the two-dimensional view surface, OpenGL retains three-dimensional information as long as possible so that operations such as hidden-surface removal, lighting, and texture mapping can be done as late as possible in the pipeline. Finally, the entities that are visible are mapped by the viewport transformation to **window coordinates**, where the units are in pixels.

5.10 Modeling with Transformations

Although transformations can be applied to either the model-view matrix or the projection matrix, in practice, transformations are used primarily to model objects via the model-view matrix. We shall examine two strategies. The first uses a set of standard objects to build scenes. Each object must be sized, oriented, and placed in the scene individually. In the second, we build objects that have parts that are interconnected and must move together. Here we use transformations to encapsulate these relationships.

5.10.1 Instancing

Suppose that we start with a collection of common objects, such as cubes and spheres, for which we might have the code, or they may be objects supplied by GLUT or GLU. We can build other objects by applying affine transformations to them. Often these base objects are called **symbols**, and each occurrence of one in our code is an **instance** of that symbol.

If we start with a cube, we can create an arbitrary right parallelepiped by scaling it. If we also allow shear transformations, we can create any parallelepiped from the cube. We can create any ellipsoid by nonuniformly scaling a sphere. We can then apply rotation matrices to orient these objects and translation matrices to position them. The matrix that brings the object into the model with the desired size, orientation, and position is called the **instance transformation**.

Generally the basic objects that we use to build our models are sized, located, and oriented in a convenient manner. For example, spheres are often of a unit radius with the center at the origin. Cubes may have a side of length one and their sides aligned with the coordinates axes. The GLU cylinder was aligned with the z axis and had its base in the plane $z = 0$. With such a starting point, we almost always want to scale the object to its desired size, then orient it, and finally translate it to its desired position in that order. Consequently, a typical instancing sequence looks like

```
glMatrixMode(GL_MODELVIEW);
glLoadIdentity();
glTranslatef(x, y, z);
glRotatef(theta, dx, dy, dz);
glScalef(sx, sy, sz);
```

Note again the order of the transformations.

5.10.2 Hierarchical Models

In many applications, the parts of a model depend upon each other. If we apply a transformation to one part of the model, the resulting changes cause other parts to move. In the majority of such applications, including figure animation and robotics, the models are hierarchical. The parts of such models can be organized as a tree data structure composed of nodes and links. Each node, except for the top or root node, has a parent and all nodes, except for the terminal nodes or leaves, have one or more children. Figure 5.9 shows a simple robot arm, and its hierarchical representation is shown in Figure 5.10. Figures 5.11 and 5.12 show a simple figure we might want to animate and its hierarchical representation. In these hierarchies, the position and orientation of an object can be affected by the position and orientation of its parent (and its parent's parent and so on).

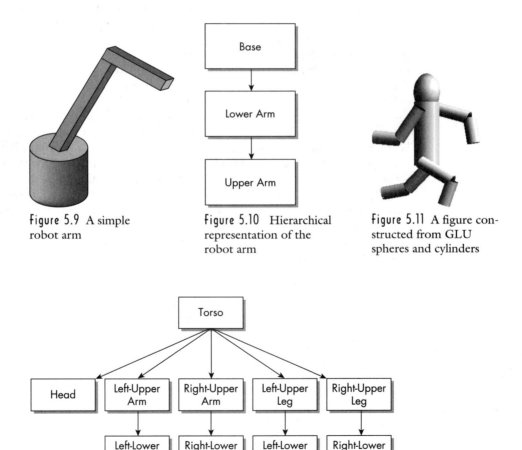

Figure 5.9 A simple robot arm

Figure 5.10 Hierarchical representation of the robot arm

Figure 5.11 A figure constructed from GLU spheres and cylinders

Figure 5.12 Hierarchical representation of the figure

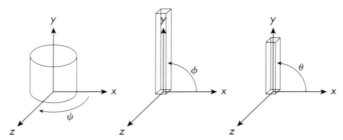

figure 5.13 Robot parts

Both of these examples have parts that are connected by joints that rotate, thus reducing animation and motion to computing a set of joint angles and then rerendering the scene when one or more of these angles change.

From an OpenGL perspective, we would like to represent these models using transformations. The instance transformations that we just presented are not quite right as they place each symbol in the scene independent of the others. However, if we recall that OpenGL transformations are applied to the current matrix, we can observe that each transformation actually represents a *relative* change from one scaling, position, and orientation to another.

Consider the simple robot. It consists of three parts: a base, a lower arm, and an upper arm. Each part can be described in its own coordinate system using standard OpenGL objects such as cylinders and scaled cubes, as shown in Figure 5.13.

Suppose that we use a cylinder for the base and scaled cubes for the upper and lower arms; then we can define the parts through three functions: `base()`, `lower_arm()`, and `upper_arm()`. Note that the quadric object has to be created within `main()` or `init()` and the various parameters describing the various lengths are defined elsewhere in the program. The use of `glPushMatrix()` and `glPopMatrix()` allows us to use the present model-view matrix to locate the entire figure while still preserving it for drawing other objects.

```
GLUquadricObj *p; /* pointer to quadric object */

void base()
{
  glPushMatrix();

/* rotate cylinder to align with y axis */

  glRotatef(-90.0, 1.0, 0.0, 0.0);

/* cylinder aligned with z axis, render with five slices for
base and five along length */

  gluCylinder(p, BASE_RADIUS, BASE_RADIUS, BASE_HEIGHT, 5, 5);
  glPopMatrix();
}
```

```
void upper_arm()
{
  glPushMatrix();
  glTranslatef(0.0, 0.5*UPPER_ARM_HEIGHT, 0.0);
  glScalef(UPPER_ARM_WIDTH, UPPER_ARM_HEIGHT,
    UPPER_ARM_WIDTH);
  glutWireCube(1.0);
  glPopMatrix();
}

void lower_arm()
{
  glPushMatrix();
  glTranslatef(0.0, 0.5*LOWER_ARM_HEIGHT, 0.0);
  glScalef(LOWER_ARM_WIDTH, LOWER_ARM_HEIGHT,
    LOWER_ARM_WIDTH);
  glutWireCube(1.0);
  glPopMatrix();
}
```

The base can rotate independently of the rest of the robot. The lower arm is attached to the base and can rotate relative to it. However, when the base rotates, it also rotates the lower arm. The upper arm can rotate with respect to the lower arm, but it is also affected by the rotation of the base and the lower arm. The lower arm is also positioned on top of the base so it must be translated up. The upper arm has to be translated up the height of the base and the length of the lower arm. The following display callback captures all these relationships. The code is incremental. Because the transformations describe the changes when each part is added to a parent, the code demonstrates that most matrices need not be recomputed when one part is changed or moved.

```
void display(void)
{

  glClear(GL_COLOR_BUFFER_BIT);
  glMatrixMode(GL_MODELVIEW);
  glLoadIdentity();
  glColor3f(1.0, 0.0, 0.0);
  glRotatef(theta[0], 0.0, 1.0, 0.0);
  base();
  glTranslatef(0.0, BASE_HEIGHT, 0.0);
  glRotatef(theta[1], 0.0, 0.0, 1.0);
  lower_arm();
  glTranslatef(0.0, LOWER_ARM_HEIGHT, 0.0);
  glRotatef(theta[2], 0.0, 0.0, 1.0);
  upper_arm();
  glutSwapBuffers();
}
```

We can add animation to this program in a number of ways. One method is to use a menu attached to one (of three) mouse buttons to choose which angle to change and use the other two buttons to increase or decrease that angle. Alternately, we could use the keyboard to choose an angle and increment or decrement it either with the keyboard or the mouse.

Our first example did not require us to save any information about the model-view matrix as we went through the display callback because the transformations accumulated. If we look at the tree in Figure 5.10, we see that it is a very simple one in which no node has more than one child. The figure model in Figure 5.11 is more complex. It comprises parts connected to a torso. Each arm and leg comprises two parts. The position and orientation of each arm and leg depend on the location and orientation of the torso but not on any other arm or leg. Let's assume that we can build the individual parts and put that information in a set of functions, such as head(), torso(), and left_upper_arm(). Each part can be located with respect to its parent by a translation and one or more rotations, depending on how the part is connected to its parent.

The display callback must **traverse** the tree in Figure 5.12. That is, we must visit every node, drawing the objects for that node using the correct model-view matrix. A standard preorder traversal travels down the left of the tree visiting each node. When we can go no further, we back up to the first right branch and repeat the process recursively. Let us see how that process works with the figure model.

First we draw the torso. It has one angle associated with it, which allows us to rotate the torso about an axis in the y direction. We then go on to the head. However, we note that we will have to come back up to the torso to get to the arms and legs. Any matrix that we apply to draw the head is not required for the arms or legs. Rather than recompute the matrix that we apply at the torso node, we can save it on the stack with a glPushMatrix(). We can then go to the node for the head, changing the model-view matrix as necessary to draw the head (which uses two joint angles). When we come back to the torso node, we recover the model-view matrix with a glPopMatrix(). We will have to come back up to the torso after dealing with the left arm, so we must to a glPushMatrix() immediately after the pop to keep a copy of the same model-view matrix. Although the code below may appear somewhat convoluted, the rule is actually very simple. Every time we go to the left at a node with another unvisited right child, we do a push, and every time we return to that node we do a pop. Note that we must do a pop at the end so that the number of pushes and the number of pops is the same.

```
void display()
{
  glClear(GL_COLOR_BUFFER_BIT | GL_DEPTH_BUFFER_BIT);
  glMatrixMode(GL_MODELVIEW);
  glLoadIdentity();
  glColor3f(1.0, 0.0, 0.0);

  glRotatef(theta[0], 0.0, 1.0, 0.0);
  torso();
  glPushMatrix();
```

```
glTranslatef(0.0, HEADX, 0.0);
glRotatef(theta[1], 1.0, 0.0, 0.0);
glRotatef(theta[2], 0.0, 1.0, 0.0);
glTranslatef(0.0, HEADY, 0.0);
head();

glPopMatrix();
glPushMatrix();
glTranslatef(LUAX, LUAY, 0.0);
glRotatef(theta[3], 1.0, 0.0, 0.0);
left_upper_arm();

glTranslatef(0.0, LLAY, 0.0);
glRotatef(theta[4], 1.0, 0.0, 0.0);
left_lower_arm();

glPopMatrix();
glPushMatrix();
glTranslatef(RUAX, RUAY, 0.0);
glRotatef(theta[5], 1.0, 0.0, 0.0);
right_upper_arm();

glTranslatef(0.0, RLAY, 0.0);
glRotatef(theta[6], 1.0, 0.0, 0.0);
right_lower_arm();

glPopMatrix();
glPushMatrix();
glTranslatef(LULX, LULY, 0.0);
glRotatef(theta[7], 1.0, 0.0, 0.0);
left_upper_leg();

glTranslatef(0.0, LLLY, 0.0);
glRotatef(theta[8], 1.0, 0.0, 0.0);
left_lower_leg();

glPopMatrix();
glPushMatrix();
glTranslatef(RULX, RULY, 0.0);
glRotatef(theta[9], 1.0, 0.0, 0.0);
right_upper_leg();

glTranslatef(0.0, RLLY, 0.0);
glRotatef(theta[10], 1.0, 0.0, 0.0);
right_lower_leg();

glPopMatrix();
glutSwapBuffers();
}
```

We can complete this program and animate in a manner similar to the robot example. For example, we can use a menu to choose which of the 11 angles to change, and either two mouse buttons or two keys to increment and decrement the chosen angle.

We can generalize this code by defining a node data structure such as the left-child right-sibling structure:

```
typedef struct treenode
{
  GLfloat m[16];
  void(*f)();
  struct treenode *sibling;
  struct treenode *child;
} treenode;
```

This structure allows us to store the matrix that is applied to the parent at each node and the function to be drawn at the node. For example, we can define the torso node by using OpenGL to compute the rotation matrix that we used above and storing it in a node, along with the other information.

```
treenode torso_node;
glLoadIdenity();
glRoatef(theta[0], 0.0, 1.0, 0.0);
glGetFloatv(GL_MODELVIEW_MATRIX), torso_node.m);
torso_node.f = torso;
torso_node.sibling = NULL;
torso_node.child = &head_node;
```

Once we have defined all the nodes, such as in init(), we can traverse the data structure in the display callback by calling code such as

```
void traverse(treenode *root)
{
  if(root == NULL)return;
  glPushMatrix();
  glMultMatrix(root -> m);
  root -> f();
  if(root.child != NULL)traverse(root -> child);
  glPopMatrix();
  if(root -> sibling(!= NULL)traverse(root -> sibling);
}

void display()
{
  glClear(COLOR_BUFFER_BIT | GL_DEPTH_BUFFER_BIT);
  glMatrixMode(GL_MODELVIEW);
  glLoadIdentity();
  traverse(&torso_node);
  glutSwapBuffers();
}
```

We can also create dynamic structures by using dynamically created nodes. For example, we can define

```
typedef treenode* tree_ptr;
```

and then

```
tree_ptr torso_ptr;
torso_ptr = malloc(sizeof(treenode));
```

Tree nodes are defined in almost the same way, using pointers. and the traversal accomplished recursively in same way as before:

```
traverse(torso_ptr);
```

One advantage of using this approach is that we can create and delete nodes within the application program, allowing us great flexibility in how we can work with our models.

5.11 Programming Exercises

1. Redo the rotating square program to work with a single mouse button. Add the ability to stop and start the rotation.
2. Write an interactive program that will display a cube and use the mouse buttons to rotate, translate, and scale it. You might, for example, have the right mouse button rotate about one axis if you move it left or right of the center of the screen and about another axis if you move up or down from the center.
3. Write a program that will have a menu of some of the GLUT and GLU objects. The user should be able to select any of the objects and place them in the scene at any desired size and orientation.
4. Using simple primitives, write a program that displays a simple house of your own design. Make the program interactive so that a user can walk through the house.

Lights and Materials

The colors that we see in the real world are based on the interaction between the materials of which the objects are composed and the lights that illuminate them. OpenGL mimics this process, using a lighting model that incorporates diffuse, specular, ambient, and emissive terms. OpenGL allows us to define a variety of light sources and material properties. We shall also consider the fourth color component in an RGBA color, the alpha value, and show how to use it to display semi-transparent surfaces.

6.1 Light-Material Interactions

Thus far, we have achieved color in a scene by simply setting a color as part of the OpenGL state and allowing this color to be associated with one or more vertices. If we do not change the color while we are defining a visible object, then this color is the one that we display. This situation is not physically realistic. The colors that we see in the real world are based on the interaction between light coming from light sources and the materials of which the objects are made. What is perhaps worse is that if we assign a fixed color to a three-dimensional object, we risk not seeing its three-dimensionality in the image. In a two-dimensional photograph or painting, objects appear to be three-dimensional because we see small variations, or **shades**, in the colors of rendered objects. These shades are determined by light-material interactions. If we simply display a red sphere in OpenGL by giving it a single color, it will appear as a uniformly colored circle. What we need to add to our OpenGL functionality is the ability to shade objects in a manner that is visibly close to what we see in images created by photographs.

In the physical world, the shades that we see are the result of a multitude of complex interactions between lights and materials. Light from sources strikes objects. Some of this light is absorbed by the surfaces and some is reflected. Objects appear in a color due to the colors of the lights striking them and which frequencies in the light are reflected. The light that is reflected from an object can be over a narrow or broad range of angles depending on the smoothness of the surface. Reflected light may then strike other surfaces, where in turn it is partially absorbed and partially reflected. If we have highly reflective materials in the scene, a significant percentage of the light will go through many such reflections before most of it is absorbed.

Consequently, for a renderer to do physically correct shading, we need a global calculation, one that uses information about all the objects and lights in the scene to compute the shade for any point. Such a calculation is beyond the capabilities of real-time rendering. In addition to the amount of calculation, global shading requires that the entire database of objects be available for the calculation. Some rendering strategies, such as ray tracing, can do global calculations for limited types of materials but these renderers are not capable of real-time performance.

OpenGL does not work globally. It uses a pipeline architecture in which each primitive is passed down the pipeline independently and, if visible, is rendered independently of all other primitives. Thus in OpenGL, shading must be done locally on a vertex-by-vertex basis.

In most situations we can do a reasonably good job with OpenGL, although scenes full of highly reflective objects probably will not render well. There are also many tricks that we can use within OpenGL to give good approximations to global calculations. For example, shadows for general scenes require a global calculation. However, we saw in the previous chapter that for the special case of a shadow on a flat surface, we could do a second rendering to obtain shadows. Nevertheless, for scenes consisting of objects that are not highly reflective, we can do a fairly good job of shading on a vertex-by-vertex basis.

6.2 The Phong Model

There are many physically based models of how light interacts with materials. Unfortunately, these models are too complex for real-time graphics. Phong proposed an approximate lighting model that is easy to compute and has been very useful in computer graphics. OpenGL uses a modified Phong model for its shading calculations and is implemented in hardware on commodity graphics cards.

Suppose that we start with the light from a point in three-dimensional space that illuminates a surface. Consider a location **P** on that surface. The Phong model is based on using the four vectors in Figure 6.1. The direction to the light source

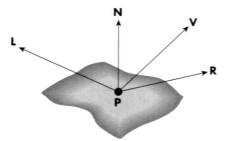

figure 6.1 Vectors used in the Phong model

from **P** is given by the vector **L**. The viewer is located in the direction **V** from **P**. Note that either the viewer or the light source could be an infinite distance from the surface. The direction that reflected light leaves the surface depends on both the direction it came from and the orientation of the surface. The local orientation at a point on the surface is given by the **normal** vector **N**, which is the perpendicular to the surface at that point. If the surface is highly reflective, it will act like a mirror and most of the light will go off in the direction of a perfect reflector **R**. In OpenGL, the direction **V** is known from the viewing specifications. We will specify **L** through our light source functions. The local normal **N** will have to be supplied by the user program. The vector **R** can be computed from **N** and **L**.

The Phong model considers four types of contributions to the shade at a point: **diffuse reflections**, **specular reflections**, **ambient reflections**, and **emissive light** from the material. The Phong model uses RGB color and is applied independently to each of the primaries. Because the light model is additive, light from multiple sources can be added together. Thus, the Phong model is computed once for each point source and the shade is determined by the sum of the contributions from all the sources.

6.2.1 Diffuse Reflection

Incoming light that strikes a surface is partially absorbed by the material and partially reflected or scattered. In a diffuse interaction, the reflected light is scattered equally in all directions. Consequently, a diffuse surface appears the same to all viewers, so the calculation of the diffuse contribution to a shade does not depend on **V**. However, the amount of the contribution does depend on the angle between the light source and the normal (Figure 6.2). A viewer will see the maximum contribution from a diffuse reflection when the light source is in the same direction as the normal. Diffuse surfaces tend to look dull like plastic. We characterize the surface by the fraction of the incoming light that is reflected by each of the RGB components. A surface has a color (when illuminated by white light) because it absorbs more light at some frequencies than at others. In the Phong model, there can be different properties for each of the RGB components. We can also modify the shading calculation to take into account the attenuation of the light due to the distance between the light source and the surface.

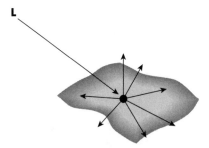

Figure 6.2 Diffuse reflections

6.2.2 Specular Reflections

A specular surface also absorbs some of the light striking it and reflects the rest. However, a specular surface is smooth and the reflected light is concentrated along the direction **R** that a perfect reflection would travel. Because this reflected light is concentrated, what the viewer sees depends on the angle between **R** and **V** (see Figure 6.3).

The smoother the surface is, the more concentrated is the reflected light. The Phong model characterizes this concentration with a **shininess coefficient**. We must also specify what fraction of the incoming light is reflected. Specular surfaces include polished materials, such as metals, and are responsible for the bright highlights that we often see in images. However, for efficiency OpenGL uses a modification of the Phong model that replaces **R** by **L** + **V**, thus avoiding the calculation of **R**.

6.2.3 Ambient Reflection

The Phong model is based on using ideal point light sources. However, the real world is characterized by sources that have a finite area. In addition, global phenomena such as multiple reflections result in light from many directions striking each point. One way to deal with this light, in a simple way, is to add a constant amount of light to every point in the scene. We call this light **ambient light**, and it is similar to the effect that we see in a room with multiple lights and diffusers that spread out the light. Ambient light is also partially absorbed and partially reflected, but the light that we see does not depend on any of the four vectors, only on the incoming light and the fraction that is reflected.

6.2.4 Emission

In the real world, light sources have a finite area and thus often are visible in a scene. In addition, a surface may both emit light and reflect light that strikes it. In the Phong model, we can add on an emissive term that is not affected by incoming light and can help model visible light sources or glowing objects. The emissive contribution from a surface is not used to calculate shading. Thus, a purely emis-

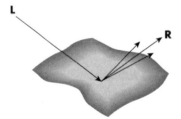

Figure 6.3 Specular reflections

sive surface appears the same regardless of any other sources or materials. Emissive light is unaffected by the position of the viewer.

6.3 OpenGL Lighting

A real light source has a finite area and a set of frequencies with corresponding strengths at which it emits light. In addition, the source may emit light differently in different directions. Such sources are far too difficult to model in a system that tries to do lighting calculations in real time. Consequently, OpenGL provides a limited variety of light sources and leaves it to the user to approximate the world by carefully controlling these sources.

In OpenGL, we can have point sources, spotlights, and ambient sources. Sources can be located either at a finite distance from the objects or at infinity. Each source can have separate diffuse, specular, and ambient properties.

For each source there are separate diffuse, specular, and ambient RGB parameters. It may appear strange that there are multiple parameter sets for each light. After all, a real light source has but one color and cannot be characterized as being both a blue diffuse source and a white ambient source. However, because we cannot do global lighting in OpenGL, we can use this added flexibility to give better approximations. For example, suppose that we have a white light in a red room. The light that hits a surface directly from the source will be white, but reflections from the red wall will add an ambient component that is red or pink. We can model this global contribution in OpenGL by using white diffuse and specular components and a red ambient component for the light source.

Materials are modeled in a complementary manner. For each surface, we must give separate ambient, diffuse, and specular components (or use default values). These parameters are the fraction of the incoming light of each type that is reflected. We can also give an emissive component to the surface. Each parameter has separate RGB values.

Lighting calculations must be enabled and each light source must be enabled individually. For a single source, we could use

```
glEnable(GL_LIGHTING);
glEnable(GL_LIGHT0);
```

Enabling lighting asks OpenGL to do the shading calculations. All colors will be assigned based on light sources and material properties rather than by glColor*(). Individual lights must be turned on and off separately.

> Once lighting is enabled, colors assigned by glColor*() are no longer used.

Light and material properties are part of the OpenGL state. So are normal vectors. Thus, the user generally must supply the normal vectors through glNormal*(). Some functions such as glutSolidTeapot() will compute normals for you. Normals are usually computed for each vertex or once for each polygon.

> **void glNormal3{bsidf}(TYPE dx, TYPE dy, TYPE dz)**
>
> **void glNormal3{bsidf}v(TYPE *v)**
>
> defines the present normal to be the vector (**dx, dy, dz**) of **TYPE** or a pointer to the array **v** of **TYPE**.

6.4 Specifying a Light Source

The main function for specifying light sources is `glLight*()`. The two forms are for scalar and vector (array) parameters. These functions will be invoked multiple times to set all the available options.

> **void glLight{if}(GLenum light, GLenum param, TYPE value)**
>
> **void glLight{if}v(GLenum light. GLenum param, TYPE *value)**
>
> sets scalar and vector parameters for OpenGL light source **light**, parameter **param** to **value**.

For a point source, we can set its (x, y, z) location (**GL_POSITION**) and its diffuse (**GL_DIFFUSE**), specular (**GL_SPECULAR**), and ambient (**GL_AMBIENT**) RGBA components. The colors properties use RGBA colors. Because we will be working with opaque surfaces for a while, we will set the fourth component to 1.0.

The defaults are slightly different for light 0 and all the other sources. The default for all lights is no ambient light. For light source 0, the default is white, (1.0, 1.0, 1.0, 1.0), for the diffuse and specular components. For all the other light sources, these defaults are black, (0.0, 0.0, 0.0, 1.0). These values allow simple lighting from one source without even specifying parameters. The default value of the position is (0.0, 0.0, 1.0, 0.0). This value is in eye coordinates, so it is behind the default camera. Note that this position is in homogeneous coordinates and the zero for the w component indicates that the source is at infinity because $w = 0$ indicates it is the representation of direction rather than of a point. We call such a source a **directional light**, and it corresponds to parallel light from the specified direction. We can define a spotlight by giving it a direction and an angle as in Figure 6.4.

The parameter name for the direction is **GL_SPOT_DIRECTION** and its default is in the negative z direction in eye space. Note that the direction is specified by the triplet (dx, dy, dz). A spotlight has an angle (**GL_SPOT_CUTOFF**) that is measured from the spotlight direction and forms a cone of light. The default is 180 degrees, for which the spotlight is a point source. The amount of

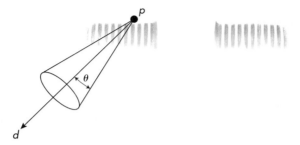

Figure 6.4 Specifying a spotlight

light within a spotlight can be made to drop off exponentially from its center by giving it a nonzero value for **GL_SPOT_EXPONENT**.

The light from a physical point light source drops off as the inverse of the distance squared from the light to the surface. This attenuation should be applied to the specular and diffuse terms. However, an ideal point source is only an approximation to real distributed light sources, and use of a purely quadratic dropoff can produce images with too much contrast. A softer, more realistic image can be obtained by using the more general form $1/(a + bd + cd^2)$ where d is the distance as computed by OpenGL and a, b, and c are the constant (**GL_CONSTANT_ATTENUTATION**), linear (**GL_LINEAR_ATTENUAT-ION**), and quadratic (**GL_QUADRATIC_ATTENUATION**) factors. The default is no attenuation ($a = 1$, $b = c = 0$).

6.4.1 Light Sources and Transformations

The position of a near light source and the direction of a distant one are given in homogeneous coordinates and are passed down the OpenGL pipeline just as are other geometric entities. Thus, they are subject to the model-view transformation in effect when they are defined. Consequently, depending on where in the code we define a light source's position or direction, we can have a light source fixed in position as the viewer or objects move, have a light source that moves around while the objects and viewer are stationary, or have the viewer, the objects, and the light source all moving independently.

Consider the following code fragments for an application with an initialization function, `init()`; an idle callback, `idle()`; and a display callback, `display()`. If we want the light source to remain stationary, we set its location in `init()` and never change it.

```
void init()
{
  GLfloat light_pos[] = {1.0, 2.0, 3.0, 1.0};
    /* rest of init() */
```

```
        glEnable(GL_LIGHTING);
        glEnable(GL_LIGHT0);
        glMatrixMode(GL_MODELVIEW);
        glLoadIdentity();
        glLightfv(GL_LIGHT0, GL_POSITION, light_pos);
    }
```

The position of both the camera and the objects can be altered later in the program by altering the model-view matrix but the light position is defined only in init(), so it will not change.

Now suppose that we have an idle callback that simply increments an angle and we want to rotate the light source about the objects.

```
GLfloat dx = 1.0; dy = 1.0; dz = 1.0;
GLfloat light_pos[] = {1.0, 2.0, 3.0, 1.0};
GLfloat theta = 0.0;

void idle()
{
  angle += 2.0;
  if(angle > 360.0) angle -= 360.0;
}

void display()
{
  glClear(COLOR_BUFFER_BIT | GL_DEPTH_BUFFER_BIT);
  glMatrixMode(GL_MODELVIEW);
  glLoadIdentity();
  glLookAt(1.0, 1.0, 1.0, 0.0, 0.0, 0.0, 0.0, 1.0, 0.0);
  glPushMatrix();
  glRotatef(angle, dx, dy, dz);
  glLightfv(GL_LIGHT0, GL_POSITION, light_pos);
  glPopMatrix();

    /* draw objects here */

  glutSwapBuffers();
}
```

In this code, we push the model-view matrix before we add the rotation. After the rotation, we set a new light position that is altered by the rotation and the previous model-view matrix. We pop the matrix before we draw the objects, so they are unaffected by the rotation.

If we removed the push and pop in the code, both the light source and the objects would have rotated. By altering the model-view matrix in different parts of the code and inserting pushes and pops, we can have both the objects and the light source move in different ways.

Suppose that we position the light source at the origin before we set the model-view transformation, so that the model-view transformation is an identity matrix. We have then fixed the location of the light source at the origin in eye coordinates or, equivalently, at the eye point. If we then use a gluLookAt() in the form

```
gluLookAt(eyex, eyey, eyez, 0.0, 0.0, 0.0, upx, upy, upz);
```

the effect will be the same as keeping the viewpoint at the origin in eye coordinates and moving the objects by (-eyex, -eyey, -eyez), but because we have not changed the position of the light source, which was already at the origin in eye coordinates, we have effectively tied the light source to the eye point. Of course, simply repositioning the light source at the eye point each time that it changed would accomplish the same effect.

In the following code, we set up a light source which has bright red diffuse component, a bright white specular component, and a small amount of gray ambient light. The source is at infinity and shines from behind the camera in the upper-right corner.

```
GLfloat position0[] = {1.0, 1.0, 1.0, 0.0};
GLfloat diffuse0[] = {1.0, 0.0, 0.0, 1.0};
GLfloat specular0[] = {1.0, 1.0, 1.0, 1.0};
GLfloat ambient0[] = {0.1, 0.1, 0.1, 1.0};

glEnable(GL_LIGHTING);
glEnable(GL_LIGHT0);

glMatrixMode(GL_MODELVIEW);
glLoadIdentity();
glLightfv(GL_LIGHT0, GL_POSITION, position0);
glLightfv(GL_LIGHT0, GL_DIFFUSE, diffuse0);
glLightfv(GL_LIGHT0, GL_SPECULAR, specular0);
glLightfv(GL_LIGHT0, GL_AMBIENT, ambient0);
```

A few additional calls to glLight*() will change the source from a point source to a spotlight and add attenuation.

6.5 Specifying a Material

Materials properties match the lighting properties. A material has reflectivity properties for each type of light. However, while there are light properties for each light source in the OpenGL state, there is only one set of material properties in the state. The functions for setting these properties are glMaterial*().

void glMaterial{if}(GLenum face, GLenum name, TYPE value)

void glMaterial{if}v(GLenum face, GLenum name, TYPE *value)

sets scalar and vector parameters for materials for the face (**GL_FRONT, GL_BACK, GL_FRONT_AND_BACK**). Parameter **name** is of **TYPE**.

As we have seen, polygons have both front and back faces. These faces can have the same or different properties. For each we can set its diffuse (GL_DIFFUSE), specular (GL_SPECULAR), and ambient (GL_AMBIENT) properties. Often the ambient and diffuse properties are the same and can be set together using GL_AMBIENT_AND_DIFFUSE. These parameters are RGBA color values. Here the fourth component is the opacity, which can be used to simulate translucent materials. This component is 1.0 for opaque surfaces. The default surface parameters correspond to a gray surface with a small amount of ambient reflection (0.2, 0.2, 0.2, 1.0), high diffuse reflectivity (0.8, 0.8, 0.8, 1.0), and no specular reflectivity (0.0, 0.0, 0.0, 1.0). Each surface can also emit light (GL_EMISSION). This term is not subject to lighting calculations and thus appears the same regardless of the light sources. Finally, there is a shininess parameter (GL_SHININESS). The higher the value of this parameter, the shinier the material appears as the specular highlights are concentrated in a smaller area near the angle of a perfect reflection.

We can make individual function calls for each property. If we change materials often, for example when we have many objects or each face of an object has different properties, we can put the calls that set parameters inside functions. Another strategy is to set up a structure that contains the material properties

```
typedef struct materialStruct {
  GLfloat ambient[4];
  GLfloat diffuse[4];
  GLfloat specular[4];
  GLfloat shininess;
} materialStruct;
```

Now we set up our materials.

```
materialStruct brassMaterials = {
  {0.33, 0.22, 0.03, 1.0},
  {0.78, 0.57, 0.11, 1.0},
  {0.99, 0.91, 0.81, 1.0},
  27.8
};
materialStruct redPlasticMaterials = {
  {0.3, 0.0, 0.0, 1.0},
  {0.6, 0.0, 0.0, 1.0},
  {0.8, 0.6, 0.6, 1.0},
  32.0
};
materialStruct whiteShineyMaterials = {
  { 1.0, 1.0, 1.0, 1.0 },
  { 1.0, 1.0, 1.0, 1.0 },
  { 1.0, 1.0, 1.0, 1.0 },
  100.0
};
```

and a function to assign them to the faces

```
void materials(materialStruct *materials)
{
  /* define material properties for front face of all polygons */
  glMaterialfv(GL_FRONT_AND_BACK, GL_AMBIENT,
        materials -> ambient);
  glMaterialfv(GL_FRONT_AND_BACK, GL_DIFFUSE,
        materials -> diffuse);
  glMaterialfv(GL_FRONT_AND_BACK, GL_SPECULAR,
        materials -> specular);
  glMaterialf(GL_FRONT_AND_BACK, GL_SHININESS,
        materials -> shininess);
}
```

Now when we want to set up the material properties for, say, the red plastic material, we can make the single function call

```
materials(&redPlasticMaterials);
```

The same strategy will work if we have light sources whose properties change during the execution of the program.

6.6 Shading the Rotating Cube

We can now change our rotating cube program from Chapter 5 to demonstrate OpenGL lights and materials. If we still want to use the mouse to select the direction of rotation, we can use the keyboard to change light and material properties. We can place the definition of the brass, red plastic, and white shiny materials with the data structure at the beginning of the program. We can do the same for light source properties using a fixed position with a directional light.

```
typedef struct lightingStruct {
  GLfloat ambient[4];
  GLfloat diffuse[4];
  GLfloat specular[4];
} lightingStruct;

lightingStruct whiteLighting = {
  {0.0, 0.0, 0.0, 1.0},
  {1.0, 1.0, 1.0, 1.0},
  {1.0, 1.0, 1.0, 1.0}
};

lightingStruct coloredLighting = {
  {0.2, 0.0, 0.0, 1.0},
  {0.0, 1.0, 0.0, 1.0},
  {0.0, 0.0, 1.0, 1.0}
```

```
};
GLfloat light0_pos[4] = {0.90, 0.90, 2.25, 0.00};
```

Next we define two pointers that we will use to change among different materials and light sources:

```
materialStruct *currentMaterials;
lightingStruct *currentLighting;
```

We need a normal for each face for the shading calculation. We put this information in an array

```
GLfloat normals[][3] = {{0.0, 0.0, -1.0}, {0.0, 1.0, 0.0},
    {-1.0, 0.0, 0.0}, {1.0, 0.0, 0.0}, {0.0, 0.0, 1.0},
    {0.0, -1.0, 0.0}};
```

We can draw the cube using the new cube function

```
void colorcube()
{
    glNormal3fv(normals[0]);
    polygon(0, 3, 2, 1);
    glNormal3fv(normals[1]);
    polygon(2, 3, 7, 6);
    glNormal3fv(normals[2]);
    polygon(0, 4, 7, 3);
    glNormal3fv(normals[3]);
    polygon(1, 2, 6, 5);
    glNormal3fv(normals[4]);
    polygon(4, 5, 6, 7);
    glNormal3fv(normals[5]);
    polygon(0, 1, 5, 4);
}
```

Note how each glColor3vf() from our previous example is replaced by a glNormal3fv(). Because the normals are processed as are other geometric objects, they are affected by the model-view matrix and thus rotate with the cube. We have to define some initial properties and enable lighting in our init() function.

```
void init()
{
  glEnable(GL_LIGHTING);
  glEnable(GL_LIGHT0);

  currentMaterials = &redPlasticMaterials;

  glMaterialfv(GL_FRONT, GL_AMBIENT,
        currentMaterials -> ambient);
  glMaterialfv(GL_FRONT, GL_DIFFUSE,
        currentMaterials -> diffuse);
  glMaterialfv(GL_FRONT, GL_SPECULAR,
```

```
            currentMaterials -> specular);
    glMaterialf(GL_FRONT, GL_SHININESS,
            currentMaterials -> shininess);

    currentLighting = &whiteLighting;

    glLightfv(GL_LIGHT0, GL_AMBIENT,
            currentLighting -> ambient);
    glLightfv(GL_LIGHT0, GL_DIFFUSE,
            currentLighting -> diffuse);
    glLightfv(GL_LIGHT0, GL_SPECULAR,
            currentLighting -> specular);
    glLightfv(GL_LIGHT0, GL_POSITION, light0_pos);
}
```

Finally, we use the keyboard callback to allow us to change the shading parameters and stop the rotation:

```
void key(unsigned char k, int x, int y)
{
switch(k)
{
    case '1':
      glutIdleFunc(NULL);
      break;
    case '2':
      glutIdleFunc(spinCube);
      break;
    case '3':
      currentMaterials = &redPlasticMaterials;
      break;
    case '4':
      currentMaterials = &colorCubeMaterials;
      break;
    case '5':
      currentMaterials = &brassMaterials;
      break;
    case '6':
      currentLighting = &whiteLighting;
      break;
    case '7':
      currentLighting = &coloredLighting;
      break;
    case 'q':
      exit(0);
      break;
}

    glMaterialfv(GL_FRONT, GL_AMBIENT,
            currentMaterials -> ambient);
    glMaterialfv(GL_FRONT, GL_DIFFUSE,
```

```
                currentMaterials -> diffuse);
    glMaterialfv(GL_FRONT, GL_SPECULAR,
            currentMaterials -> specular);
    glMaterialf(GL_FRONT, GL_SHININESS,
            currentMaterials -> shininess);

    glLightfv(GL_LIGHT0, GL_AMBIENT,
            currentLighting -> ambient);
    glLightfv(GL_LIGHT0, GL_DIFFUSE,
            currentLighting -> diffuse);
    glLightfv(GL_LIGHT0, GL_SPECULAR,
            currentLighting -> specular);

    glutPostRedisplay();
}
```

6.7 Controlling the Shading Calculation

Shading calculations require a significant amount of resources. In many situations, OpenGL can avoid some of the calculations with little or no effect on the resulting image. The functions glLightModel*() allows us to tell OpenGL how to carry out its lighting calculations.

---

void glLightModel{if}(GLenum param, TYPE value)

void glLightModel{if}v(GLenum param, TYPE *value)

sets light model properties for **param** (**GL_LIGHT_MODEL_AMBIENT**, **GL_LIGHT_MODEL_LOCAL_VIEWER**, or **GL_LIGHT_MODEL_TWO_SIDE**).

Recall that because normals are reversed for back faces and the front and back faces can have different material properties, calculating shading for back faces can require extra work. In many situations, we work with models in which back faces are not displayed. For example, we saw earlier that for convex objects, we cannot see any back faces. OpenGL can take advantage of this situation and not do any lighting calculations for back faces. If we really need two-sided lighting calculations, for example, when we can see inside an object, we can request OpenGL to do the correct calculation by

```
glLightModeli(GL_LIGHT_MODEL_TWO_SIDE, GL_TRUE);
```

| Shading for back faces will not be correct unless the light model is set to two-sided. |

OpenGL can make additional simplifications that are appropriate for some circumstances. For example, if the viewer is far from the objects, the vector from any point on the object to the viewer, which is used for calculating the specular term, is almost unchanged as we move along the object. Thus, if we tell OpenGL the viewer is an infinite distance from the scene by

```
glLightModeli(GL_LIGHT_MODEL_LOCAL_VIEWER, GL_TRUE);
```

this part of the lighting calculation can be simplified.

When we discussed ambient light, it was part of each light source. The reasoning was that a physical light source causes ambient light because much of the light that it emits reflects from surfaces in the environment. Thus, if all light sources are disabled, there will be no ambient light. However, often we would like there to be a small amount of ambient light even when all the sources are turned off. We achieve this affect by setting up a global ambient light source through

```
glLightModelfv(GL_LIGHT_MODEL_AMBIENT, global_ambient);
```

where the array `global_ambient` contains the RGBA values.

6.8 Smooth Shading

Lighting calculations are made on a vertex-by-vertex basis. OpenGL uses the current state to compute vertex colors using the modified Phong model. If the shading model, set by glShadeModel(), is set to flat (GL_FLAT), a color is computed only for the last vertex in a polygon and each polygon will appear in a solid color. This situation is appropriate when we are working with objects, such as the cube, that are composed of flat polygons. In this case, even if the object has the same material properties, each polygon will have a different shade as each has a different orientation with respect to the lights and the viewers.

However, if the polygons are being used to approximate a curved object, such as with the GLU quadrics, giving each polygon a constant shade will only emphasize that what we see is a polygonal approximation to a curved surface. However, OpenGL can interpolate vertex colors across polygons. Consequently, if we set the parameter in glShadeModel() to GL_SMOOTH, then OpenGL will perform the lighting calculation at each vertex and will then interpolate these vertex colors across the polygon. Figure 6.5 shows the difference between smooth and flat shading for a polygonal approximation to a sphere. Note that GL_SMOOTH is the default.

You may be disappointed with smooth shading if you are using large polygons. Suppose that we use one large rectangle for a wall in a room and want it to show variations of light across its surface. Hence, we use smooth shading. What we may see is that the center of the wall is very dark compared with the corners. This appearance is a consequence of the interpolation of the colors at the four corners, all of which can be further from the viewer than the center. The usual solution to such problems is to tessellate large polygons into smaller ones.

Figure 6.5 Flat and smooth shading polygonal
approximations to a sphere

Shading may be unsatisfactory if you use large polygons due to the interpolation of vertex shades across a large area.

6.9 Working with Normals

To a large degree, the quality of our shading depends on the normals, which we usually have to compute ourselves. A flat polygon has a constant normal across its surface, which can be computed from the first three vertices. However, when we want smooth shading, the normal for each polygon is not what we need.

Smooth shading is sometimes called **Gouraud shading**. This is a slight misnomer. What Gouraud proposed is that we compute a normal at each vertex that is the average of the normals of the polygons that meet at that vertex. Because OpenGL processes each polygon independently, OpenGL does not have the information to compute vertex normals based on surrounding polygons. Thus, it is the application that must "know" about the surrounding polygons and compute normals correctly. For the smooth image in Figure 6.5, we were able to use the fact that we were trying to approximate a sphere to obtain the exact normals at the vertices, which for the sphere always point directly out from its center to the points on its surface.

The lighting calculations require that the normal vector have unit length; that is, the sum of the squares of the three components must equal one. Usually it is more efficient to enforce this requirement within the application program. However, we can also use enable automatic normalization by

```
glEnable(GL_NORMALIZE);
```

Because this function will be executed every time on each normal when we go through our display process, there is a performance penalty for using it.

When we do transformations, rotations and translations do not affect the length of the normals but scalings do. Consequently, the normals may no longer have unit length and the shading calculations will be wrong.

Lighting calculations require that normals have unit length.

Scaling changes the lengths of normals.

6.10 Transparency

We now turn to working with the fourth color component, the A in RGBA color. This component is also called the **alpha value**. In normal rendering, this value is ignored. If we first enable blending, by

```
glEnable(GL_BLEND);
```

then the alpha value will have meaning. Although we can use the alpha values in many ways, the usual use is to use this value to determine the degree of opacity of a color or material. An opacity of 1.0 indicates that a material is opaque and hides anything behind. A value of 0.0 indicates that the material is completely transparent and cannot be seen. Values in between indicate that the material is semi-transparent and some of the color of objects behind it blend with its color, the value of alpha determining the weight of its contribution to the color assigned at a point in the image.

The use of alpha allows for many additional capabilities but also there are more options and a few places where one has to be careful. The basic problem is that when we blend together semi-transparent polygons for display, the order in which they are rendered matters. In contrast, when we render only opaque polygons, the z-buffer algorithm for hidden-surface removal ensures that we get the same image regardless of the order in which the polygons are rendered.

Suppose that we have two polygons that we want to blend together. Let's start without lighting and assume that each polygon has an RGB color and an A (alpha) value. We start with a color buffer that has been cleared to the clear color set by glClearColor(). Recall that the clear color is an RGBA color, so if we have enabled blending, then the initial display, before we render any polygons, may be semi-transparent and show other windows behind the OpenGL window. For now, we can assume that the initial window color was set by

```
glClearColor(0.0, 0.0, 1.0, 1, 0);
```

so it is blue and opaque. Now suppose that the first polygon is defined by the code

```
glColor3f(1.0, 0.0, 0.0, 0.5);
glBegin(GL_POLYGON);

/* vertices go here */

glEnd();
```

Assuming that this polygon is visible, its color must be blended with the color that is already in the color buffer so that it appears semi-transparent. We must decide not only on a new RGB to put in the color buffer where the polygon is rendered, but also a new A. The new A will indicate how translucent is the blending of the polygon and the background color. OpenGL provides a variety of constants that determine how to blend colors and alpha values. The model is based on the idea that the color buffer is the **destination** where we place our colors, and the values from the state that are used for the polygon colors is the **source**. When blending is disabled, the source color simply replaces the destination color. However, when blending is enabled the new destination color is a combination of the old destination color, and the source color as shown in Figure 6.6.

Suppose that the color buffer contains the values (R_d, G_d, B_d, A_d) at some point where the polygon is to be rendered. Let (R_s, G_s, B_s, A_s) be the polygon color. By blending, we form a new destination color by multiplying the source color by a **source blending factor**, multiplying the destination color by a **destination blending factor**, and adding the results together. Suppose that (S_r, S_g, S_b, S_a) and (D_r, D_g, D_b, D_a) are the source and destination blending factors, respectively. The new destination color is $(S_r R_s + D_r R_d, S_g G_s + D_g G_d, S_b B_s + D_b B_d, S_a A_s + D_a A_d)$. In OpenGL, we set these factors by the function `glBlendFunc()`.

void glBlendFunc(GLenum source, GLenum destination)

sets the **source** and **destination** blending factors.

Of the 15 possible blending factors, some can apply only to the source, some to the destination, and others to either. We shall consider some of the most important cases.

When we draw polygonal surfaces, the most common choices for the source factor and destination factors are `GL_SRC_ALPHA` and `ONE_MINUS_SRC_ALPHA`, respectively. Consider what happens when initially the color buffer is cleared to an opaque color $(R_c, G_c, B_c, 1)$. When we blend in a polygon with color (R_s, G_s, B_s, A_s), the resulting destination color where the polygon is rendered is $(A_s R_s + (1 - A_s)R_c, A_s G_s + (1 - A_s)G_c, A_s B_s + (1 - A_s)B_c, A_s^2 + (1 - A_s)A_c) = (R_d, G_d, B_d, A_d)$. We can establish a few important properties of the new color. If the original color components are each in the range $(0.0, 1.0)$, so are the new RGBA values. Thus, we can never overflow or underflow a color. If the polygon is transparent $(A_s = 0)$, then the new color is the same as the background color. If the polygon is

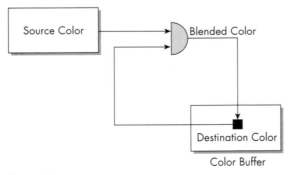

Figure 6.6 Writing model for blending

opaque, the new color is the same as the polygon color. These results are what we would expect from real materials. Now suppose that we add in a second polygon with color $(R_{s'}, G_{s'}, B_{s'}, A_{s'})$. The color where the two polygons overlap will be $(A_{s'}R_{s'} + [1 - A_{s'}][A_sR_s + (1 - A_s)R_c], A_{s'}G_{s'} + [1 - A_{s'}][A_sG_s + (1 - A_s)G_c],$ $A_{s'}B_{s'} + [1 - A_{s'}][A_sB_s + (1 - A_s)B_c], A_{s'}^2 + [1 - A_{s'}][A_s^2 + (1 - A_s)A_c])$. Although this expression is a bit messy, we can verify that the new values of RGB and A will still be in the range (0.0, 1.0). However, the order in which we render the polygons matters. If we switch the order in which we render the two polygons, we get slightly different final colors. Not only is the situation physically unrealistic, but because we usually cannot guarantee the order in which polygons will flow down the OpenGL pipeline, we get different images when the order changes.

We can ensure that the rendering does not depend on the order in which the polygons pass down the pipeline by using the source and destination factors GL_SRC_ALPHA and GL_ONE, respectively. Consider our same example. When we blend in the first polygon, over the opaque background we obtain the color $(A_sR_s + R_c, A_sG_s + G_c, A_sB_s + B_c, A_s^2) = (R_d, G_d, B_d, A_d)$. These colors could overflow but we can avoid the problem by setting the clear color to black, resulting in the colors $(A_sR_s, A_sG_s, A_sB_s, A_s^2)$. When we blend in the second polygon, we obtain $(A_sR_s + A_{s'}R_{s'}, A_sG_s + A_{s'}G_{s'}, A_sB_s + A_{s'}B_{s'}, A_s^2 + A_{s'}^2)$. The problem here is that the resulting image can be dimmer if the As are small because the color components are scaled rather than blended. If the values of A are large, then the colors can overflow.

As far as realism is concerned, the most difficult situation occurs when some of the polygon are opaque and others are translucent. While we may be willing to accept the order dependency of blending translucent polygons, we must handle opaque polygons correctly. Every opaque polygon must block all polygons behind it.

We can use the depth buffer to keep track of whether or not a polygon is in front of all polygons that have been rendered so far. However, we must handle translucent polygons differently with respect to changing the values in the depth buffer. When a translucent polygon goes down the pipeline, it will be rendered if it is in front of any polygon found thus far. However, such a polygon should not affect the contents of the depth buffer as it does not block polygons in behind it. OpenGL provides a function glDepthMask(), which can make the depth buffer read-only (GL_FALSE) or writeable (GL_TRUE).

---

void glDepthMask(GLboolean flag)

makes the depth buffer read-only (**GL_FALSE**) or writeable (**GL_TRUE**), the default.

Suppose that we consider the color cube again but this time some of the sides are translucent. We can define the vertices as before, but this time use RGBA color for the sides, making the first three colors translucent.

```
GLfloat vertices[][3] = {{-1.0, -1.0, 1.0}, {-1.0, 1.0, 1.0},
    {1.0, 1.0, 1.0}, {1.0, -1.0, 1.0}, {-1.0, -1.0, -1.0},
    {-1.0, 1.0, -1.0}, {1.0, 1.0, -1.0}, {1.0, -1.0, -1.0}};
```

```
GLfloat colors[][4] = {{1.0, 0.0, 0.0, 0.5},
  {0.0, 1.0, 1.0, 0.5}, {1.0, 1.0, 0.0, 0.5},
  {0.0, 1.0, 0.0, 0.5}, {0.0, 0.0, 1.0, 1.0},
  {1.0, 0.0, 1.0, 1.0}};
```

We can render the cube as before using the functions `polygon()` and `cube()`, making sure that we check each polygon to see if is opaque before we render it.

```
void polygon(int a, int b, int c , int d)
{
  glColor4fv(colors[a]);
  if(colors[a][4] != 1.0) glDepthMask(GL_FALSE);
    else glDepthMask(GL_TRUE);
  glBegin(GL_POLYGON);
    glVertex3fv(vertices[a]);
    glVertex3fv(vertices[b]);
    glVertex3fv(vertices[c]);
    glVertex3fv(vertices[d]);
  glEnd();
}

void cube()
{
  polygon(0, 3, 2, 1);
  polygon(2, 3, 7, 6);
  polygon(3, 0, 4, 7);
  polygon(1, 2, 6, 5);
  polygon(4, 5, 6, 7);
  polygon(5, 4, 0, 1);
}
```

We must remember to enable blending and set the blending factors in `main()` or `init()`:

```
glEnable(GL_BLEND);
glBlendFactor(GL_SRC_ALPHA, GL_ONE_MINUS_SRC_ALPHA);
```

6.11 Programming Exercises

1. Apply shading to the tessellated triangle that we introduced in Chapter 2. Investigate the relationship between the degree of tessellation and the smoothness of the shading.
2. Write a program that will display one or more curved objects (spheres, disks, cones) and shade them interactively. You might use slide-bars to adjust lighting and material parameters or use menus with a selection of fixed choices.

Images

Thus far, we have worked with geometric entities that flow down OpenGL's geometric pipeline and are subject to the model-view and projection transformations. OpenGL also allows us to work directly with bits and groups of bits, or pixels, which flow down a parallel pipeline to the frame buffer. We can read bits from the frame buffer (or framebuffer) and write bits to the frame buffer. We can also take advantage of a variety of features that OpenGL provides within the pixel pipeline.

7.1 Pixels and Bitmaps

The back end of every graphics system is the frame buffer where the image is formed. The frame buffer is really a collection of buffers. For each x, y value in screen space, there is a corresponding group of bits that can be thought of as a generalized picture element or **pixel**.[1] Such a pixel might have 32 bits for the front buffer RGBA values, 32 bits for the back buffer RGBA values, and 32 bits for the depth values. If the implementation supports other buffers, such as the accumulation buffer, stencil buffer, and extra color buffers, there will be many more bits to a pixel. We can envision the frame buffer as in Figure 7.1. It consists of a one-bit planes, each of which has the resolution of the screen. Groups of planes correspond to the various OpenGL buffers. All the bits for a given x, y in screen coordinates form a pixel.

From the perspective of an application program that wants to access these buffers directly, we need the ability to read and write rectangular arrays of pixels. However, we usually manipulate only specific groups of bits in the generalized

---

1. Most graphics textbooks use the term *frame buffer* to refer to the buffer in which the RGB or RGBA image is formed. A *pixel* is then a group of bits that give the RGB or RGBA value for an x, y location in screen space. OpenGL uses *color buffer* to refer to these bits and the *frame buffer* (or framebuffer) is the collection of all the buffers, including the color buffer(s) and the depth buffer. OpenGL usage of the terms is closer to how graphics systems are actually implemented.

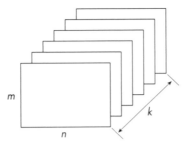

Figure 7.1 $n \times m$ frame buffer shown with k parallel bit planes

pixel at one time, namely those that correspond to one of the OpenGL buffers. Consequently, we shall use the term *pixel* to denote a group of bits, usually an integral number of bytes, at an *x, y* location in the frame buffer. With this definition, we can write depth pixels or RGBA pixels depending on where in the frame buffer we do the write operation. Our OpenGL functions will allow us to read or write rectangular blocks of such pixels with a single function execution, an operation called a **bit block transfer operation** or a **bitblt**.

We also want to be able to work with rectangular arrays of bits, called **bitmaps**. Although bitmaps can be thought of as special types of pixel rectangles, they are used in very different ways and thus there are separate functions for manipulating pixels and bitmaps. In OpenGL, pixels and bitmaps are the two fundamental nongeometric primitives.

Figure 7.2 shows a simple view of the architecture of a graphics system. The application program runs in the standard processor, as does any other program. The graphics subsystem enters the picture when the application program executes a function that alters the state of the graphics subsystem or generates a graphics primitive, such as a vertex. Geometric primitives flow down the geometric pipeline that handles transformations (viewing, modeling, projection), lighting, and clipping. Eventually, those geometric primitives that are visible are rasterized into a color buffer. Nongeometric primitives flow through a parallel pipeline. The two pipelines merge at the rasterization stage.

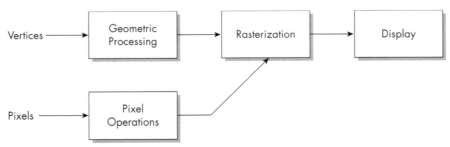

Figure 7.2 Simplified OpenGL architecture showing parallel pipelines

At a conceptual level, working with bitmaps and pixels is simple. We can define them in our programs or read them in from files. Then, we move them to the desired place in the frame buffer. Reading pixels involves going to the correct place in the frame buffer and extracting the values that we find there. Unfortunately, things are not quite so simple in the real world. We have to worry about the differences in how pixels are formatted in the application program, within files, and inside the frame buffer. We also have to worry about the complications due to different architectures storing discrete data in different ways.

We will also have to account for the different types of pixels. From the perspective of the application program, a pixel might represent an RGB color, an RGBA color, a luminance value, or a depth value. On the application side, these values may be represented in a multitude of ways. For example, colors may be given as bytes, integers, or floats.

In addition, OpenGL has a sequence of operations that can be performed within the pixel pipeline, each with multiple options. For example, we can rescale pixels as they flow down the pipeline. We can also write into the frame buffer in different ways. Fortunately, we will be able to use the default settings for many parameters and we can get started without introducing too much complexity.

7.2 Bitmaps

Bitmaps are rectangular arrays of bits. Their most common use is for displaying raster text, which is text composed of characters that are defined by small rectangular blocks of bits. Figure 7.3 shows a few bitmapped characters. Each fits inside a 7×9 rectangular array. As we saw in Chapter 2, depending on whether we are working with a fixed-width or proportional font, the boxes may be of different sizes. Also, a character may have extra bits around it to aid in spacing the characters correctly when we want to display strings of characters.

Bitmaps are also used for entities such as cursors and crosshairs in interactive applications. They can also be used as **masks** that determine if something else should happen at a location. For example, we might want to form a bitmap that has the same dimensions as the screen window and use its values to determine if corresponding pixels in a color buffer should be displayed or not.

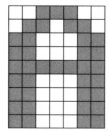 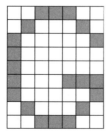

Figure 7.3 Bitmapped characters

7.2.1 Displaying a Bitmap

The simplest thing that we can do with a bitmap is to display it as a two-dimensional pattern. Suppose that we have a bitmap that we define in our program. We put the bits into a one-dimensional array for easier use with OpenGL. For example, the following code generates 4096 bits that describe an 8×8 checkerboard. That is, if we arrange the 4096 bits as a 64×64 array, we get alternating 8×8 blocks of zeros and ones.

```
GLubyte wb[2] = {0x00, 0xff};
GLubyte check[512];
int i, j;
for(i = 0; i < 64; i++) for(j = 0; j < 8; j++)
  check[i*8+j] = wb[(i/8+j)%2];
```

When we display these bits through glBitmap(), we display them as a two-dimensional bitmap where we can decide how many rows and columns to use. If we choose to display a square map (64 rows and 64 columns), then we obtain the display shown in Figure 7.4.

We display this pattern by the function call

```
glBitmap(64, 64, 0.0, 0.0, 0.0, 0.0, check);
```

Each bit in the bitmap is mapped to a pixel on the display. The question is which pixels? The current raster position can be set by the function glRasterPos*() that we introduced in Chapter 2. The third and fourth parameters (x0 and y0) are offsets that are added to the current raster position to determine where in the color buffer the lower-left corner of the bitmap is drawn. After the bitmap is drawn, the raster position is incremented by the fifth and sixth parameters (xi and yi). In our example, the pattern is simply drawn starting at the present raster position and the raster position is left unchanged.

The major reason for adding these parameters has to do with creating text. Bitmap characters are stored as rectangular patterns. Some fonts use the same-sized boxes; others use different sizes for different characters. However, even if all the characters are stored in the same-sized box, for example as a 5×7 characters set,

Figure 7.4 64×64 bitmap displayed as an 8×8 checker board pattern

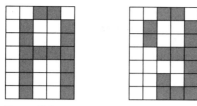

Figure 7.5 Two 5 × 7 characters

there are potential complications. For example, a possible upper case "A" is shown in Figure 7.5. The **base line** of the text, where we would want to start printing it, is at the lower-left corner. Note that this character has a column of blank space at the beginning of the character; that space would separate the character from the previous character. Hence, for the "A" a choice of 0.0 for both x0 and y0 would seem appropriate. Now consider the lower case "g" in Figure 7.5. It also fits in the 5 × 7 box but the character has a **descender**, which indicates that part of the character should be below the base line. Thus, for this character to appear correctly, we need a negative value of y0. The exact value of y0 depends on the viewing conditions as they affect the raster position. We shall return to this issue in the next section. Note that we could have used a larger character set in which the baseline of the characters differed among characters. But such a character set would require more blank spaces within each character box and require more storage. It is more efficient to use x0 and y0.

When we want to display a string of characters, we have to space them. Here is where xi and yi enter the picture. They are used to increment the raster position after each call to glBitmap(). If we execute glBitmap() for each character with the correct increments, the raster position is set automatically at the beginning of the next character.

There are a few additional subtleties that control where a bitmap appears on the screen and how it appears. First, we address the issue of where the bitmap appears.

void glBitmap(GLsizei c, GLsizei r, GLfloat xb, GLfloat yb, GLfloat xi, GLfloat yi, GLubyte *bits)

draws a bitmap of width **r** and height **c** from the array **bits**. The bitmap is started offset by **x0, y0** from the current raster position. After the bitmap is drawn, the current raster position is incremented by **xi, yi**.

7.2.2 Mixing Bitmaps and Geometry

Recall from Chapter 2 that the raster position can be specified in two, three, or four dimensions, using floats or integers. This position passes through the geometric pipeline. Thus, the raster position is transformed by both the model-view and projection matrices before it eventually yields a position in screen coordinates. If the resulting position does not lie within the viewport, the bitmap will not be drawn. Note that there is a mixing of the geometric pipeline, which determines the raster position, and the pixel pipeline, through which the bitmap flows, that affect where and whether a bitmap appears. If we want to display only pixels and bitmaps, we could use a window and viewport that match the screen. For example, if w and h are the width and height of the viewport as set by the reshape callback, then we could use

```
gluOrtho2D(0.0, (GLfloat) w, 0.0, (GLfloat) h);
```

Now, if the model-view matrix is left as an identity matrix, the raster position as set by

```
glRasterPos2i(x, y);
```

sets a position in window coordinates that is the same as the position in the viewport where the generating of the bitmap will begin.

If we want to use both raster primitives and geometric primitives in the same program, setting the raster position can be tricky as the proper viewing condition for the polygons in the scene may not make it clear how to increment the raster position to place characters in the correct position. One solution to this problem is to use two sets of viewing conditions, one for the geometry and the other for the bitmaps. Within the application program, we can redefine the necessary transformations as needed or use the matrix stacks to save and recover transformations.

7.2.3 Colors and Masks

In our example, we regarded one bits as black and zero bits as white. Actually, the bitmap is a **mask**. Where there is a one in the bitmap, we see a color based upon the current **raster color** that is part of the OpenGL state. Where there is a zero, the color of the bitmap does not affect the corresponding pixel in the frame buffer, thus we see what is "underneath" a zero bit when the bitmap is placed on top of the color buffer. Suppose that we clear the color buffer to red and set the present drawing color to green. If we clear the screen and draw the bitmap, as in the code

```
glClearColor(1.0, 0.0, 0.0, 1.0);
glColor3f(0.0, 1.0, 0.0);
glClear(GL_COLOR_BUFFER_BIT);
glBitmap(64, 64, 0.0, 0.0, 0.0, 0.0, check);
```

then we will see a red and green checkerboard.

In the above code, we set the raster color in the same manner that we set the color in our geometric programs and here it affected the color of the bitmap.

OpenGL stores *both* a present drawing color and a present raster color as part of its state. Both colors are set by glColor*(). However, the present raster color is locked by the use of glRasterPos*(). Thus, in the code

```
glColor3f(1.0, 0.0, 0.0);
glBegin(GL_POLYGON);
  .
  .
  .
glEnd();
glRasterPos2i(xr, yr);
glColor3f(0.0, 1.0, 0.0);
glBitmap(64, 64, 0.0, 0.0, 0.0, 0.0, check);
glBegin(GL_POLYGON);
  .
  .
  .
glEnd();
```

the first polygon is drawn in red and the second in green. The checkerboard is drawn in red because the raster color is the color that was in effect the last time that the function glRasterPos2i() was executed.

7.3 Drawing Modes

In our examples thus far, the set bits in the bitmap became pixels colored with the current raster color. We have made two assumptions. First, the buffer that we draw into is the same color buffer into which we draw our geometric primitives. Unless we alter the "drawing buffer" explicitly, this will be the case by default. Second, when we draw a pixel using the current color, this color is the one that goes into the frame buffer. Again, this is the default case, but we have more control over how bits and pixels are drawn into the frame buffer.

OpenGL uses a drawing model similar to that shown in Figure 7.6. This model is essentially the same as the model we used for blending in Chapter 6. When we

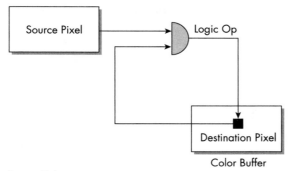

Figure 7.6 Writing model for bitmaps

want to write pixels or bitmaps, we first look at what is contained in the location at which we wish to draw. What we draw can depend on the value that we find there. Consider a single bit from the bitmap. When we render the bitmap, each bit in the bitmap corresponds to a pixel on the screen. We call this bit the **source bit**. If this bit is one, OpenGL uses the present raster color to affect the destination pixel. We can think of this color as the **source color** that is the color of a **source pixel** that matches the source bit. The corresponding pixel in the frame buffer is called the **destination pixel**. In the simplest case, for each location in the frame buffer that corresponds to a bit in the bitmap, the corresponding source color replaces the color of the destination pixel in the frame buffer. However, if we can first look at the color of the destination pixel, we can make the new value of the destination pixel be some function of the source and destination colors. In OpenGL, this function operates on a bit-by-bit basis between the source and destination colors. We can apply any of the 16 possible logical operations between two bits using the function glLogicOp() to select the function.

---

void glLogicOp(GLenum op)

selects which of the 16 logical operations between the source and destination pixels are combined in the frame buffer if logic operations (**GL_COLOR_LOGIC_OP**) are enabled. Choices include **GL_COPY** (the default), **GL_OR**, and **GL_XOR**.

We must first enable logic operations by

glEnable(GL_COLOR_LOGIC_OP);

The default (GL_COPY) produces the same result as we would get without enabling logic operations; the source pixel simply replaces the destination pixel. The other possible operations are more interesting. For example, we could always replace the source pixel by the logical OR of the two pixels (taken bitwise) using GL_OR or by the complement of the source (again taken bitwise) using GL_COPY_INVERTED. Many of these options may leave unexpected colors on the display because logic operations are applied bit by bit. If we use GL_OR between a red pixel and a yellow pixel, the resulting color may not have any clear relationship to either red or yellow.

Logic operations combine the source and destination colors bitwise. Consequently, for more than one-bit pixels, the resulting colors may be odd visually.

Of all the operations, the most interesting and useful is the exclusive OR operation (GL_XOR). Most of its applications are dependent on the property that if we apply the operation twice we get back to the starting state. Thus, if $\oplus$ denotes XOR and x and y are bits,

$$x = x \oplus y \oplus y$$

Hence, if x is the value of a bit in the frame buffer and we draw bit y at the same place using the exclusive OR mode, we get the value $x \oplus y$. When we draw y a second time, we get the value x again.

Suppose that we want to remove an object from the screen. We could clear the color buffer and then redraw all the other objects. This strategy requires that we either go through all the code that defines the other objects or use display lists. If we use XOR, we simply draw the same object a second time at the same place that we drew it the first time. The second draw undoes the first. Here is a simple mouse callback that redraws the checkerboard at the original mouse position each time that the left mouse button is clicked and then draws it again at the position of the mouse:

```
void mouse(int btn, int state, int x, int y)
{
    if(btn == GLUT_LEFT_BUTTON && state == GLUT_DOWN)
    {
        glBitmap(64, 64, 0.0, 0.0, 0.0, 0.0, check);
        glRasterPos2i(x, hh-y);
        glBitmap(64, 64, 0.0, 0.0, 0.0, 0.0, check);
        glFlush();
    }
}
```

Here ww is the height of the viewport and window as set in the reshape callback, which are saved as global variables.

```
void reshape(int w, int h)
{
    glViewport(0, 0, w, h);
    glMatrixMode(GL_PROJECTION);
    glLoadIdentity();
    gluOrtho2D(0.0, (GLfloat) w, 0.0, (GLfloat) h);
    hh = h;
    glMatrixMode(GL_MODELVIEW);
    glLoadIdentity();
}
```

The mode was set in main() as

```
glEnable(GL_COLOR_LOGIC_OP);
glLogicOp(GL_XOR);
```

In this sample code, the bitmap is drawn initially at the lower-left corner of the window in the display callback:

```
void display()
{
  glClear(GL_COLOR_BUFFER_BIT);
  glColor3f(1.0, 0.0, 0.0);
  glRasterPos2f(0.0, 0.0);
  glBitmap(64, 64, 0.0, 0.0, 0.0, 0.0, check);
  glFlush();
}
```

Subsequently, each time the left mouse button is clicked, the checkerboard pattern is drawn in the old position first, because the raster position has not yet been changed. This operation erases the previous instance of the checkerboard. Then the raster position is updated to match the mouse location, and the checkerboard is rendered in the new position.

Applications of this simple idea include moving a cursor around the screen, rubberbanding lines and rectangles, and implementing pop-up menus. All involve drawing an object, perhaps on top of other objects, and then returning the screen to its original state.

7.4 Reading and Writing Pixels

We now turn to reading and writing arrays of multibit pixels in the frame buffer. Conceptually, the process is simple. Consider writing. We have image data that are either defined in the application program or read from a file. We have to move these data to the frame buffer. We can use the OpenGL function glDrawPixels(). Reading is the inverse process. We move pixels from the frame buffer to the application using glReadPixels(). However, there is a host of small problems about which we must worry. Most arise from the differences between how pixels are represented within the frame buffer and how they are represented within system memory. These problems are exacerbated by the differences in how numbers are represented on different architectures. In addition, we want to be able to use multiple ways of representing pixel data in our applications, including ints, bytes, and floats, regardless of how our data are eventually stored in the frame buffer.

We can envision the process as in Figure 7.7. Pixels pass through a pipeline where, as they go from the application program to the frame buffer, they are **unpacked** from their original format in system memory. Pixels can be altered as they go from the program to the frame buffer through **pixel transfer operations**. For example, we might want to scale them to go over the range allowed in the frame buffer. We can also apply **pixel mapping** operations, which will allow us to use lookup tables to map pixel values to other values. We might use mapping operations for color conversion operations between different color systems or to

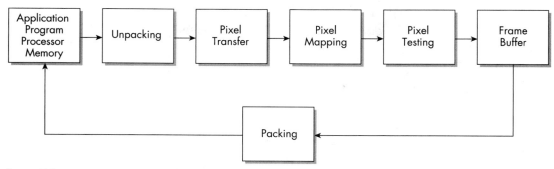

Figure 7.7 Pixel pipeline

do color balancing to adjust for the properties of our display. We can then apply scaling operations to the pixels to replicate pixels as they are placed in the frame buffer. Finally, there is a series of tests that are performed on each pixel before it is placed in the frame buffer.

A similar process applies when we read pixels from the frame buffer. Of particular concern is the format conversion (**packing**) that determines how information in the frame buffer is placed in processor memory.

We can also choose which buffers to use for reading and writing. We can write RGB or RGBA pixels to the front or back color buffers, we can read or write depth values, and we can read pixels from one of the buffers that comprise the frame buffer and write to another buffer, even the one from which we are reading. This architecture suggests that not only can we use OpenGL to display discrete data such as pictures and text, but we can also use OpenGL to process images.

7.4.1 Writing Pixels

The fundamental pixel-writing function is `glDrawPixels()`, which draws pixel rectangles at the current raster position. We must specify the format of the pixels that we are drawing. For example, if we have an RGB image that we form in our program of the form

```
GLubyte image[WIDTH][HEIGHT][3];
```

then we use `GL_RGB` for the format, `GL_UNSIGNED_BYTE` for the type, and draw by

```
glDrawPixels(WIDTH, HEIGHT, GL_RGB, GL_UNSIGNED_BYTE, image);
```

This format specifies that the data are RGB triplets. If the data are provided in separate arrays, we can use `GL_RED`, `GL_GREEN`, and `GL_BLUE` and access three arrays. Other formats include `GL_RBGA` and `GL_DEPTH_COMPONENT` (to write into the depth buffer). The type parameter can be most of the standard types (GL_INT, GL_FLOAT) or be of some packed types that are used to compress image data. For example, the type GL_UNSIGNED_BYTE_3_3_2 corresponds to some situations where one byte is used to store an RGB value using 3 bits each for red and green, and two bits for blue.

**void glDrawPixels(GLsizei w, GLsizei h, GLenum format,
     GLenum type, GLvoid *array)**

draws a **w** × **h** rectangle of pixels from **array** at the current raster position. The pixels are in the specified **format** using data of **type**.

7.4.2 Reading Pixels

We can move pixels from the frame buffer to memory with glReadPixels(). The parameters are the same as for glDrawPixels() but used in the reverse way. Thus, the function call

```
glReadPixels(0, 0, columns, rows,
GL_RGB, GL_UNSIGNED_BYTE, image);
```

will read rows * columns RGB pixels starting at the lower-left corner of the frame buffer. These values will be returned as three unsigned bytes per pixel regardless of how pixels are represented in the frame buffer.

**void glReadPixels(GLint x, GLint y, GLsizei w, GLsizei h,
     GLenum format, GLenum type, GLvoid *array)**

reads a **w** × **h** rectangle of pixels from the frame buffer starting at (**x, y**) into **array**. The pixels are in the specified **format** and written as data of **type**.

Reading pixels returns values that are limited by the resolution of the frame buffer. When we write pixels, usually we can specify a color and not worry about how many bits are in the frame buffer for storing and displaying the color. The implementation will do the best it can with whatever resolution it has. Many systems use a method called **dithering** that varies low-order bits as they are placed in the frame buffer to smooth out transitions between colors that would otherwise be visible in a display with few bits per color component. However, when we read from a color buffer, what is returned depends on how many bits really are in the hardware. Hence, we might write a pixel where the red has a value in the program between 0 and 255 but read back only 16 different values because the frame buffer only has 4 bits for red. If the display is dithered and we write the same value over a large area, we will read back a variety of slightly different values because of the dithering. In addition, the number of bits in the display may be different for single- and double-buffered displays on the same system.

When reading pixels, make sure that you know the color resolution of the display and account for possible dithering.

How pixels are stored within an OpenGL implementation may bear little relation to how they are stored in processor memory.

Hence, when we read pixels, we should first check the number of bits of resolution. For example, we can use the inquiry function

```
glGetIntegerv(GL_RED_BITS, &nbits);
```

to determine the number of bits. If the display is dithered, we should turn off dithering by

```
glDisable(GL_DITHER);
```

so that we will always get the same quantized value back for a given color that we write.

7.4.3 Copying Pixels

Sometimes, we want to move pixels from one part of the frame buffer to another. We could do a glReadPixels() followed by a glDrawPixels(), but that would require using system memory for a frame-buffer-to-frame-buffer operation. The function glCopyPixels() allows us to accomplish this operation without going through system memory. We set the starting point of the copy as in glReadPixels(), using the present raster position to determine where to place the copy. If we are working with RGB or RGBA colors, the buffer parameter is set to GL_COLOR.

void glCopyPixels(GLint x, GLint y, GLsizei w, GLsizei h,
    GLenum buffer)

copies a **w** × **h** block of pixels starting at (**x, y**) from **buffer** starting at the current raster position.

7.5 Selecting Buffers

When we read and write RGBA values, we are working with a color buffer in the frame buffer. When we work in single-buffer mode, by default, reading and writing will be in the front color buffer (GL_FRONT). In double-buffer mode, by default, we draw into the back color buffer (GL_BACK). These are the same buffers where normally geometric primitives are placed.

However, most OpenGL implementations support additional color buffers. For example, if the implementation supports double-buffered stereo images, there are four color buffers, GL_RIGHT_FRONT, GL_LEFT_FRONT, GL_RIGHT_BACK, and GL_LEFT_BACK (or just GL_RIGHT and GL_LEFT for single-buffered stereo). We might also have auxiliary color buffers (GL_AUX0 ... GL_AUXn) that can be used for other purposes. For example, when we discussed picking in Chapter 3, we saw that picking required an extra rendering. Often one of these extra buffers is a convenient place to put the results of the extra rendering pass.

We can select which buffer to use for reading by glReadBuffer() and which to use for writing by glDrawBuffer().

---

void glReadBuffer(GLenum buffer)

selects **buffer** for reading.

void glDrawBuffer(GLenum buffer)

selects **buffer** for drawing.

There are cases in interactive applications where we want to write into both the front and back buffers. We can do so by selecting GL_FRONT_AND_BACK for the drawing buffer.

There are many ways we can use extra buffers. One example is an alternate picking mechanism to the one that we presented in Chapter 3. In this mechanism, we render each object in a distinct color into a color buffer, one that is not displayed. We can then use the mouse position returned in the mouse callback to determine where to read a color in this color buffer. We then map the color that we read to the identifier of the object. Consider, for example, a shaded sphere. The sphere that we see on the display will show many shades, while the rendering of the sphere into the other buffer will be in a constant shade. This technique requires an extra rendering but provides a simple picking strategy. We could also have rendered the scene twice into the back buffer before swapping buffers, once in distinct colors for the picking and the second time as we wish to display the objects.

Another application is when we need renderings using multiple cameras. For example, if there is a mirror in a scene, we can first render the scene with a camera behind the mirror into an extra buffer. We can then read that buffer and texture map it—as we shall discuss in Chapter 8—to the face of the mirror when we render the scene normally.

7.6 Pixel Store Modes

Depending on your system, moving data between system memory and the frame buffer may or may not work correctly. The problem is that OpenGL may need additional information about how bytes are arranged in processor memory. For example, systems differ in which are the most significant bytes in a short or in an int. Some machines may require that data be aligned on four byte boundaries in memory. In some cases, although there may be more than one allowable method of arranging image data, there may be great differences in efficiency among them. OpenGL provides the function glPixelStore*() to allow programs to adapt to how image data are stored in the processor.

> **void glPixelStore{fd}(GLenum param, TYPE value)**
>
> sets the pixel store mode parameter **param** to **value**.

There are many values of the parameters to account for the many possible situations on different machines. Two of the more common options are

```
glPixelStorei(GL_UNPACK_SWAP_BYTES, GL_TRUE);
glPixelStorei(GL_PACK_SWAP_BYTES, GL_TRUE);
```

These functions reorder the bytes from least significant to most significant for shorts and ints without changing the order of bits in a byte. Two other important options are

```
glPixelStorei(GL_UNPACK_ALIGNMENT, 1);
glPixelStorei(GL_PACK_ALIGNMENT, 1);
```

which packs and unpacks the data always using the next byte. Note that we can control the reading of pixels from the frame buffer (packing) and the writing of pixels to the frame buffer from processor memory (unpacking) independently.

> If imaging functions give unexpected results, check your pixel store modes.

Fortunately, if you are working on single architecture, usually you need not worry about these options and can use the default values for parameters. You can also often avoid problems, as we did in our program, by using unsigned bytes whenever possible.

7.7 Displaying a PPM Image

When we use images from external sources, they are usually in some standard format such as JPEG, TIFF, GIF, or PPM. The multiplicity of these formats is due, in large part, to the multiple types of image data. Images can be RGB, indexed color, RGBA, or luminance. The data may be stored as integers, bytes, or floats. In addition, the data may be compressed to reduce the size of the image file. One of the reasons that OpenGL lacks functions to handle images in standard formats is that there are so many formats. Consequently, we often have to write our own code to read image files and to take images that we form in the frame buffer and save them in a standard format. Often, we can use standard software, such as Photoshop or the xv image viewer, to convert from one standard format to another, rather than creating a large number of image readers and writers.

We can illustrate the basic ideas, as well as the use of various pixel functions in OpenGL, by writing a program that will read an image in a standard format and use OpenGL to display it. We will do this for a Portable Pixel Map (PPM) file. This format is uncompressed and very simple. The example will cover most issues for uncompressed formats. Working with compressed formats is, however, beyond the scope of this book.

PPM files, like most image files, start with a header that identifies the type of the file, the size and format of the image, and some optional comments. The header is followed by the data. PPM files store RGB images as successive RGB pixels, each component represented by an integer in ASCII form. The header looks like

```
P3
# comment 1
# comment 2
       .
# comment n
rows columns max
```

The P3 identifies the file as a PPM file. It is followed by an arbitrary number of comment lines: each begins with a # and can be at most 70 characters long. The next three values are integers for the number of rows and columns, and the maximum value of the RGB values in the data. The minimum value is assumed to be zero. These are followed by the data as a sequence of RGB values; each RGB value is a string of ASCII characters for three integers. The PPM format uses one or more white space characters (spaces, tabs, new lines) to separate values.

We will write the program so it prompts the user for the filename of the PPM file. There are a few tricks in reading the header because we do not know how many comment lines there will be. We allocate a buffer into which we can read data.

```
FILE *fd;
char c;
char b[70];

printf("enter file name\n");
```

```
scanf("%s", b);
fd = fopen(b, "r");

fscanf(fd, "%[^\n] ", b);
if(b[0] != 'P' || b[1] != '3')
{
   printf("%s is not a PPM file!\n", argv[1]);
   exit(0);
}
```

After we read the first line, we check if the first two characters are P3. Then, we read the first character on the next line. If it is a #, we know it is a comment line and we can read the rest of the line into the buffer. If this character is not a #, we can put it back into the file stream using ungetc(). Now, we can read the three integers for the number of rows and columns and for the maximum value of the color components.

```
fscanf(fd, "%c", &c);
while(c == '#')
{
   fscanf(fd, "%[^\n]", b);
   printf("%s\n", b);
   fscanf(fd, "%c", &c);
}
ungetc(c,fd);
fscanf(fd, "%d %d %d", &n, &m, &k);
```

We can use the rows and columns to set the size of the window:

```
glutInitWindowSize(n, m);
```

We use a dynamic array so that the program will work for any size image. We now allocate a one-dimensional array of 3*rows*columns unsigned bytes.

```
GLubyte *image;
nm = n*m;
image = malloc(3*sizeof(GLuint)*nm);
```

When using dynamic arrays with OpenGL, it is important to allocate one-dimensional arrays of data rather than arrays of pointers to arrays of data. If we tried the latter, we could not pass the array to an OpenGL function such as glDrawPixels(). We will use an array of unsigned bytes to store the image data. Although OpenGL can use a variety of types, we usually cannot see at a greater resolution, even if the display has more than eight bits per color component. However, the data are given as integers so we must scale them by the factor

```
float s = 255.0/k;
```

We can now read the data. If the value of s is 1.0 (as it often is for PPM files), we can skip the scaling step.

```
if (k == 255) for(i = 0; i < nm; i++)
{
   fscanf(fd, "%d %d %d", &red, &green, &blue);
   image[3*nm-3*i-3] = red;
   image[3*nm-3*i-2] = green;
   image[3*nm-3*i-1] = blue;
}
else for(i = 0; i < nm; i++)
{
   fscanf(fd,"%d %d %d", &red, &green, &blue);
   image[3*nm-3*i-3] = red*s;
   image[3*nm-3*i-2] = green*s;
   image[3*nm-3*i-1] = blue*s;
}
```

Finally, we can display the image in the display callback:

```
void display()
{
   glClear(GL_COLOR_BUFFER_BIT);
   glRasterPos2i(0, 0);
   glDrawPixels(n, m, GL_RGB, GL_UNSIGNED_BYTE, image);
   glFlush();
}
```

OpenGL uses one-dimensional arrays to store two-dimensional information. When using dynamic arrays in an application, it is safer to use one-dimensional arrays to hold image data.

Note that there are no geometric functions in this program. By choosing the OpenGL window to match the size of the image, we fill the window when we display the image, as in Figure 7.8. However, when we resize the window, we will see only part of the image if we make the window smaller, or extra blank space if we make the window larger, as in Figure 7.9. We can avoid this problem if we use glPixelZoom() that we will discuss in Section 7.10. This situation is fundamentally different from what is possible for displaying geometric entities. When we display a scene with polygons, we can change the projection matrix within the reshape callback whenever the window is resized, so that the entire image fills the viewport. The present situation is due to pixels flowing through their own pipeline, which is unaffected by the projection and model-view matrices.

We can rescale images so that they change size when we change the window if we use the images to define texture maps, the topic of the next chapter.

Image rectangles and bitmaps are placed exactly in the frame buffer so their sizes on the screen are unaffected by the reshape callback.

Figure 7.8 Display of PPM image where window size matches image size

Figure 7.9 Display of PPM image after window size has been changed

One tempting change to our program would be to use integers rather than bytes for the array image

```
GLuint *image;
nm = n*m;
image = malloc(12*sizeof(GLuint)*nm);
```

and then use `glDrawPixels()` with integers:

```
glDrawPixels(n, m, GL_RGB, GL_UNSIGNED_INT, image);
```

We could then use pixel transfer operations

```
glPixelTransferf(GL_RED_SCALE, s);
glPixelTransferf(GL_GREEN_SCALE, s);
glPixelTransferf(GL_BLUE_SCALE, s);
```

so that the scaling would be done by OpenGL rather than inside the application. However, we must be sure we are using the correct pixel store mode.

Here is the PPM reader again, using pixel transfer and pixel store operations. The code prints the contents of the header.

```
#include <stdio.h>
#include <stdlib.h>

#include <GL/glut.h>

int n;
int m;

GLuint *image;

void display()
{
  glClear(GL_COLOR_BUFFER_BIT);
  glRasterPos2i(0, 0);
  glDrawPixels(n, m, GL_RGB, GL_UNSIGNED_INT, image);
  glFlush();
}

void myreshape(int w, int h)
{
  glMatrixMode(GL_PROJECTION);
  glLoadIdentity();
  gluOrtho2D(0.0, (GLfloat) n, 0.0, (GLfloat) m);
  glMatrixMode(GL_MODELVIEW);
  glLoadIdentity();
  glViewport(0, 0, w, h);
}

int main(int argc, char **argv)
{
  FILE *fd;
  int k, nm;
  char c;
  int i;
  char b[71];
  float s;
  unsigned int red, green, blue;

  printf("enter file name\n");
  scanf("%s", b);
  fd = fopen(b, "r");
  fscanf(fd, "%[^\n]", b);
  if(b[0] != 'P' || b[1] != '3')
  {
    printf("%s is not a PPM file!\n", b);
    exit(0);
```

```
    }
    printf("%s is a PPM file\n", b);
    fscanf(fd, "%c", &c);
    while(c == '#')
    {
        fscanf(fd, "%[^\n]", b);
        printf("%s\n", b);
        fscanf(fd, "%c", &c);
    }
    ungetc(c, fd);
    fscanf(fd, "%d %d %d", &n, &m, &k);

    printf("%d rows %d columns max value = %d\n", n, m, k);

    nm = n*m;

    image = malloc(3*sizeof(GLuint)*nm);

    s = 255./k;

    for(i = 0; i < nm; i++)
    {
        fscanf(fd, "%u %u %u", &red, &green, &blue);
        image[3*nm-3*i-3] = red;
        image[3*nm-3*i-2] = green;
        image[3*nm-3*i-1] = blue;
    }
    printf("read image\n");
    glutInit(&argc, argv);
    glutInitDisplayMode(GLUT_SINGLE | GLUT_RGB);
    glutInitWindowSize(n, m);
    glutInitWindowPosition(0, 0);
    glutCreateWindow("image");
    glutReshapeFunc(myreshape);
    glutDisplayFunc(display);
    glPixelTransferf(GL_RED_SCALE, s);
    glPixelTransferf(GL_GREEN_SCALE, s);
    glPixelTransferf(GL_BLUE_SCALE, s);
    glClearColor(1.0, 1.0, 1.0, 1.0);
    glutMainLoop();
}
```

7.8 Using Luminance

In many applications, we work with images that consist only of shades of gray. Often these images are referred to as **luminance** images. Luminance images can be stored in an array using only scalars for the elements rather than RGB triplets. Such grayscale images are often captured from the real world, and the grayscale values can be related to the red, green, and blue color components that we might measure with a black-and-white camera. Equivalently, the gray values can be thought of as the values we might see on a monochrome television.

The relationship between luminance and the color components of a standard RGB display is defined by the perceptually-based equation

$$L = .30\ R + .59\ G + .11\ B$$

Thus, what we see on a monochromic display is dominated by the green component. This equation is determined both by the characteristics of the display, such as the relative strengths of the phosphors in a CRT, and the properties of our visual systems. We have very low sensitivity to blue, which is at the end of the visible part of the spectrum, but very high sensitivity to green. Consequently, to handle luminance correctly, we can use pixel scaling with the correct factors when we go between RGB and luminance.

7.9 Pixel Mapping

One weakness of our use of RGB color is that it does not take account of the differences among the RGB systems used in display technologies, including CRTs, film, and projectors. A RGB pixel in a color buffer can appear differently when displayed on two different output devices due to differences between, for example, film dyes and CRT phosphors. We can compensate for some of these problems in OpenGL by **pixel mapping**. This feature allows each pixel to be altered by a user-defined table. We can apply the features in a variety of modes. We can use a separate table for each of red, green, blue, and alpha. Thus, the blue table would alter each blue value as it goes into the frame buffer. If we wish to use the color maps, first we use

```
glPixelTransferi(GL_MAP_COLOR, GL_TRUE);
```

Then we set up the maps using `glPixelMap*v()`.

---

void glPixelTransfer{if}(GLenum name, TYPE value)

sets the pixel transfer mode parameter **name** to **value**. Various options allows enabling color mapping (**GL_MAP_COLOR**) and scaling and biasing the scaling.

void glPixelMap{ui us f}v(GLenum map, GLint size, TYPE *array)

sets up a pixel map for pixels of type (unsigned int, unsigned short, or float) to map from pixel as specified by **map**. The map is of length **size** with values in **array**. The values of **map** include **GL_PIXEL_MAP_I_TO_R** (or **G** or **B**) for mapping color indices to colors and **GL_PIXEL_MAP_R_TO_R** (or **G_TO_G** or **B_TO_B**) for rescaling RGB colors. **Size** must be a power of 2.

Generally, the size parameter is determined by how much memory is allocated for each component of a pixel. Thus, if we use eight bits for each RGB component and we want to map blue values to blue values, we might see a function call of the form

```
float bluemap[256];
glPixelMapfv(GL_PIXEL_MAP_B_TO_B, 256, bluemap);
```

Here, the values of blue on both the input to and output from the map would normally be in the range (0, 1). We would have similar lines of code for the green and red maps.

Another common example of the use of pixel maps occurs with **pseudocolor**. Here we start with a luminance image but use color to display the gray values. This technique has many similarities to using indexed color; however, the processing is done on luminance values that have meaning within the application. A typical use might look something like

```
for(i = 0; i < 256; i++)
{
   redmap[i] = i/255.0;
   if(i < 128) greenmap[i] = i/128.0;
   else greenmap[i] = 1.0-(i-128.0)/127.0;
   blue_map[i] = 1.0-i/255.0;
}
glPixelMapfv(GL_PIXEL_MAP_I_TO_R, 256, redmap);
glPixelMapfv(GL_PIXEL_MAP_I_TO_R, 256, greenmap);
glPixelMapfv(GL_PIXEL_MAP_I_TO_R, 256, bluemap);
```

Here black is mapped to blue, white is mapped to red, and grays in the middle are mapped to colors that are shades of green.

7.10 Pixel Zoom

When we are working with pixels, most geometric transformations, such as rotation and translation, are not practical because pixels are discrete entities and must lie at fixed locations in the frame buffer. If we were to rotate a block of pixels, we could only approximate their appearance on the display. However, the scaling of blocks of pixels along the directions of the window can make sense. For example, if we have a raster set of characters and we want to make a character twice as large, we can **replicate** its pixels; that is, we can render each pixel in the font four times as in Figure 7.10.

OpenGL provides the function glPixelZoom() for this purpose. We can use it to replicate pixels, thus enlarging the image. We can also use it for reducing the

Figure 7.10 Replicating pixels to form larger characters

size of the image. If a scale factor is negative, we also flip the image with respect to the corresponding direction on the display.

---

void glPixelZoom(GLfloat sx, GLfloat sy)

magnifies or reduces pixels by the scale factors **sx** and **sy** when pixels are drawn. Negative values flip the image in that direction, in addition to the magnification or reduction. Pixel zoom does not apply to bitmaps.

Note that although fractional factors are allowed, you may notice defects in the image when the pixels are rendered. If we look back at our example of the PPM reader, we flipped and mirrored the image as we read it to account for how OpenGL displays its pixels. Instead, we could have read the pixels in order by the code

```
for(i = 0; i < nm; i++)
{
    fscanf(fd, "%d %d %d", &red, &green, &blue);
    image[3*i] = red;
    image[3*i+1] = green;
    image[3*i+2] = blue;
}
```

and then used the pixel zoom

```
glPixelZoom(-1.0, -1.0);
```

In some applications, we have images of one size but need to work with images of another. For example, when we work with textures in the next chapter, all the texture maps must have sizes that are powers of 2. We could use a combination C code and OpenGL functions to produce these images, but there is a function in the utility library to help us.

---

void gluScaleImage(GLenum format, GLint win, GLint hin,
     GLenum typein, void *imagein, GLint wout, GLint hout,
     GLenum typeout, void *imageout)

takes a **win** × **hout** image **imagein** of **format** and **typein** and produces a **wout** × **hout** image **imageout** of **format** and **typeout**.

7.11 Image Processing in OpenGL

With this wealth of functionality, we can write programs to use OpenGL to accomplish many of the operations that are associated with digital image processing, including histogram computations, filtering (convolution), and color table

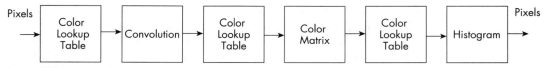

Figure 7.11 The imaging pipeline

manipulation. Although all these operations could be done within the user program, we would like to use the OpenGL processing capabilities that are often implemented in hardware. One reason is that we want to use the imaging capabilities that are supported within the hardware of many commodity graphics cards. Another is that we would like to avoid multiple transfers of images between processor memory and memory on the graphics card.

Image-processing systems usually work on a stream of pixels and perform operations including

- Color lookup tables that map input pixel values (colors and luminance) to other values
- Convolution or filtering that replaces a pixel value by a linear function of the surrounding pixel values
- Color matrix operations that multiply an RGBA color by a 4×4 matrix, creating another RGBA color
- Histogram calculations that compute the distribution of pixel values in an image

One approach to doing image processing in OpenGL is to create a set of functions using the pixel functions that we have just presented. Much of this has already been done and comprises the **imaging subset** of OpenGL, which is documented in the OpenGL *Programming Guide*. These functions are an OpenGL extension and thus are not supported on all OpenGL implementations. However, they are so useful that they are supported on many. The functions are based on an image-processing pipeline as in Figure 7.11.

Another approach to image processing is to use texture maps, the topic of the next chapter. Texture mapping combines the pixel and geometric pipelines and allows us to use our transformation capabilities on pixels by first converting our images to textural maps.

7.12 Programming Exercises

1. If you wrote a drawing program from the exercises at the end of Chapter 3, then use logic operations to add rubberbanding. For example, if you want to draw a line segment, the pushing down of a mouse button fixes one end point of the line segment. As long as the button is held down, new lines are drawn from the initial point to the location of the mouse. When the mouse button is released, the final position of the

mouse determines the second endpoint of the line segment. A similar strategy can be used for circles and rectangles.

2. The histogram of an image is a table of the occurrences of each luminance or color component level in an image. Write a program to compute the histogram of a luminance image with 256 levels. Use the histogram to construct a lookup table such that when it is applied to the same image, the resulting image will have a histogram in which each level occurs the same number of times.

3. The appearance of many images can be improved by altering the distributions of the luminance or color components through lookup tables. Write a program that will allow you to change the values in color tables interactively. One approach might be to allow users to construct piecewise linear curves of input to output values with three or four segments and then approximate these curves with pixel maps.

Texture Mapping

Texture mapping combines pixels with geometric objects to provide images of seemingly great complexity but without the overhead of building large geometric models. Implementation of texture mapping uses both the geometric and pixel pipelines. Although the basics of how we apply texture maps to objects are simple, doing it well requires the careful setting of a variety of parameters. We shall start with a simple example and then add to it in subsequent sections.

8.1 What Is a Texture Map?

At this point, we have two fundamental ways to display objects on the screen. We can either model them as geometric objects, typically as polygons in three dimensions, and pass them through the geometric pipeline; or we can display blocks of pixels. Each approach has its limitations. Pixels can show great detail but lack three-dimensional properties. Although we can process polygons at rates measured in millions of polygons per second on systems that implement the geometric pipeline in hardware, even these systems cannot process polygons fast enough to model many natural phenomena, such as fire, grass, water, or clouds.

What we can do, however, is attempt to combine the best features of each approach, using a method called **texture mapping**. Suppose that we have an $n \times m$ array of pixels. Instead of regarding the array as discrete elements, we can think of it as a continuous array. A point in this array is defined by variables s and t. Thus, as in Figure 8.1, for each (s, t) pair we have a value that is the value of a pixel, usually either a luminance value or an RGB or RGBA value. This continuous array is a two-dimensional **texture**. When we refer to the original elements we call them **texels**, or texture elements, rather than pixels.

Now consider a geometric object in three dimensions. Each point on its surface corresponds to coordinates (x, y, z) in three-dimensional world-coordinate space. Now, if we can associate each (x, y, z) point in world coordinates with a point (s, t) in **texture coordinates** through a pair of functions

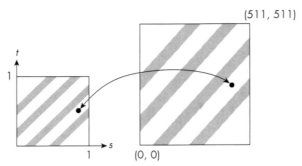

figure 8.1 Texture map as a continuous image in (s, t) space and as a discrete image

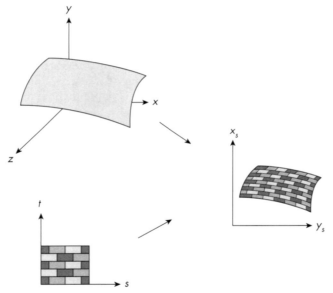

Figure 8.2 Combining a texture with a surface to color pixels in window coordinates

$$s = f(x, y, z)$$
$$t = g(x, y, z)$$

then we could use the color or luminance from the texture to determine the color that we use for the point on the surface (if it is visible). This process is shown in Figure 8.2 and shows the essence of texture mapping.

At this point, texture mapping is rather abstract and not coupled to how OpenGL processes pixels and geometry. The main difficulty is that pixels (texels) and geometry flow forward through different pipelines, and at the point at which we need the texture value we are in the rasterization stage. Thus, it is not clear how we match points on the surface with texels. OpenGL handles this problem by forcing the application program to define texture coordinates for each vertex. More specifically, texture coordinates, like colors and normals, are part of the OpenGL state and when a vertex is defined, it uses the current texture coordinates. Thus, we never define functions f and g explicitly. Rather we provide samples of their values in our programs by defining texture coordinates for vertices. OpenGL uses interpolation to determine the texture coordinates that it needs during rasterization.

8.2 Constructing a Texture Map

Using a texture map requires three basic steps. First, we must identify the image that we want to use for the texture map. This image can be one that we read in, as in Chapter 7, or it can be defined within the application program. The texture image can also be copied from one of the OpenGL color buffers. Second, we define parameters that determine how the texture should be applied. Finally, we define texture coordinates for the vertices in the program.

However, like other OpenGL functionality, there is a large variety of options available that affects both the efficiency of the process and the appearance of the image. Let's proceed with a simple example and then we can worry about the options.

OpenGL supports one-, two-, and three-dimensional texture mapping. Two-dimensional texture mapping is the most familiar case. Here we map images to the surfaces of geometric objects, such as polygons. However, we could also use a one-dimensional texture to create a pattern of colors for a line segment or curve. Three-dimensional textures use three-dimensional volumes of texels (sometimes called **voxels** or volume elements). OpenGL then maps the values in this texture volume to surfaces. Conceptually, a three-dimensional texture map is similar to sculpting the shape of a three-dimensional object from a block of material with the specified texture.

Suppose that we have a two-dimensional RGB image in our program. We need not worry from where this image came. We can make this image into a two-dimensional texture map by

```
GLubyte myimage[64][64][3];
glEnable(GL_TEXTURE_2D);

glTexImage2D(GL_TEXTURE_2D, 0, GL_RGB, 64, 64, 0, GL_RGB,
  GL_UNSIGNED_BYTE, myimage);
```

First, texture mapping must be enabled. Note that we have to separately enable one-, two-, and three-dimensional mapping. Next, we use glTexImage2D() to specify the texture image. Most of the parameters should be clear. But let's examine them in order

GL_TEXTURE_2D: tells OpenGL that we are specifying a two-dimensional texture. There is only one other possible option here, GL_PROXY_TEXTURE_2D, which is useful if we want to determine if we have the resources available to support the size texture that we want to use.

0: This parameter sets the level of the texture map. OpenGL supports a facility called *mipmapping*, which we will discuss later, that enables us to use a sequence of texture images at different resolutions to increase efficiency. Level 0 is the highest level and we specify this value when we do not want to use mipmapping.

GL_RGB: Gives the internal format of the image data. The constant GL_RGB identifies the image data as coming from an RGB image. Other values allow us to specify that the image data are in luminance form (GL_LUMINANCE), RGBA (GL_RGBA), or one of many other formats that store image data using other than eight bits per component.

64: Number of rows in the texture. The number of rows (and columns) must be a power of 2.[1]

64: Number of columns in the texture.

0: Border width. A texture map optionally can have a border of one pixel around it that can be used to create smooth texture maps when two texture maps meet.

GL_RGB: The type of texels that are to be used. This parameter and the next have the same options as for pixel data that we discussed in Chapter 7.

GL_UNSIGNED_BYTE: The format of the texels to be used.

myimage: Pointer to the array of image data.

---

void glTexImage2D(GLenum target, GLint level, GLint iformat, GLsizei width, GLsizei height, GLint border, GLenum format, GLenum type, GLvoid *texels)

sets up a two-dimensional texture of **height** × **width texels** of **type** and **format**. A border of **b** texels can be specified. The image data is of format **iformat**.

Although there are many parameters in this function, most of what we are doing here is similar to what we did for images. Texture mapping takes image data from the application program and passes them through the pixel pipeline, just as we do when we draw pixels. Thus, OpenGL must know how these data are formatted in processor memory before it takes them and puts them into texture memory. Consequently, we may also have to set up options via glPixelStore*(). However, there are a few differences at the end of the pixel pipeline. First, texels go into tex-

---

1. Although powers of 2 are part of the OpenGL specification, newer graphics cards allow for an arbitrary texture size.

ture memory rather than the frame buffer. Depending on the implementation, texture memory may be part of the same memory that is used for the frame buffer or it might be special memory. But just as with the frame buffer, OpenGL can use its own format to store texels, and the transfer of texels from the application program to texture memory can take a significant amount of time for large textures. Moreover, texture memory may be a limited resource. Newer graphics cards have many megabytes of texture memory. We shall see in Section 8.9 that OpenGL supports multiple textures through texture objects.

The dimensions of texture images must be powers of 2.

It may take a significant amount of time to move a texture image from processor memory to texture memory.

We can set up one- and three-dimensional texture maps in a similar manner, using `glTexImage1D()` and `glTexImage3D()`. Each must be enabled separately (`GL_TEXTURE_1D` or `GL_TEXTURE_3D`).

> **void glTexImage1D(GLenum target, GLint level, GLint iformat,**
>   **GLsizei width, GLint border, GLenum format, GLenum type,**
>   **GLvoid *texels)**
>
> **void glTexImage3D(GLenum target, GLint level, GLint iformat,**
>   **GLsizei width, GLsizei height, GLsizei depth, GLint border,**
>   **GLenum format, GLenum type, GLvoid *texels)**
>
> sets up one- and three-dimensional texture maps.

8.3 Texture Coordinates

The mapping between points on geometric objects and texels is through the functions `glTexCoord*()`. Texture coordinates are part of the OpenGL state. Just as with vertices, texture coordinates are represented internally in four dimensions that conventionally use the letters (s, t, r, q) to denote the coordinates. If we specify fewer than the full four dimensions, the defaults are $t = r = 0$, $q = 1$.

> **void glTexCoord{1234}{sifd}(TYPE scoord, TYPE tcoord, ...)**
>
> **void glTexCoord{1234}{sifd}v(TYPE *vcoord)**
>
> sets the current texture coordinates to **scoord, tcoord,** . . . or through the array **vcoord.**

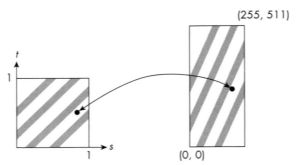

Figure 8.3 Texture coordinates and texture array for a
256×512 image

In two dimensions, the array of texels that we specified in `glTexImage2D()` is assumed to range over the continuous (s, t) rectangle with coordinates in the range $(0, 1)$. Thus even if the array does not have the same number of rows and columns, it still has texture coordinates such that $(0, 0)$ is the lower-left corner and $(1, 1)$ is the upper-right corner as in Figure 8.3.

Now suppose that we want to map our entire texture to a quadrilateral. We set the texture coordinates before each specification of a vertex as in the code

```
glBegin(GL_QUADS);
    glTexCoord2f(0.0, 0.0);
    glVertex3fv(vertex[0]);
    glTexCoord2f(0.0, 1.0);
    glVertex3fv(vertex[1]);
    glTexCoord2f(1.0, 1.0);
    glVertex3fv(vertex[2]);
    glTexCoord2f(1.0, 0.0);
    glVertex3fv(vertex[3]);
glEnd();
```

Effectively, we have assigned a texture coordinate to each vertex. During rendering, OpenGL obtains texture values for interior points by interpolating the values in the array of texels. This method is similar to how OpenGL constructs smooth colors and shades. However, because the texels are discrete, we might see some artifacts of the interpolation. OpenGL provides some parameters that give us some control over the interpolation, texture sampling, and texture smoothing. We shall discuss these parameters in the next section.

Figure 8.4 shows two examples of checkerboard textures mapped to a quadrilateral. Checkerboards are especially useful for demonstrating the various options and seeing how OpenGL implements texture mapping. If the quadrilateral is a square aligned with the viewer, we get the image on the left. If we move one of the corners of the quadrilateral so it is no longer a square, we get the image on the right. In both cases, the texture map is stretched to fit the quadrilateral and the

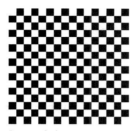

Figure 8.4 Applying a checker board texture to quadrilaterals

interior values are obtained from the texture map by interpolation. But, as we can see from Figure 8.4, the interpolation can cause distortions to the texture. We see that OpenGL renders the quadrilateral as two triangles, which results in the distinct distortion pattern that we see when the texture is mapped to the quadrilateral on the right of Figure 8.4. Of course, we could have chosen different texture coordinates for the vertices of the quadrilateral and avoided the noticeable distortion. However, in practice it is not always clear how to pair texture coordinates with vertices.

Internally, texture coordinates are stored in four dimensions, as are vertices. To complete the analogy with vertices, there is a 4×4 texture matrix, initially set to an identity matrix, that multiplies the present texture coordinates. We can alter this matrix by setting the matrix mode

```
glMatrixMode(GL_TEXTURE);
```

and using the same techniques that we used for the model-view and projection matrices. Thus, we can use the texture matrix to rotate, translate, and scale a given texture by transforming texture coordinates.

8.4 Texture Parameters

Although `glTexCoord*()` and `glTexImage*()` are the essential routines in texture mapping, we must also set some additional required parameters. There are also other optional parameters that give us more control over how the texture is applied to the surface. These parameters are set by `glTexParameter*()`.

void glTexParameter{if}(GLenum target, GLenum name, TYPE value)

void glTexParameter{if}v(GLenum target, GLenum name, TYPE *value)

set the parameter **name** to **value** for texture of type **target (GL_TEXTURE_1D, GL_TEXTURE_2D, or GL_TEXTURE_3D)**.

The required parameters determine what happens when values of s, t, r, or q go outside the range $(0, 1)$ and how sampling and filtering are applied.

Although the texture map is assumed to be defined for values of s, t, r, and q over $(0, 1)$, we can use any values in $\texttt{glTexCoord*()}$. We use the parameters $\texttt{GL\_TEXTURE\_WRAP\_*}$ to tell OpenGL what to do if values are out of that range. The two possibilities are to let the values repeat ($\texttt{GL\_REPEAT}$); that is, to use the fractional part for positive values and to increase any negative values by the smallest integer that makes them positive. We can make separate decisions for each texture coordinate. The second option is to clamp the values ($\texttt{GL\_CLAMP}$) at 0.0 and 1.0; that is, negative values use 0.0 and values greater than 1.0 use 1.0. A typical usage for two-dimensional texture might look like

```
glTexParameteri(GL_TEXTURE_2D, GL_TEXTURE_WRAP_S, GL_REPEAT);
glTexParameteri(GL_TEXTURE_2D, GL_TEXTURE_WRAP_T, GL_REPEAT);
```

Mapping of a texture map to a surface takes place during rendering. Hence, it is not really applied to the surface but rather to a pixel that is the projection (in window coordinates) of a small region of the surface. Looked at another way, each pixel corresponds to a small area of a geometric surface *and* to a small region of texture space—sometimes called the **preimage** of the pixel. Depending on the values of the texture coordinates, the size of the surface, and the viewing conditions, each texel may cover multiple pixels (**magnification**) or each pixel may cover multiple texels (**minification**), as in Figure 8.5.

The situation is further complicated because the pixels and texels need not be aligned and if we are working with perspective or with curved surfaces, the preimage of a texel may not be rectangular. The simplest solution to this problem is through **point sampling**. The center of each pixel is mapped to a point in texture space (using interpolation) and OpenGL uses the value at this point. Although this method is simple and fast, it can lead to unacceptable visual effects that are an example of an aliasing error. A smother appearance can be obtained by using the average of a group of texels around the point sample to obtain the value of the texture. This averaging is a form of linear filtering. OpenGL uses a 2×2 array of neighboring texels for its filter. We specify these options separately for magnification and minification. The parameters are $\texttt{GL\_TEX\_MAG\_FILTER}$, and

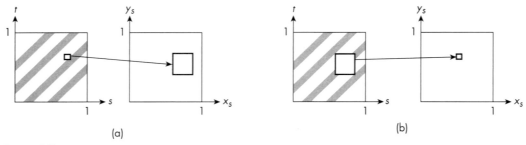

Figure 8.5 (a) Magnification and (b) minification

GL_TEX_MIN_FILTER, and we can choose between GL_NEAREST and GL_LINEAR. If we want the fastest implementation, we would set these parameters as follows in our initialization

```
glTexParameteri(GL_TEXTURE_2D, GL_TEXURE_MAG_FILTER,
   GL_NEAREST);
glTexParameteri(GL_TEXTURE_2D, GL_TEXURE_MIN_FILTER,
   GL_NEAREST);
```

Texture mapping presents the programmer with many choices between efficiency and smooth textures. A problematic area is with perspective viewing. The fastest methods of interpolating textures do not handle the shape distortion caused by the perspective transformation. Most of the time you probably will not notice the problem, but you might with regular textures, such as stripes and checkerboards. Some OpenGL implementations can adjust their renderers for perspective if asked. The function glHint() can be used to ask the implementation to produce a better-looking image, even if the rendering is slower.[2]

```
glHint(GL_PERSPECTIVE_CORRECTION_HINT, GL_NICEST);
```

The option GL_FASTEST is the alternative to GL_NICEST. Recent graphics hardware can do perspective-correct texturing without a performance penalty.

---

void glHint(GLenum option, GLenum hint)

requests that the **hint** be applied to **option**.

Hints can be requested for other rendering options such as for antialiasing lines and polygons (GL_LINE_SMOOTH_HINT, GL_POLYGON_SMOOTH_HINT).

8.5 A Rotating Cube with Texture

Here is a simple program that puts a checkerboard texture on the rotating cube that we used in previous chapters. Note that very few changes are needed to add texture if we use the standard defaults.

```
#include <stdlib.h>
#include <GL/glut.h>
```

---

2. Modern graphics cards support many options in hardware so that filtering any perspective correction may be automatic or not incur a performance penalty.

```
GLfloat vertices[][3] = {{-1.0, -1.0, 1.0}, {-1.0, 1.0, 1.0},
   {1.0, 1.0, 1.0}, {1.0, -1.0, 1.0}, {-1.0, -1.0, -1.0},
   {-1.0, 1.0, -1.0}, {1.0, 1.0, -1.0}, {1.0, -1.0, -1.0}};

GLfloat colors[][3] = {{{1.0, 0.0, 0.0},
   {0.0, 1.0, 1.0}, {1.0, 1.0, 0.0}, {0.0, 1.0, 0.0},
   {0.0, 0.0, 1.0}, {1.0, 0.0, 1.0}};
   {0.0, 0.0, 0.0}, {1.0, 1.0, 1.0}};

void polygon(int a, int b, int c, int d)
{

/* draw a polygon via list of vertices */

  glBegin(GL_POLYGON);
    glColor3fv(colors[a]);
    glTexCoord2f(0.0, 0.0);
    glVertex3fv(vertices[a]);
    glColor3fv(colors[b]);
    glTexCoord2f(0.0, 1.0);
    glVertex3fv(vertices[b]);
    glColor3fv(colors[c]);
    glTexCoord2f(1.0, 1.0);
    glVertex3fv(vertices[c]);
    glColor3fv(colors[d]);
    glTexCoord2f(1.0, 0.0);
    glVertex3fv(vertices[d]);
  glEnd();

}

void colorcube()
{

/* map vertices to faces */

  polygon(0, 3, 2, 1);
  polygon(2, 3, 7, 6);
  polygon(3, 0, 4, 7);
  polygon(1, 2, 6, 5);
  polygon(4, 5, 6, 7);
  polygon(5, 4, 0, 1);
}

static GLfloat theta[] = {0.0, 0.0, 0.0};
static GLint axis = 2;
```

```
void display(void)
{

  glClear(GL_COLOR_BUFFER_BIT | GL_DEPTH_BUFFER_BIT);
  glLoadIdentity();
  glRotatef(theta[0], 1.0, 0.0, 0.0);
  glRotatef(theta[1], 0.0, 1.0, 0.0);
  glRotatef(theta[2], 0.0, 0.0, 1.0);

  colorcube();

  glutSwapBuffers();
}

void spinCube()
{

  theta[axis] += 2.0;
  if(theta[axis] > 360.0) theta[axis] -= 360.0;
  glutPostRedisplay();
}

void mouse(int btn, int state, int x, int y)
{
  if(btn == GLUT_LEFT_BUTTON & state == GLUT_DOWN)
    axis = 0;
  if(btn == GLUT_MIDDLE_BUTTON & state == GLUT_DOWN)
    axis = 1;
  if(btn == GLUT_RIGHT_BUTTON & state == GLUT_DOWN)
    axis = 2;
}

void myReshape(int w, int h)
{
  glViewport(0, 0, w, h);
  glMatrixMode(GL_PROJECTION);
  glLoadIdentity();
  if(w <= h)
    glOrtho(-2.0, 2.0, -2.0 * (GLfloat) h / (GLfloat)
      w, 2.0 * (GLfloat) h / (GLfloat) w,
        -10.0, 10.0);
  else
    glOrtho(-2.0 * (GLfloat) w / (GLfloat) h,
        2.0 * (GLfloat) w / (GLfloat) h, -2.0, 2.0,
        -10.0, 10.0);
  glMatrixMode(GL_MODELVIEW);
}
```

```
int main(int argc, char **argv)
{
  GLubyte image[64][64][3];
  int i, j, r, c;
  for(i = 0; i < 64; i++)
  {
    for(j = 0; j < 64; j++)
    {
      c = (((((i&0x8) == 0)^((j&0x8)) == 0))*255;
      image[i][j][0] = (GLubyte) c;
      image[i][j][1] = (GLubyte) c;
      image[i][j][2] = (GLubyte) c;
    }
  }
  glutInit(&argc, argv);
  glutInitDisplayMode(GLUT_DOUBLE | GLUT_RGB |
    GLUT_DEPTH);
  glutInitWindowSize(500, 500);
  glutCreateWindow("colorcube");

  glutReshapeFunc(myReshape);
  glutDisplayFunc(display);
  glutIdleFunc(spinCube);
  glutMouseFunc(mouse);
  glEnable(GL_DEPTH_TEST);
  glEnable(GL_TEXTURE_2D);

  glTexImage2D(GL_TEXTURE_2D, 0, GL_RGB, 64, 64, 0, GL_RGB,
    GL_UNSIGNED_BYTE, image);

  glTexParameterf(GL_TEXTURE_2D, GL_TEXTURE_WRAP_S, GL_CLAMP);
  glTexParameterf(GL_TEXTURE_2D, GL_TEXTURE_WRAP_T, GL_CLAMP);
  glTexParameterf(GL_TEXTURE_2D, GL_TEXTURE_MAG_FILTER,
    GL_NEAREST);
  glTexParameterf(GL_TEXTURE_2D, GL_TEXTURE_MIN_FILTER,
    GL_NEAREST);
  glutMainLoop();
}
```

8.6 Applying Textures to Surfaces

We have not yet addressed how textures are applied in the rendering process and how texture mapping interacts with shading. If you run the above program, you will notice that the color at each point is a mixture of the interpolated colors from the vertex colors and the colors in the texture matrix. But this is not the only option. You might also try combining texture with blending by redefining the colors to have four components with translucency by

```
GLfloat colors[][4] = {{1.0, 0.0, 0.0, 0.5},
  {1.0, 1.0, 0.0, 0.5}, {0.0, 1.0, 0.0, 0.5},
  {0.0, 0.0, 1.0, 0.5}, {1.0, 0.0, 1.0, 0.5},
  {0.0, 1.0, 1.0, 0.5}};
```

Then we would use glColor4f() in our polygon function, not enable depth buffering but enable blending

```
glEnable(GL_BLEND);
glBlendFunc(GL_SRC_ALPHA, GL_ONE_MINUS_SRC_ALPHA);
```

We would then see a more interesting mixture of the texture and polygon colors. Recall, however, from Chapter 7, that blending is order dependent.

The default mode of operation is called **modulation**. Here the texture color multiplies the color computed for each face. There are other methods that can be set by glTexEnv*(). The most important mode is **replacement** mode where only the texture color determines the color we see in the frame buffer. We set these modes through the function glTexEnv*().

---

void glTexEnv{if}(GLenum target, GLenum param, TYPE value)

void glTexEnv{if}v(GLenum target, GLenum param, TYPE *value)

set texture parameter **param** to **value**; **target** must be **GL_TEXTURE_ENV**.

The default modulation mode is equivalent to executing

```
glTexEnvi(GL_TEXTURE_ENV, GL_TEXTURE_ENV_MODE, GL_MODULATE);
```

If we use GL_REPLACE rather than GL_MODULATE, we use only the texture color. There are other options including GL_BLEND and GL_DECAL that determine how blending takes place if you are also using the alpha channel or you specify a texture environment color through

```
glTexEnvfv(GL_TEXTURE_ENV, GL_TEX_ENV_COLOR, color);
```

that combines with the object shade and the texture color.

8.7 Borders and Sizing

One difficulty that arises when we use linear filtering is what happens at the edges of the texture where we lack one or more texels to use in the filtering. One solution to this problem is to specify texture map with a border of one additional texel on each side through `glTexImage*()`. Thus, a texture map must be of size $2^m + 2b \times 2^n + 2b$ where b is either 0 or 1.

Alternately, we can specify a border color that will be used automatically by

`glTexParameter3fv(GL_TEXTURE_2D, GL_TEXTURE_BORDER_COLOR, color);`

OpenGL requires that textures have sizes (less any border) that are a power of 2. As we pointed out in Chapter 7, we can use the GLU function `gluScaleImage()` to convert an image to acceptable size for a texture map. We can also obtain a texture map from an image in the frame buffer by the function `glCopyTexImage2D()`.

> **void glCopyTexImage2D(GLenum target, GLint level, GLint iformat, GLint x, GLint y, GLsizei w, GLsizei h, GLint border)**
>
> copies an **w** × **h** image from the present drawing buffer to texture memory. The parameters are as in **glCopyPixels()**, and **target** is **GL_TEXTURE_2D**. The parameter **level** is 0 except if using mipmaps.

You can also copy pixels into parts of an existing texture using the function `glTexSubImage2D()`.

> **void glTexSubImage2D(GLenum target, GLint level, GLint xoffset, GLint yoffset, GLsizei w, GLsizei h, GLenum format, GLenum type, GLvoid *texels)**
>
> copies a **w** × **h** array of **texels** described by **type** and **format** into texture memory starting at (**xoffset, yoffset**).

The function `glCopyTexSubImage2D()` replaces part of a texture from the frame buffer.

> **void glCopyTexSubImage2D(GLenum target, GLint level, Glint xoffset, Glint yoffset, GLint x, GLint y, GLsizei w, GLsizei h)**
>
> copies a **w** × **h** array of pixels from the frame buffer starting at (**x, y**) to texture memory. The other parameters are as in **glTexSubImage2D()**.

8.8 Mipmaps

One of the difficulties with texture maps is that when a large part of a texture array corresponds to a single pixel in the image, simple filtering gives a poor approximation. This situation happens, for example, in perspective viewing when a small object is far from the camera. In addition, whether we use point sampling or filtering, the value that we get from the texture map is still only an approximation to the desired texture values. What we would prefer is to have a texture value that is the average of the texels values over a large area of the texture. One possible way we could accomplish this would be to form smaller texture maps by averaging groups of texels. For example, we could create a 32×32 texture map from a 64×64 texture map by average groups of 4 texels. We could then create a 16×16 texture map by repeating the process. However, once we created these new texture arrays, it would then be problematic to determine which of these maps to use. OpenGL has an option called **mipmapping** which automates this process.

Suppose that we create a sequence of images, each time halving the height and width by merging four pixels into one. If we start with a 64×64 image, we create 32×32, 16×16, 8×8, 4×4, 2×2, and 1×1 images.[3] The first image has level 0, the second has level 1, and so on. We can now call glTexImage2D() for each of these images, each with its own level and dimensions, as in the code

```
GLubyte image0[64][64][3];
GLubyte image1[32][32][3];
.

.
Glubyte image5[1][1][3];
glTexImage2D(GL_TEXTURE_2D, 0, GL_RGB, 64, 64, GL_RGB,
    GL_UNSIGNED_BYTE, image0);
glTexImage2D(GL_TEXTURE_2D, 1, GL_RGB, 32, 32, GL_RGB,
    GL_UNSIGNED_BYTE, image1);
.

.
glTexImage2D(GL_TEXTURE_2D, 5, GL_RGB, 1, 1, GL_RGB,
    GL_UNSIGNED_BYTE, image5);
```

To use these images, we just need to set the minification filter

```
glTexParameteri(GL_TEXTURE_2D, GL_TEXTURE_MIN_FILTER,
    GL_NEAREST_MIPMAP_NEAREST);
```

This is the lowest quality option. OpenGL will use the closest image in which the texel size matches the pixel size and it will use the closest texel. We can, sometimes at a speed penalty, use the closest image and linear filtering (GL_LINEAR_MIPMAP_NEAREST), use the closest texel but linear filter between the closest images (GL_NEAREST_MIPMAP_LINEAR), or do both (GL_LINEAR_MIPMAP_LINEAR). Although the usual use of mipmapping employs a set of images that are reduced-size versions of the one image, there is no reason

---

3. If the original image is not square, we halve each dimension, until the smaller is reduced to 1 and then continue halving the other.

we need to do so. Hence, we can do something such as use a simple texture when a surface projects to a small area on the screen, but have a detailed view revealed when we move the viewer closer by using different images at different levels.

However, if we want to start with one image and produce a set of mipmaps from it, we can use OpenGL to produce these images through the GLU function `gluBuild2DMipmaps()`. This function loads the images into texture memory, so we need not call `glTexImage2D()`. Because the mipmap images are in texture memory, there is no extra storage required in the application.

---

int gluBuild2DMipmaps(GLenum target, GLint iformat, GLint w, GLint h, GLenum format, GLenum type, void *texels)

builds and loads set of mipmaps. The parameters are the same as for **glTexImage2D()**.

8.9 Automatic Texture Coordinate Generation

Although there are many parameters that we can set to use texture maps efficiently, the essence of two-dimensional texture mapping is fairly simple: we map an image to a surface. Once you become familiar with the parameters and options, the most difficult problem is in determining texture coordinates for vertices. There are both practical and theoretical problems. There are two helpful analogies to keep in mind: maps of the Earth and wallpapering.

One problem in mapping the Earth is in trying to represent something that is round on a flat surface. We cannot do this mapping without some shape distortion. In the standard Mercator projection, we put the majority of the shape distortion at the poles. However, if you look at an atlas, you will find other types of maps that handle the distortion in other manners. The two-dimensional texture mapping problem is the inverse of this map problem. Given a rectangular "map," how do we wrap it around a curved surface? There must be some distortion. How we assign texture coordinates determines where the distortion takes place and how we distribute the errors.

Wallpapering also has problems with distortion if we try to put wallpaper on a curved surface. But even on a flat surface, wallpapering has the problem of what to do when we have to use another roll. Matching the new roll to edges of the old roll is problematic. We saw that the use of borders in texture mapping can help, but there is an additional issue related to the size of the areas that we want to wallpaper or texture map. In graphics, we often work with surfaces that are defined by groups of polygons. Although we may have a simple method for assigning texture coordinates to any polygon, each polygon may have a different size. Imagine how distorted an image we would obtain if the same checkerboard texture were mapped to each polygon, regardless of its size.

Consider again the problem of generating texture maps for a sphere. One way of describing the points on the sphere is through the equations

$$x(u, v) = r \cos u \sin v$$
$$y(u, v) = r \cos u \cos v$$
$$z(u, v) = r \sin v$$

As u goes over 360 degrees and v goes over 180 degrees, we generate a sphere of radius r centered at the origin. We can generate polygons from these equations by taking evenly spaced values in u and v. This is what is done by the GLU and GLUT quadric objects. Constant values of u and v generate lines of longitude and latitude. If we want to use a single texture to cover the sphere, then we could use texture coordinates

$$s = u/360.0$$
$$t = v/180.0$$

This assignment will work, but there will be distortion of the texture at the poles. If we used some other method to generate the sphere, then we would see a different distortion pattern.

All quadric surfaces can be described by two parameter functions similar to those for the sphere. Because an OpenGL quadric is displayed as a polygonal approximation to specified quadric with all the vertices located on the actual surface of the quadric, OpenGL can evaluate the correct texture coordinates for each vertex. We use the GLU function `gluQuadricTexture()` to enable automatic generation of texture coordinates.

> **void gluQuadricTexture(GLUquadricObj *obj, GLboolean mode)**
>
> turns on (**GL_TRUE**) or off (**GL_FALSE**) automatic texture coordinate generation for quadric object **obj** based on the value of **mode**.

Figure 8.6 (a) shows a quadric cone that is formed by using a GLU cylinder with the top radius set to zero and the polygons displayed by their edges

```
GLUquadricObj *cone;
cone = gluNewQuadric();
glEnable(GL_CULL_FACE);
gluQuadricDrawStyle(cone, GLU_FILL);
glPolygonMode(GL_FRONT_AND_BACK, GL_LINE);
gluCylinder(cone, 1.0, 0.0, 2.0, 20, 20);
```

If we define our checkerboard texture as before, we can have it placed on the cone by the code

```
GLUquadricObj *cone;
cone = gluNewQuadric();
glEnable(GL_CULL_FACE);
```

```
glPolygonMode(GL_FRONT_AND_BACK, GL_FILL);
glEnable(GL_TEXTURE_2D);
gluQuadricDrawStyle(cone, GLU_FILL);
gluQuadricTexture(cone, GL_TRUE);
glTexEnvi(GL_TEXTURE_ENV, GL_TEXTURE_ENV_MODE,
    GL_MODULATE);
gluCylinder(cone, 1.0, 0.0, 2.0, 20, 20);
```

The result is shown in Figure 8.6 (b). Note that alternate black and white areas become smaller as we move toward the apex of the cone because the polygons that OpenGL uses to approximate the cone become smaller as we go up the cone. Although we might be satisfied with this appearance, in other applications we want to preserve the size of the texture as it is mapped onto the surface.

OpenGL provides another option for automatic texture coordinate generation. Often, the desired texture coordinates can be expressed in terms of points in (x, y, z) space. OpenGL allows us to generate texture coordinates that are measured as distances from a plane in either object space or eye space. Remember that vertices are represented internally in four-dimensional homogeneous coordinates. Hence, internally every vertex is stored as (x, y, z, w) where usually, but not always, w is equal to one. The value $ax + by + cz + dw$ is proportional to the distance from (x, y, z, w) to the plane determined by (a, b, c, d). For example, consider the plane

$$x + 2y + 3z + 4 = 0$$

It has coefficients $(1, 2, 3, 4)$. For any point (x_0, y_0, z_0, w_0) in homogenous coordinates, $x_0 + 2y_0 + 3z_0 + 4w_0$ is proportional to the distance to this plane.

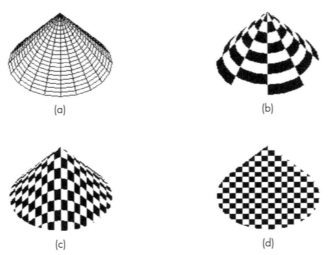

(a)

(b)

(c)

(d)

Figure 8.6 Automatic texture generation on a cone using GLU cylinder (a) cylinder with polygon edges (b) displayed using gluQuadricTexture (c) displayed using glTexGen with GL_OBJECT_LINEAR and (d) displayed using glTexGen with GL_EYE_LINEAR

OpenGL allows us to generate a texture value for any texture coordinate (s, t, r, or q) using this formula, each with its own plane. Such a mapping is equivalent to each of the texture coordinates being determined by a simple linear equation of the form

$$s = a_s x + b_s y + c_s z + d_s w$$
$$t = a_t x + b_t y + c_t z + d_t w$$

Suppose that we have a square in the plane $z = 0$ whose opposite corners are at $(-1, -1, 0)$ and $(1, 1, 0)$, and we want to map a two-dimensional texture to this square. The equations

$$s = x/2 + 1/2$$
$$t = y/2 + 1/2$$

represent this mapping. These two equations correspond to using the planes determined by the coefficients $(1/2, 0, 0, 1/2)$ and $(0, 1/2, 0, 1/2)$. We have to enable this facility independently for each texture coordinate

```
glEnable(GL_TEXTURE_GEN_S);
glEnable(GL_TEXTURE_GEN_T);
```

We use the function `glTexGen*()` to set up the required parameters and identify the planes.

---

void glTexGen{ifd}(GLenum texcoord, GLenum param, TYPE value);

void glTexGen{ifd}v(GLenum texcoord, GLenum param, TYPE *plane);

sets up automatic texture generation for texture coordinate **texcoord**. The parameter **param** specifies either the mode (**GL_TEXTURE_GEN_MODE**) or which space (**GL_OBJECT_LINEAR, GL_EYE_LINEAR**) the plane determined by the array **plane** is specified. If mode is **GL_TEXTURE_GEN_MODE**, then **value** is either **GL_OBJECT_LINEAR** or **GL_EYE_LINEAR**.

Thus, for the above example we would use the four function calls

```
GLfloat planes[] = {0.5, 0.0, 0.0, 0.5};
GLfloat planet[] = {0.0, 0.5, 0.0, 0.5};
glTexGeni(GL_S, GL_TEXTURE_GEN_MODE, GL_OBJECT_LINEAR);
glTexGeni(GL_T, GL_TEXTURE_GEN_MODE, GL_OBJECT_LINEAR);
glTexGenfv(GL_S, GL_OBJECT_LINEAR, planes);
glTexGenfv(GL_T, GL_OBJECT_LINEAR, planet);
```

We still would use all the other texture functions to define the required texture parameters, but we would not use glTexCoord*().

Hence, we generated the texture-mapped cylinder in Figure 8.6 (c) by following these six lines of code with

```
gluCylinder(cone, 1.0, 0.0, 2.0, 20, 20);
```

If we use GL_OBJECT_LINEAR mode, then the texture map is fixed to the surface and if we move the surface, we move the texture with it. Thus, the texture appears painted to the surface. If we use the GL_EYE_LINEAR mode, texture coordinates are based on the vertex positions in eye space so that when we move the object, the texture coordinates assigned to vertices change. Thus, the texture changes as we move the object. Figure 8.8 (d) was generated with the same code as Figure 8.6 (c) except that we used GL_EYE_LINEAR instead of GL_OBJECT_LINEAR.

8.10　Texture Objects

In the default mode of operations, there is a "current texture" that is part of the OpenGL state. This texture is moved to OpenGL's texture memory from system memory when we execute to glTexImage*(). If we have only a single texture map, we incur the overhead of the move only once. However, if we have multiple textures in our program, then we may have a problem. Suppose that each object has its own texture. Then, just as with material properties, every time that we render a different object, we must reload its texture. With any sizable texture dimensions, performance can suffer dramatically.

OpenGL provides an alternative: **texture objects**. The idea is simple. We form an object that consists of a texture and its parameter values. We can then fill texture memory with multiple objects and have OpenGL use a texture determined by the identifier of the object. As long as there is sufficient memory to hold the texture objects, we can avoid reloading of texture maps. If there is not sufficient memory for all the textures that we need, we can prioritize the texture objects to minimize the amount of data movement from the processor to texture memory.

> In most systems, texture memory is a limited resource and we want to minimize the reloading of textures into texture memory.

Just as with display lists, texture identifiers are integers. We can use the function glGenTextures() to find a set of unused integers.

---

void glGenTextures(GLsizei n, GLuint *name)

returns in **name**, the first integer of **n** unused integers for texture object identifiers.

The function g⁻IsTexture() allows us to check if a given id is already in use.

> **GLboolean glIsTexture(GLunint name)**
>
> returns **GL_TRUE** if **name** is already a texture id, and **GL_FALSE** if it is not.

There is a single function, glBindTexture(), that both switches between texture objects and forms new texture objects.

> **void glBindTexture(GLenum target, GLuint name)**
>
> binds **name** to texture of type **target**. (**GL_TEXTURE_1D**, **GL_TEXTURE_2D**, or **GL_TEXTURE_3D**).

If we call glBindTexture() with name and name has not been used before, the subsequent calls to the various texture functions define the texture object with the id name. If name already exists from a previous call to glBindTexture(), then that texture object becomes the present texture and is applied to surfaces until the next call to glBindTexture().

If glBindTexture() is called with name set to 0, then the normal texture calls apply and the present texture that is part of the OpenGL state and the current values of the texture parameters both apply.

We can get rid of texture objects and free the resource that they consume through glDeleteTextures().

> **void glDeleteTextures(GLsizei n, GLunint *namearray)**
>
> deletes **n** texture objects from **namearray**, which holds texture-object names.

If there is not enough room for all our textures in texture memory, we can set a priority for each texture object

```
glTexParameterf(GL_TEXTURE_2D, GL_TEXTURE_PRIORITY, priority);
```

where the value of priority is in the range (0.0, 1.0) with 0.0 being the lowest priority. When OpenGL needs room for a texture, the lowest priority texture is removed from texture memory.

8.11 Texture Maps for Image Manipulation

Often, texture maps are easier to work with than pixels. Because they are mapped to geometric objects, we can manipulate the geometric object and OpenGL will "stretch" the texture to fit the projection of the object. For example, suppose that we want to reshape an image. This problem arises when we have two (or more) images taken with different cameras or from different angles. We then have to stretch one of the images to fit over the other. The traditional approach to this problem was to find matching points in the two images and then to find mathematical functions to map points in one to points in the other. A simpler solution is to let OpenGL do the work with texture maps. We can make texture maps of the two images, map each to a quadrilateral, and then manipulate the corners of the quadrilaterals interactively until we obtain the desired stretching.

Another example of the advantage of using texture maps is that the objects onto which we map our images are subject to the transformations in the OpenGL geometric pipeline. Thus, when we display an image as a texture map and then resize the window, we can use the reshape callback to keep the entire image in the resized window. Here is the PPM display program from Chapter 7, rewritten to use texture maps.

```c
#include <stdio.h>
#include <stdlib.h>
#include <GL/glut.h>

int n;
int m;

GLuint *image;

void display()
{

  glClear(GL_COLOR_BUFFER_BIT);
  glBegin(GL_QUADS);
    glTexCoord2f(0.0, 0.0);
    glVertex2i(0, 0);
    glTexCoord2f(0.0, 1.0);
    glVertex2i(0, m-1);
    glTexCoord2f(1.0, 1.0);
    glVertex2i(n-1, m-1);
    glTexCoord2f(1.0, 0.0);
    glVertex2i(n-1, 0);
  glEnd();
  glFlush();
}


void myreshape(int w, int h)
{
  glMatrixMode(GL_PROJECTION);
```

```
    glLoadIdentity();
    gluOrtho2D(0.0, (GLfloat) n, 0.0, (GLfloat) m);
    glMatrixMode(GL_MODELVIEW);
    glLoadIdentity();
    glViewport(0, 0, h, w);
}

int main(int argc, char **argv)
{
    FILE *fd;
    int k, nm;
    char c;
    int i;
    char b[100];
    float s;
    unsigned int red, green, blue;

    printf("enter file name\n");
    scanf("%s", b);
    fd = fopen(b, "r");
    fscanf(fd, "%[^\n]", b);
    if(b[0] != 'P' || b[1] != '3')
    {
        printf("%s is not a PPM file!\n", b);
        exit(0);
    }
    fscanf(fd, "%c", &c);
    while(c == '#')
    {
        fscanf(fd, "%[^\n]", b);
        fscanf(fd, "%c", &c);
    }
    ungetc(c, fd);
    fscanf(fd, "%u %u %u", &n, &m, &k);
    nm = n*m;
    image = malloc(3*sizeof(GLuint)*nm);
    s = 255./k;

    for(i = 0; i < nm; i++)
    {
        fscanf(fd, "%d %d %d", &red, &green, &blue);
        image[3*nm-3*i-3] = red;
        image[3*nm-3*i-2] = green;
        image[3*nm-3*i-1] = blue;
    }
    glutInit(&argc, argv);
    glutInitDisplayMode(GLUT_SINGLE | GLUT_RGB);
    glutInitWindowSize(n, m);
    glutInitWindowPosition(0, 0);
    glutCreateWindow("image");
```

```
glutReshapeFunc(myreshape);
glutDisplayFunc(display);
glPixelTransferf(GL_RED_SCALE, s);
glPixelTransferf(GL_GREEN_SCALE, s);
glPixelTransferf(GL_BLUE_SCALE, s);
glPixelStorei(GL_UNPACK_SWAP_BYTES, GL_TRUE);
glPixelStorei(GL_UNPACK_ALIGNMENT, 1);
glEnable(GL_TEXTURE_2D);
glTexImage2D(GL_TEXTURE_2D, 0, GL_RGB, n, m, 0, GL_RGB,
  GL_UNSIGNED_INT, image);
glTexParameterf(GL_TEXTURE_2D, GL_TEXTURE_WRAP_S,
  GL_CLAMP);
glTexParameterf(GL_TEXTURE_2D, GL_TEXTURE_WRAP_T,
  GL_CLAMP);
glTexParameterf(GL_TEXTURE_2D, GL_TEXTURE_MAG_FILTER,
  GL_NEAREST);
glTexParameterf(GL_TEXTURE_2D, GL_TEXTURE_MIN_FILTER,
  GL_NEAREST);
glClearColor(0.0, 0.0, 0.0, 1.0);
glColor3f(1.0, 1.0, 1.0);
glutMainLoop();
}
```

Notice that as you resize the window, the relative size of the image in the window remains the same.

8.12 Programming Exercises

1. Apply automatic texture generation to a rotating quadric or the Utah teapot. Your program should allow you to switch between object linear and eye linear mapping.
2. Write a program that displays the interior of a room in which the surface of each wall is a texture map from a digital image. Experiment with how moving a light source affects the image.

CHAPTER 9

Curves and Surfaces

Until now, all our OpenGL geometric primitives, such as lines and polygons, have been flat. Even when we worked with OpenGL quadrics, these surfaces were rendered using flat polygons. OpenGL provides curves and surfaces through a mechanism called evaluators that allows us to generate Bézier curves and surfaces. This mechanism is flexible as we can generate polynomial curves of an arbitrary degree and convert other types of polygonal curves and surfaces into Bézier curves and surfaces.

9.1 Parametric Curves

In many applications in computer graphics, the best choice for curves is based on **parametric polynomial curves**. With such curves, we can represent a curve in two, three, or four dimensions, using a separate equation for each spatial variable using independent variable (or parameter) u

$$x = x(u) = a_{x0} + a_{x1}u + a_{x2}u^2 + \cdots\cdots\cdots + a_{xn}u^n$$
$$y = y(u) = a_{y0} + a_{y1}u + a_{y2}u^2 + \cdots\cdots\cdots + a_{yn}u^n$$
$$z = z(u) = a_{z0} + a_{z1}u + a_{z2}u^2 + \cdots\cdots\cdots + a_{zn}u^n$$
$$w = w(u) = a_{w0} + a_{w1}u + a_{w2}u^2 + \cdots\cdots\cdots + a_{wn}u^n$$

where n is the degree of the polynomials. For a curve in two dimensions, we use only x and y; in three dimensions, x, y, and z; and for four dimensions, we use x, y, z, and w. If we only use two or three, then the standard defaults for the others ($z = 0$, $w = 1$) are applied.

Parametric curves give a point in homogeneous coordinate space ($x(u)$, $y(u)$, $z(u)$, $w(u)$) for each value of u. Generally, we define a **curve segment**, a finite piece of a curve, by allowing u to range over the values

$$u_{\min} \geq u \geq u_{\max}$$

Figure 9.1 shows that the individual curves for the spatial variables are combined to form the three-dimensional curve $\mathbf{p}(u) = (x(u), y(u), z(u))$.

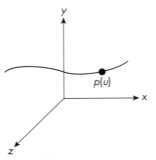

Figure 9.1 Parametric curve

Figure 9.2 Interpolating curves through p_0, p_1, p_2, p_3

For now, we shall consider only curves for which we need to specify x, y, and z, fixing $w = 1$. If we want a curve for a particular n, we must define $3(n + 1)$ coefficients. We can do so by providing $3(n + 1)$ independent conditions that we would like the curve to satisfy. Each type of condition that we apply determines a distinct type of curve. For example, we can provide a set of three-dimensional points that the curve must pass through. Such a curve is said to **interpolate** the set of points as Figure 9.2.

We shall work with cubic polynomials of the form

$$q(u) = a_0 + a_1u + a_2u^2 + a_3u^3$$

with u conventionally varying over the range $(0, 1)$. We can obtain other ranges of u by a simple scaling and translation. Cubics are, by far, the most popular curves with which to work as they provide a good combination of flexibility and efficiency. Here, q can be x, y, z, or w. Thus, we need four independent conditions to determine each set of coefficients for a curve. For interpolation, we must provide four points through which the curve must pass. However, in computer graphics, interpolating curves usually are not the most useful type due to their lack of smoothness.

If we work with cubics, four conditions are not enough to control a curve over a significant part of space. Rather than work with higher-order polynomials that are more expensive to compute and harder to control, we can define many short curve segments, each defined by a subset of the conditions that we would like to impose on the whole curve. For example, in the two segments in Figure 9.3, each is valid over a small part of space corresponding to its values of u between 0 and 1. Each is determined by the data locally. In computer graphics, this type of local control of the shape of a curve is of great importance. However, when we work with multiple curve segments, we must be careful of what happens at the **join points**, the places where adjacent segments meet. Simply ensuring that two seg-

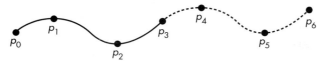

Figure 9.3 Two interpolating curve segments sharing with join point at P_3

ments meet reduces the flexibility in curve design. For the example in Figure 9.3, we see that if we use P_0, P_1, P_2, and P_3 as the data for the first curve, we must use P_3 as the first data point in the second curve segment to be sure we have a continuous curve at the join point.

Once we decide on the conditions that we would like our curves to satisfy, we have three sets of $n + 1$ equations for the $n + 1$ coefficients for x, y, and z. These conditions are generally stated in terms of points in space called **control points** that are supplied by the user, often interactively.

9.2 Parametric Surfaces

Whereas curves are defined by functions of a single variable u, parametric surfaces are defined by functions of two variables u and v. Each coordinate is defined by a separate function

$$x = x(u, v)$$
$$y = y(u, v)$$
$$z = z(u, v)$$
$$w = w(u, v)$$

Thus each value of u and v gives one point in three- or four-dimensional space as in Figure 9.4. Here, $\mathbf{p}(u, v) = (x(u, v), y(u, v), z(u, v))$.

In computer graphics, these functions usually are bicubic polynomials, each of the form

$$q(u, v) = a_{00} + a_{10}u + a_{01}v + a_{11}uv + a_{20}u^2 + a_{02}v^2 + a_{21}u^2v + a_{12}uv^2 + a_{22}u^2v^2 + a_{30}u^3 + a_{03}v^3 + a_{31}u^3v + a_{13}uv^3 + a_{32}u^3v^2 + a_{23}u^2v^3 + a_{33}u^3v^3$$

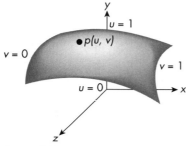

Figure 9.4 Parametric surface patch

defined for both u and v over the range $(0, 1)$. Again, q can be x, y, z, or w. There are 16 coefficients, so we need 16 conditions in each variable to determine each **surface patch**. For example, if we want to interpolate a set of control points, each patch would pass through 16 points. Thus, to determine an (x, y, z) surface patch with $w = 1$, we have to determine 48 coefficients.

9.3 Bézier Curves and Surfaces

In computer graphics and CAD, we are willing to only come close to some of the control points rather than interpolating them, if the resulting curve is smoother than the curve that interpolates all the control points. Although there are many ways we could define "close," the most popular choice is the **Bézier curves** and **surfaces**.

Figure 9.5 shows a cubic Bézier polynomial $q(u)$ where again q can be x, y, z, or w. This curve is determined by the four control points Q_0, Q_1, Q_2, and Q_3. The cubic Bézier curve interpolates Q_0 and Q_3 and uses the line segments between Q_0 and Q_1 and Q_2 and Q_3 to determine the slope of the curve at the endpoints. Such curves are very smooth and the curve is confined to lie in the box formed by the control points called the **convex hull**, which is also shown in Figure 9.5.

For a sequence of control points, the next curve segment uses Q_3, Q_4, Q_5, and Q_6, thus ensuring continuity at the join point.

Bézier surfaces are defined in a similar manner. For bicubic surfaces, we use 16 control points $\{Q_{ij}\}$ for i and j ranging from 0 to 3. The surface patch interpolates the four corner points, Q_{00}, Q_{03}, Q_{30}, and Q_{33}, and fits in the convex hull of the 16 control points. Bézier surfaces are actually extensions of Bézier curves. For a constant value of u (or v), the surface $\mathbf{p}(u, v)$ reduces to a Bézier curve in v (or u).

When we go to higher-order curves and surfaces, we need to use more control points to determine each curve segment or surface patch. For example, the Bézier curve of degree 7 uses eight control points. It interpolates the end points and uses the other control point data to approximate various derivatives at the end points. The polynomials that are used in u and v to determine these curves and surfaces are from a family of polynomials known as the **Bernstein polynomials** that can be implemented very efficiently.

If we strip away the mathematics, which is very elegant and covered in most textbooks on computer graphics, and look at the results, we can identify the prop-

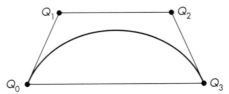

Figure 9.5 Bézier curve and its convex hull

Figure 9.6 Line segment approximation to the Bézier curve determined by Q_0, Q_1, Q_2, and Q_3.

erties of Bézier curves and surfaces that make them so important in computer graphics:

1. Bézier curves and surfaces are smooth.
2. Bézier curves and surfaces are defined locally by control points.
3. Bézier curves and surfaces of any order can be generated as accurately as desired in an efficient manner.
4. Any other polynomial curve and surface can be obtained from a Bézier curve or surface.

This last point is important as it makes it simple to obtain other types of curves and surfaces while still using the efficient algorithms for the Bézier curves and surfaces that are in OpenGL. We shall see an example of how we can do this later.

OpenGL implements Bézier curves and surfaces through a mechanism known as **evaluators**. These evaluators can compute a user-specified number of points on a Bézier curve or surface of any degree. OpenGL then uses these points on the curve or surface to generate standard OpenGL primitives, such as line segments and polygons that approximate the curve or surface. Figure 9.6 shows a cubic Bézier curve determined by control points Q_0, Q_1, Q_2, and Q_3 on which five points have been computed exactly by an evaluator. The dashed line shows an approximating polyline (GL_LINE_STRIP) that is determined by these points.

Because we can have OpenGL compute as many points as we like on the curve, we can achieve as much accuracy as we need for our application.

9.4 One-Dimensional OpenGL Evaluators

For a curve, we use a one-dimensional evaluator that we set up by glMap1*().

> **void glMap1{fd}(GLenum entity, TYPE u0, TYPE u1, GLint stride, GLint order, TYPE* data)**
>
> sets up a one-dimensional evaluator for **entity** over the range (**u0, u1**) using a Bernstein polynomial of degree **order** −1. There are **stride** variables of **TYPE GLfloat** or **GLdouble** between successive data points in the array **data**.

We can use this evaluator for a variety of entities. If we want a curve, we set entity to GL_MAP1_VERTEX_3. Every time that we use the evaluator, through functions that replace calls to glVertex*(), such as glEvalcoord1*() and glMapGrid1*(), an (x, y, z) point is evaluated. We can also form four-dimensional points (GL_MAP1_VERTEX_4), normals (GL_MAP1_NORMAL), colors (GL_MAP1_COLOR_4), and texture coordinates. Each type of entity for which we use an evaluator must be enabled with a call such as

```
glEnable(GL_MAP1_VERTEX_3);
```

We can choose the order of the Bézier curve we would like to use. The **order** of a curve is one greater than the degree of the polynomial and is equal to the number of points it takes to determine the curve. We can use any range in the parameter u in our curves because the range of values (u_0, u_1) can be scaled to $(0, 1)$ by the substitution

$$u' = (u - u_0)/(u_1 - u_0)$$

Once one or more evaluators have been enabled, we can form approximations to Bézier curves. The simplest method is to replace each call to glVertex*() with a call to glEvalcoord1*(). Rather than using a point in two, three, or four dimensions as does glVertex*(), glEvalCoord1*() passes a value of u to all enabled evaluators. The evaluators then produce a point, a normal, a color, or a texture coordinate, depending on which evaluators are enabled. For example, suppose that we want to set up and enable an evaluator for vertices using u over the range $[0, 1]$ and we want 21 points on a line strip that approximates the curve. We can use the code

```
glBegin(GL_LINE_STRIP);
  for(i = 0; i < =  20; i++) glEvalCoord1f(i / 20.0);
glEnd();
```

> **void glEvalCoord1{fd}(TYPE u)**
>
> **void glEvalCoord1{fd}v(TYPE *u)**
>
> force the evaluation of all enabled one-dimensional maps for the value **u**.

If we had defined the evaluator over another range as in

```
glMap1f(GL_MAP1_VERTEX_3, u0, u1, 3, 4, data);
```

we could have 21 points over this range by

```
glBegin(GL_LINE_STRIP);
  for(i = 0; i <= 20; i++)
    glEvalCoord1f(u0+i*(u1-u0)/20.0);
glEnd();
```

We also could have enabled a color evaluator by the code

```
glMap1f(GL_MAP1_COLOR_4, u0, u1, 3, 4, colors);
glEnable(GL_MAP1_COLOR_4);
```

The array `colors[]` should have four RGBA colors in it. As the above loop is executed, we would not only generate a line segment for each call to `glEvalCoord1f()`, but we would also generate a new color for each vertex by using a Bézier curve determined by the colors in the array. Hence, if smooth shading were enabled (`GL_SMOOTH`), we would see a smooth color change over the line strip starting with the first color in the array and ending with the last color. Note that we would come close to the second and third colors but not pass through them.

The advantage of using `glEvalCoord1*()` is that we can use any values of u, not just equally spaced values as in our example. However, if we want to use 21 values of u, then we must make 21 function calls using `glEvalCoord1*()`. OpenGL provides an alternative for equally spaced values of u. First, we use the function `glMapGrid1*()` to set up an equally spaced set of values of u. Then we use `glEvalMesh1()` to apply the evaluators over the grid with a single function execution. Thus, for 21 points from u0 to u1 we can use

```
glMap1f(GL_MAP1_VERTEX_3, u0, u1, 3, 4, data);
glEnable(GL_MAP1_VERTEX_3);
glMapGrid1f(20, u0, u1);
```

to set up the grid and

```
glEvalMesh1(GL_LINE, 0, 20);
```

to draw the line strip.

---

void glMapGrid1{fd}(GLint n, TYPE u0, TYPE u1).

sets up an equally spaced grid of **n** partitions between **u0** and **u1**.

void glEvalMesh1(GLenum mode, GLint first, GLint last)

renders in mode (**GL_LINE, GL_POINT**) all enabled evaluators from the **first** to **last** values of u defined by **glMapGrid()**.

9.5 Two-Dimensional Evaluators

Two-dimensional evaluators allow us to evaluate two-dimensional Bernstein polynomials and form Bézier surfaces. The mechanism is a direct extension of what we did for one-dimensional curves. However, we have more options in how we can display these surfaces. Surfaces are defined by two-parameter polynomials $p(u, v)$, where for a fixed u (or v) we have a parametric polynomial in the other variable.

Thus, the mechanisms for working with surfaces are very similar to the mechanisms that we introduced for curves. We define the evaluator by `glMap2*()` and then use it with `glEvalCoord2*()`.

---

void glMap2{fd}(GLenum entity, TYPE u0, TYPE u1, GLint ustride,
  GLint uorder, TYPE v0, TYPE v1, GLint vstride, GLint vorder,
  TYPE data)

defines a two-dimensional evaluator for **entity** using Bézier polynomials in *u* and *v*. The control points are stored in the array **data**.

void glEvalCoord2{fd}(TYPE u, TYPE v)

void glEvalCoord2{fd}v(TYPE *uv)

force the evaluation of all enabled two-dimensional evaluators for the specified values of **u** and **v**.

For regular spacing, we can use the functions `glMapGrid2*()` and `glEvalMesh2()` to reduce the number of function calls.

---

void glMapGrid2{fd}(GLint n, TYPE u0, TYPE u1, GLint m,
  TYPE v0, TYPE v1)

sets up a two-dimensional grid with **n** evenly spaced partitions between **u0** and **u1** in *u* and with **m** partitions between **v0** and **v1** in *v*.

void glEvalMesh2(GLenum mode, GLint ufirst, GLint ulast,
  GLint vfirst, GLint vlast)

renders in mode (**GL_LINE, GL_POINT, GL_FILL**) all enabled evaluators from the **ufirst** to **ulast** values of *u* and **vfirst** to **vlast** in *v* as defined by **glMapGrid2*()**.

9.6 An Interactive Example

The following example allows the user to enter data points from the terminal and draws cubic Bézier curves defined in the plane by each successive group of points. The program allows you to clear the screen and restart or add additional points via the keyboard and mouse.

```
#include <GL/glut.h>
#define MAX_CPTS 25

GLfloat cpts[MAX_CPTS][3];
int ncpts = 0;
```

```
static int width = 500, height = 500;

void drawCurves()
{
  int i;

  for(i = 0; i < ncpts-3; i += 3)
  {
    glMap1f(GL_MAP1_VERTEX_3, 0.0, 1.0, 3, 4, cpts[i]);
    glMapGrid1f(30, 0.0, 1.0);
    glEvalMesh1(GL_LINE, 0, 30);
  }
  glFlush();
}

static void display()
{
  int i;
  glClear(GL_COLOR_BUFFER_BIT);

  glBegin(GL_POINTS);
  for (i = 0; i < ncpts; i++)
    glVertex3fv(cpts[i]);
  glEnd();

  glFlush();
}

static void mouse(int button, int state, int x, int y)
{
  float wx, wy;

  if (button != GLUT_LEFT_BUTTON || state != GLUT_DOWN)
      return;

  wx = (2.0 * x) / (float)(width - 1) - 1.0;
  wy = (2.0 * (height - y)) / (float)(height) - 1.0;

  if (ncpts == MAX_CPTS) return;

  cpts[ncpts][0] = wx;
  cpts[ncpts][1] = wy;
  cpts[ncpts][2] = 0.0;
  ncpts++;

  glPointSize(5.0);
  glBegin(GL_POINTS);
  glVertex3f(wx, wy, 0.0);
  glEnd();
  glFlush();
}
```

```
void keyboard(unsigned char key, int x, int y)
{
  switch (key)
  {
    case 'q': case 'Q':
      exit();
      break;
    case 'c': case 'C':
      ncpts = 0;
      glutPostRedisplay();
      break;
    case 'e': case 'E':
      glutPostRedisplay();
      break;
    case 'b': case 'B':
      drawCurves();
    break;
  }
}


void reshape(int w, int h)
{
  width = w;
  height = h;
  glMatrixMode(GL_PROJECTION);
  glLoadIdentity();
  glOrtho(-1.0, 1.0, -1.0, 1.0, -1.0, 1.0);
  glMatrixMode(GL_MODELVIEW);
  glViewport(0, 0, w, h);
}


int main(int argc, char **argv)
{
  glutInit(&argc, argv);
  glutInitDisplayMode(GLUT_RGB);
  glutInitWindowSize(width, height);
  glutCreateWindow("Bézier Curve");
  glutDisplayFunc(display);
  glutMouseFunc(mouse);
  glutKeyboardFunc(keyboard);
  glutReshapeFunc(reshape);
  glClearColor(1.0, 1.0, 1.0, 1.0);
  glColor3f(0.0, 0.0, 0.0);
  glPointSize(5.0);
  glEnable(GL_MAP1_VERTEX_3);
  glutMainLoop();
}
```

This program uses the first four control points to define the first curve segment. It then takes groups of three successive control points and combines them with the final control point of the just-drawn segment to define the next segment. This strategy ensures that the resulting set of curve segments is continuous. However, there is no guarantee of any more smoothness at the join points.

9.7 Other Types of Curves

A Bézier curve is a polynomial that is defined by a set of control points and a set of conditions that we impose on the curve. If we use the same control points and a different set of conditions, we obtain another type of curve. For example, if we require that the curve pass through the control points, then we obtain an interpolating curve. If we want such a curve, we do not have to give up on OpenGL and generate other types of curves with our own code. We need only look at things a little differently.

Suppose that we have a cubic Bézier polynomial. If we pick four points on this curve, they define an interpolating cubic polynomial that must be the same polynomial with which we started. In other words, a cubic polynomial is both a Bézier curve and an interpolating curve for different sets of control points. If we want a cubic interpolating polynomial and have the four control points that define it, we can convert these four points to four other control points (actually, two are the same in this case) that define a Bézier polynomial that is identical. The advantage of this strategy is that we can use OpenGL evaluators on these new control points to generate the desired curve efficiently. For each type of curve that we want, there is a matrix that we can apply to its control points to create the desired Bézier control points. For the cubic interpolating curve, the matrix is

$$M = \begin{bmatrix} 1 & 0 & 0 & 0 \\ -\frac{5}{6} & 3 & -\frac{3}{2} & \frac{1}{3} \\ \frac{1}{3} & -\frac{3}{2} & 3 & -\frac{5}{6} \\ 0 & 0 & 0 & 1 \end{bmatrix}$$

We form a $4 \times n$ array of the control points, where n is the number of dimensions (two, three, or four) and multiply M on the right by this array, forming a new $4 \times n$ array of the new control points.

9.7.1 B-Splines

Bézier curves and surfaces are members of a family of curves and surfaces called **splines**. Each type of spline is defined by a slightly different set of conditions involving the control points and the type of continuity that we want to enforce at

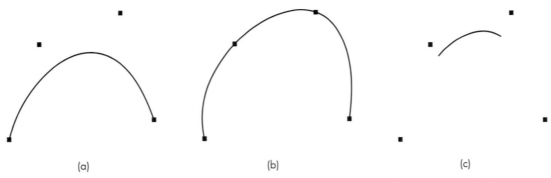

(a)   (b)   (c)

Figure 9.7 (a) Bézier curve, (b) interpolating curve, and (c) B-spline curve for same control points

the join points. The most popular type of spline is the cubic B-spline, which has the continuity of the first and second derivatives at the join points. To obtain this degree of smoothness, a new B-spline curve segment is defined for each additional control point. Thus, if control points Q_0, Q_1, Q_2, and Q_3 define the first segment, Q_1, Q_2, Q_3, and Q_4 define the second. Each curve segment is rendered only between the two middle control points.

The matrix

$$
M = \begin{bmatrix}
\frac{1}{6} & \frac{2}{3} & \frac{1}{6} & 0 \\
0 & \frac{2}{3} & \frac{1}{3} & 0 \\
0 & \frac{1}{3} & \frac{2}{3} & 0 \\
0 & \frac{1}{6} & \frac{2}{3} & \frac{1}{6}
\end{bmatrix}
$$

converts a set of control points for a cubic B-spline to a set of control points for a cubic Bézier curve that is identical.

The following code contains the major modifications to our previous example to draw the three types of curves from the same control points. The desired type of curve could be entered interactively. Figure 9.7 shows the three types of curves from the same set of control points.

```
typedef enum
{
  BÉZIER,
  INTERPOLATED,
  BSPLINE
} curveType;
```

```c
void vmult(float m[4][4], float v[4][3], float r[4][3])
{
  int i, j, k;
  for(i = 0; i < 4; i++) for(j = 0; j < 3; j++)
  {
  r[i][j] = 0;
  }
    for(k = 0; k < 4; k++) r[i][j] += m[i][k] * v[k][j];
}

/*interpolating to Bézier matrix */

static float minterp[4][4] =
{
  {1.0, 0.0, 0.0, 0.0},
  {-5.0/6.0, 3.0, -3.0/2.0, 1.0/3.0},
  {1.0/3.0, -3.0/2.0, 3.0, -5.0/6.0},
  {0.0, 0.0, 0.0, 1.0},
};

/* B-spline to Bézier matrix */

static float mbspline[4][4] =
{
  {1.0/6.0, 4.0/6.0, 1.0/6.0, 0.0},
  {0.0, 4.0/6.0, 2.0/6.0, 0.0},
  {0.0, 2.0/6.0, 4.0/6.0, 0.0},
  {0.0, 1.0/6.0, 4.0/6.0, 1.0/6.0},
};

/* identity matrix for Bézier polynomial */

static float midentity[4][4] =
{
  {1.0, 0.0, 0.0, 0.0},
  {0.0, 1.0, 0.0, 0.0},
  {0.0, 0.0, 1.0, 0.0},
  {0.0, 0.0, 0.0, 1.0}
};

/* calculate the matrix used to transform the control points */

void computeMatrix(curveType type, float m[4][4])
{
  int i, j;
  switch (type)
  {
    case BÉZIER:
    /* Identity matrix */
      m = midentity;
```

```
        break;
        case INTERPOLATED:
          m = minterp;
        break;
        case BSPLINE:
          m = mbspline;
        break;
    }
}

/* draw the indicated curves using the current control points */

static void drawCurves(curveType type)
{
    int i, j;
    int step;
    GLfloat newcpts[4][3];

    float m[4][4];

        /* set the control point computation matrix and the step size */

    computeMatrix(type, m);

    if(type == BSPLINE) step = 1;
    else step = 3;

        /* using global color matrix */

    glColor3fv(colors[type]);

/* draw the curves */

    i = 0;
    while (i + 3 < ncpts)
    {

        /* calculate the appropriate control points */

        vmult(m, &cpts[i], newcpts);

        /* draw the curve using OpenGL evaluators */

        glMap1f(GL_MAP1_VERTEX_3, 0.0, 1.0, 3, 4,
            &newcpts[0][0]);
        glMapGrid1f(30, 0.0, 1.0);
        glEvalMesh1(GL_LINE, 0, 30);

        /* advance to the next segment */

        i += step;
    }
    glFlush();
}
```

9.7.2 NURBS

NURBS (*Non Uniform Rational B-Spline*) curves and surfaces are a very flexible family of curves and surfaces that are supported through the GLU library. A NURBS curve is based on using four-dimensional parametric polynomials $(x(u)$, $y(u)$, $z(u)$, $w(u))$, where each component can be obtained by OpenGL evaluators. The desired three-dimensional points are obtained by dividing the first three terms by $w(u)$ forming a vertex $(x(u)/w(u), y(u)/w(u), z(u)/w(u))$ for each value of u.

9.8 The Utah Teapot

The best-known object in computer graphics is the Utah teapot. It was created over 30 years ago to test rendering algorithms. The teapot is composed of 32 cubic Bézier surface patches, defined by 306 distinct control points. The data set is widely available and usually is given as 32 lines, each of 16 integers in the range of 1–192. Each integer is a pointer to one of the 306 (x, y, z) values. The teapot can be displayed easily using two-dimensional evaluators. We shall develop a simple program that will draw the teapot with line segments.

We can make the code clearer and shorter if we put the data in two files: vertices.h and patches.h. The first file is simply a long line that gives the locations of the vertices and that begins with the code

```
GLfloat vertices[306][3] = {{1.4, 0.0, 2.4},
```

Likewise, the second file defines the patches with one line of code that begins

```
int indices[32][4][4] = {{1, 2, 3, 4, 5, 6, 7, 8, 9, 10, 11, 12,
13, 14, 15, 16},
```

The numbering in this data set goes back to the days when indices began with 1 rather than 0. Thus, the first index, indices[0][0][0], which has the value 1, actually refers to vertices[0]. The rest of the code is fairly straightforward. In the main() function, we traverse the data structure and put all the data in one array data[32][4][4][3]. The function myinit() sets up a two-dimensional grid with 20 points over the range [0.0, 1.0] in each direction. The data are such that the teapot is oriented along the z axis, so we start the display callback by rotating it so the top and bottom are perpendicular to the y axis. We then do two more simple rotations to create an isometric view.

The next issue is how to set up the evaluators. In this example, we use the same equally spaced grid for each patch. This choice is not ideal as the patches are of different sizes and curvature, but it is sufficient for this simple example. When we render with line segments and glEvalCoord2*(), we want to create a grid of line segments. We set up an evaluator with the function

```
glMap2f(GL_MAP2_VERTEX_3, 0.0, 1.0, 3, 4,
        0.0, 1.0, 12, 4, &data[k][0][0][0]);
```

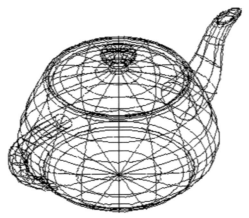

Figure 9.8 Teapot rendered using one-dimensional grids in u and v

Note that the stride is different in u and v. In u, successive control points are three floats apart in the data array because the data are stored by rows. However, in v we want to access successive points by columns and thus the next point is separated from the present point by 12 floats.

We want a series of line segments that correspond to curves with a fixed u and changing v, and another set that corresponds to curves with a fixed v and variable u. We can get a smooth uncluttered image if we draw a few polylines but evaluate many points on each polyline. We can do this by using two loops in the display function; the first draws curves of constant v and the second draws curves of constant u. For each patch, we draw five curves in u and five in v. Each curve is approximated by using the evaluator 21 times. Here is the entire program, followed by its output in Figure 9.8.

```
#include <stdlib.h>
#include <GL/glut.h>

GLfloat data[32][4][4][3];

/* 306 vertices */

#include "vertices.h"

/* 32 patches */

#include "patches.h"

void display(void)
{
  int i, j, k;

  glClear(GL_COLOR_BUFFER_BIT);
  glColor3f(1.0, 1.0, 1.0);
```

```
      glLoadIdentity();
      glTranslatef(0.0, 0.0, -10.0);
      glRotatef(-35.26, 1.0, 0.0, 0.0);
      glRotatef(-45.0, 0.0, 1.0, 0.0);
/* data aligned along z axis, rotate to align with y axis */
      glRotatef(-90.0, 1.0, 0.0, 0.0);
      for(k = 0; k < 32; k++)
      {
         glMap2f(GL_MAP2_VERTEX_3, 0, 1, 3, 4,
            0, 1, 12, 4, &data[k][0][0][0]);
         for (j = 0; j < = 4; j++)
         {
            glBegin(GL_LINE_STRIP);
            for (i = 0; i < = 20; i++)
               glEvalCoord2f((GLfloat)i/20.0,
                  (GLfloat)j/4.0);
            glEnd();
            glBegin(GL_LINE_STRIP);
            for (i = 0; i < = 20; i++)
               glEvalCoord2f((GLfloat)j/4.0,
                  (GLfloat)i/20.0);
            glEnd();
         }
      }
   glFlush();
}
void myReshape(int w, int h)
{
   glViewport(0, 0, w, h);
   glMatrixMode(GL_PROJECTION);
   glLoadIdentity();
   if (w < = h)
      glOrtho(-4.0, 4.0, -4.0 * (GLfloat) h / (GLfloat)
         w, 4.0 * (GLfloat) h / (GLfloat) w, -20.0,
         20.0);
   else
      glOrtho(-4.0 * (GLfloat) w / (GLfloat) h, 4.0 *
         (GLfloat) w / (GLfloat) h, -4.0, 4.0, -20.0,
         20.0);
   glMatrixMode(GL_MODELVIEW);
}

void myinit()
{
   glEnable(GL_MAP2_VERTEX_3);
   glClearColor(1.0, 1.0, 1.0, 1.0);
}

main(int argc, char *argv[])
```

```
{
  int i, j, k, m, n;
  for(i = 0; i < 32; i++)for(j = 0; j < 4; j++)
    for(k = 0; k < 4; k++)for(n = 0; n < 3; n++)
    {

/* put teapot data into single array for use by OpenGL */

    m = indices[i][j][k];
    for(n = 0; n < 3; n++) data[i][j][k][n] =
      vertices[m-1][n];
  }
  glutInit(&argc, argv);
  glutInitDisplayMode(GLUT_SINGLE | GLUT_RGB);
  glutInitWindowSize(500, 500);
  glutCreateWindow("teapot");
  myinit();
  glutReshapeFunc(myReshape);
  glutDisplayFunc(display);

  glutMainLoop();
}
```

As we are using a regular grid, we can take another approach to avoid all the function calls by using `glMapGrid2*()` and `glEvalMesh2()`. Thus we can define the grid as part of the initialization by

`glMapGrid2f(4, 0.0, 1.0, 4, 0.0, 1.0);`

and evaluate it by

`glEvalMesh2(GL_LINE, 0, 4, 0, 4);`

in the display callback. The resulting image is in Figure 9.9.

Figure 9.9 Teapot rendered using two-dimensional grid

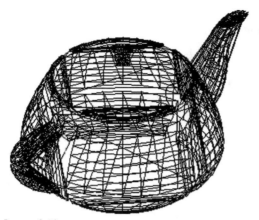

Figure 9.10 Denser rendering of teapot with two-dimensional grid

This image is not as informative as the results of the previous example because here we are using a much rougher spacing in both variables, while in the previous example we used a fine resolution on each polyline that we drew. If we were to use a higher number of curves in each direction, we would get a smoother, but denser, image. For example, with eight rather than four intervals in u and v we get the image in Figure 9.10.

If we want to display the teapot with line segments, the use of glEvalCocrd*() is probably better in spite of the extra function calls. However, the use of glEvalMesh2() should be much better if want polygons (GL_FILL) rather than line segments (GL_LINE). However, there is a problem in how we do shading.

9.9 Normals and Shading

When we want shading, we need to define normals. As we saw in Chapter 6, in OpenGL normals are usually defined in the application program using the function glNormal*(). If we want the smoothest shading, we should define a new normal before each vertex. The equivalent for surfaces would be to define a normal before each call to glEvalCoord*(). Although, in principle, we could do this, in reality we would have to compute a normal for all the vertices that were defined implicitly by the evaluators. Such a calculation would involve knowing the mathematics of parametric surfaces, something we cannot expect application programmers to possess. The situation is even worse for regular grids, where rather than make multiple calls to glEvalCoord*() within a loop, we make a single function call to glEvalMesh2(), which leaves us no place in the program to define normals.

OpenGL handles this problem by computing the normals automatically for the surfaces. To generate these normals we need only enable auto normalization by

```
glEnable(GL_AUTO_NORMAL);
```

Thus, to generate a shaded teapot, we can start with the code we used for the teapot using `glMapGrid2f()` and `glEvalMesh2()`. For example, if we want each patch to be approximated with 64 polygons, we use

```
glMapGrid2f(8, 0.0, 1.0, 8, 0.0, 1.0);
glEvalMesh2(GL_FILL, 0, 8, 0, 8);
```

Within `main()` or `init()`, we can enable auto normalization and define our lights and materials. For example, the light and material properties

```
GLfloat ambient[] = {0.2, 0.2, 0.2, 1.0};
GLfloat position[] = {0.0, 0.0, 2.0, 1.0};
GLfloat mat_diffuse[] = {0.6, 0.6, 0.6, 1.0};
GLfloat mat_specular[] = {1.0, 1.0, 1.0, 1.0};
GLfloat mat_shininess[] = {50.0};

glEnable(GL_LIGHTING);
glEnable(GL_LIGHT0);

glLightfv(GL_LIGHT0, GL_AMBIENT, ambient);
glLightfv(GL_LIGHT0, GL_POSITION, position);

glMaterialfv(GL_FRONT, GL_DIFFUSE, mat_diffuse);
glMaterialfv(GL_FRONT, GL_SPECULAR, mat_specular);
glMaterialfv(GL_FRONT, GL_SHININESS, mat_shininess);
```

produce the image in Figure 9.11.

If we use only 16 polygons per patch, we get the slightly rougher image in Figure 9.12. Note that the shading of each patch is still very smooth but that we can notice the silhouette edge around the outside because we have not used enough polygons for each patch.

Figure 9.11 Rendering of the teapot using auto normals

Figure 9.12 Rendering the teapot with fewer polygons than in Figure 9.11

9.10 Texturing Surfaces

In Chapter 8, we introduced texture mapping for quadrics using OpenGL's ability to generate texture coordinates automatically. We can apply the same techniques to Bézier surfaces. We can also use evaluators to generate normals for shading and texture coordinates. Thus, the process is automated, if we are willing to accept the scaling and distortion that is determined by our use of this particular scheme.

You can see one example of this automatic coordinate generation by using `glutSolidTeapot()` with textures. Within the definition of the teapot, a two-dimensional evaluator is created for the vertices:

```
glMap2f(GL_MAP2_VERTEX_3, 0.0, 1.0, 3, 4, 0.0, 1.0, 12, 4,
        &p[0][0][0]);
```

where the array p contains the vertex data for a single patch. A second evaluator is created by

```
glMap2f(GL_MAP2_TEXTURE_COORD_2, 0.0, 1.0, 2, 2, 0.0, 1.0, 4, 2,
        &tex[0][0][0]);
```

where the array `tex` contains the texture coordinates for the vertices. Note that because the patches are bicubic whereas the texture is two-dimensional, there are differences in the order and stride parameters in the definitions of the evaluators. The array `tex` contains only the four coordinates of the vertices of the unit square

```
float tex[2][2][2] = {{0.0, 0.0}, {1.0, 0.0},
        {0.0, 1.0}, {1.0, 1.0}};
```

Figure 9.13 Texture mapped teapot using automatic generation of texture coordinates

so that each patch has the entire texture mapped to it. `glutSolidTeapot()` enables auto normals so that we do not need a third evaluator for interpolating vertex normals.

The application program needs only to define a texture map and its parameters, enable texture mapping, and render the teapot. For the checkerboard texture, we get the image in Figure 9.13. The checks on the teapot are of different sizes because the teapot is made up of 32 separate surface patches, each of which has its own size. The automatic texture generation for the surfaces in `glutSolidTeapot()` uses the same range of s and t for each surface patch. We can also use automatic texture coordinate generation by enabling texture generation and defining the linear equations for the texture coordinates, as we did in Chapter 8.

9.11 Programming Exercises

1. Extend the interactive program for comparing Bézier, B-Spline, and interpolating curves to the corresponding surfaces.
2. Display the teapot with a checkerboard pattern so that all the mapped squares are approximately the same size.
3. Rewrite the interactive curve generation program to generate curves in three dimensions. Give careful consideration to how you would enter the control points interactively.
4. Find an array of topographic data giving heights above sea level on the web. Display a surface of Bézier patches from these data.

Putting It Together and Moving On

CHAPTER
10

In this penultimate chapter, we survey some of the features of OpenGL that we have not covered. However, we start with a last example. This example shows most of the OpenGL features that we have discussed in previous chapters and will give you the opportunity to experiment with these features, as most can be turned on and off interactively.

10.1 A Demo Program

The following program demonstrates many of the OpenGL features that we have discussed in the first nine chapters. This demonstration program has been very useful in tutorials on OpenGL that we have given in a variety of venues. The program allows the user to experiment with many of OpenGL's options for displaying a rotating cube. Options are selected using either the mouse or the keyboard. These include

lines/polygons: You can switch between using polygons and lines.
flat/smooth: You can switch between shading modes.
lighting: You can use various materials and light sources, or you can use constant colors for the polygons.
texture: You can turn on a checkerboard texture with or without mipmapping.
fog: You can add fog to the scene, which uses OpenGL blending.
hidden-surface removal: This can be turned on or off.
line smoothing: You can antialias lines in line-drawing mode.
motion: You can move either the cube or the light source.
ortho/perspective: You can switch between these viewing modes.

10.1.1 A Virtual Trackball

The only new feature of this program is the virtual trackball. The trackball is a device that has some of the characteristics of a mouse. A typical trackball is pictured in Figure 10.1. One of the advantages of an ideal frictionless trackball is that

Figure 10.1   Trackball

a user can start it spinning, giving it a constant velocity that could be used to change a position or an orientation in the program at a constant rate. If the user simply moves the trackball with her hand, then the rotation of the trackball is reflected in a change of object orientation in the program.

The program creates a virtual trackball from the physical mouse by projecting the position of the mouse upward to the virtual hemisphere, as in Figure 10.2. As the mouse moves, the program tracks the change in position on the hemisphere. Two positions on the hemisphere determine both an axis of rotation and an angle to rotate about this axis, as shown in Figure 10.3. These two positions can also be used to determine a velocity of rotation, which can be used within the idle call-back. Rotation can be terminated with a single mouse click and no motion. Note that to obtain the desired behavior, we need to use both the mouse and motion callbacks.

10.1.2 Demo Code

```
/* rotating cube demo */
/* prints out instructions */
/* both normals and colors are assigned to the vertices */
/* cube is centered at origin so that (unnormalized) normals are
the same as the vertex values */
#include <stdlib.h>
```

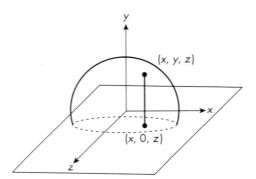

Figure 10.2   Projection position on plane to hemisphere

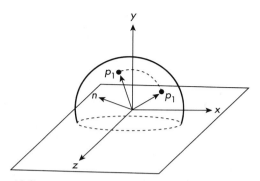

Figure 10.3 Two points and origin determining a rotation

```
#include <math.h>
#include <GL/glut.h>
#include <GL/glu.h>
#define bool int
#define false 0
#define true 1

/* global settings controlled by keyboard input */

bool texEnabled                          = false;
bool mipmapEnabled                       = false;
bool fastTexture                         = true;
bool fogEnabled                          = false;
bool depthEnabled                        = true;
bool lineAAEnabled                       = false;
bool lightingEnabled                     = false;
bool smoothEnabled                       = false;
bool drawLines                           = true;
bool idleSpin                            = true;
bool perspectiveXform                    = false;

/* global settings */

float  near = 3.0;   /* near clipping plane in eye coords */
float  far = 7.0;    /* far clipping plane in eye coords */
float  viewxform_z = -5.0;

int winWidth, winHeight;

float  angle = 0.0, axis[3], trans[3];
bool trackballEnabled = true;
bool trackballMove = false;
bool trackingMouse = false;
bool redrawContinue = false;

GLfloat lightXform[4][4] = {
```

```
  {1.0, 0.0, 0.0, 0.0},
  {0.0, 1.0, 0.0, 0.0},
  {0.0, 0.0, 1.0, 0.0},
  {0.0, 0.0, 0.0, 1.0}
};
GLfloat objectXform[4][4] = {
  {1.0, 0.0, 0.0, 0.0},
  {0.0, 1.0, 0.0, 0.0},
  {0.0, 0.0, 1.0, 0.0},
  {0.0, 0.0, 0.0, 1.0}
};
GLfloat *trackballXform = (GLfloat*)objectXform;

void display(void);
void spinCube(void);
void setMenuEntries(bool);

/*------------------------*/
/* materials setup */

typedef struct materialStruct {
  GLfloat ambient[4];
  GLfloat diffuse[4];
  GLfloat specular[4];
  GLfloat shininess;
} materialStruct;

materialStruct brassMaterials = {
  {0.33F, 0.22F, 0.03F, 1.0F},
  {0.78F, 0.57F, 0.11F, 1.0F},
  {0.99F, 0.91F, 0.81F, 1.0F},
  27.8F
};
materialStruct redPlasticMaterials = {
  {0.3F, 0.0F, 0.0F, 1.0F},
  {0.6F, 0.0F, 0.0F, 1.0F},
  {0.8F, 0.6F, 0.6F, 1.0F},
  32.0F
};
materialStruct colorCubeMaterials = {
  {1.0F, 1.0F, 1.0F, 1.0F},
  {1.0F, 1.0F, 1.0F, 1.0F},
  {1.0F, 1.0F, 1.0F, 1.0F},
  100.0F
};

materialStruct *currentMaterials = &redPlasticMaterials;

void materials( materialStruct *materials)
{
```

```
/* define material properties for front face of all polygons */
  glMaterialfv(GL_FRONT, GL_AMBIENT,
    materials->ambient);
  glMaterialfv(GL_FRONT, GL_DIFFUSE,
    materials->diffuse);
  glMaterialfv(GL_FRONT, GL_SPECULAR,
    materials->specular);
  glMaterialf(GL_FRONT, GL_SHININESS,
    materials->shininess);
}

/*-----------------------*/
/* lighting setup */

typedef struct lightingStruct {
  GLfloat ambient[4];
  GLfloat diffuse[4];
  GLfloat specular[4];
} lightingStruct;

lightingStruct whiteLighting = {
  {0.0F, 0.0F, 0.0F, 1.0F},
  {1.0F, 1.0F, 1.0F, 1.0F},
  {1.0F, 1.0F, 1.0F, 1.0F}
};
lightingStruct colorCubeLighting = {
  {0.2F, 0.0F, 0.0F, 1.0F},
  {0.0F, 1.0F, 0.0F, 1.0F},
  {0.0F, 0.0F, 1.0F, 1.0F}
};

lightingStruct *currentLighting = &whiteLighting;

void lighting(lightingStruct *lightSettings)
{
/* set up light 0 ambient, diffuse, specular, and spotlight */

  glLightfv(GL_LIGHT0, GL_AMBIENT,
    lightSettings->ambient);
  glLightfv(GL_LIGHT0, GL_DIFFUSE,
    lightSettings->diffuse);
  glLightfv(GL_LIGHT0, GL_SPECULAR,
    lightSettings->specular);

  glLightf(GL_LIGHT0, GL_SPOT_EXPONENT, 1.0F);
  glLightf(GL_LIGHT0, GL_SPOT_CUTOFF, 90.0F);
  glLightf(GL_LIGHT0, GL_CONSTANT_ATTENUATION, 1.0F);
  glLightf(GL_LIGHT0, GL_LINEAR_ATTENUATION, 0.0F);
  glLightf(GL_LIGHT0, GL_QUADRATIC_ATTENUATION, 0.0F);

  glLightModeli(GL_LIGHT_MODEL_LOCAL_VIEWER, GL_TRUE);
```

```
}
/*----------------------*/
/* light position setup */

void setLightPos()
{
  GLfloat light0_pos[4] = {0.90F, 0.90F, 2.25F, 0.00F};
  GLfloat light0_spotDir[3] = {0.0F, 0.0F, -1.0F};

  glLightfv(GL_LIGHT0, GL_POSITION, light0_pos);
  glLightfv(GL_LIGHT0, GL_SPOT_DIRECTION,
    light0_spotDir);
}

/*----------------------*/
/* initial texture settings */

void texture()
{
  GLubyte image[64][64][3];
  int i, j, r, c;
  for(i = 0; i < 64; i++)
  {
    for(j = 0; j < 64; j++)
    {
      c = ((((i&0x8) == 0)^((j&0x8)) == 0))*255;
      image[i][j][0] = (GLubyte) c;
      image[i][j][1] = (GLubyte) c;
      image[i][j][2] = (GLubyte) c;
    }
  }
  glPixelStorei(GL_UNPACK_ALIGNMENT, 1);
  glTexImage2D(GL_TEXTURE_2D, 0, 3, 64, 64, 0, GL_RGB,
    GL_UNSIGNED_BYTE, image);
  glTexParameterf(GL_TEXTURE_2D, GL_TEXTURE_WRAP_S,
    GL_CLAMP);
  glTexParameterf(GL_TEXTURE_2D, GL_TEXTURE_WRAP_T,
    GL_CLAMP);
  glTexParameterf(GL_TEXTURE_2D, GL_TEXTURE_MAG_FILTER,
    GL_LINEAR);
  glTexParameterf(GL_TEXTURE_2D, GL_TEXTURE_MIN_FILTER,
    GL_LINEAR);
  gluBuild2DMipmaps(GL_TEXTURE_2D, 3, 64, 64, GL_RGB,
    GL_UNSIGNED_BYTE, image);
}

/* set initial state */

void initSettings(void)
{
  texture();
```

```
   glLineWidth(3.0);
   setMenuEntries(true);
}

/*-----------------------*/
/* set state according to user interaction */

void userSettings(void)
{
   lighting(currentLighting);
   materials(currentMaterials);

   if (lightingEnabled)
   {
      glEnable(GL_LIGHTING);
      glEnable(GL_LIGHT0);
   }
   else
   {
      glDisable(GL_LIGHTING);
   }

   if (smoothEnabled)
      glShadeModel(GL_SMOOTH);
   else
      glShadeModel(GL_FLAT);

   if(idleSpin)
       glutIdleFunc(spinCube);
   else
      glutIdleFunc(NULL);
   if (texEnabled)
      glEnable(GL_TEXTURE_2D);
   else
      glDisable(GL_TEXTURE_2D);
   if (fastTexture)
      glHint(GL_PERSPECTIVE_CORRECTION_HINT, GL_FASTEST);
   else
      glHint(GL_PERSPECTIVE_CORRECTION_HINT, GL_NICEST);
   if (mipmapEnabled)
      glTexParameterf(GL_TEXTURE_2D,
         GL_TEXTURE_MIN_FILTER, GL_LINEAR_MIPMAP_LINEAR);
   else
      glTexParameterf(GL_TEXTURE_2D,
         GL_TEXTURE_MIN_FILTER, GL_LINEAR);

   if (fogEnabled)
   {
      float fogColor[] = {0.7, 0.6, 0.6, 1.0};

      glClearColor(fogColor[0],      fogColor[1],      fogColor[2],
```

```
      fogColor[3]);
    glEnable(GL_FOG);
    glFogi(GL_FOG_MODE, GL_LINEAR);
    glFogf(GL_FOG_DENSITY, 1.0);
    glFogf(GL_FOG_START, near);
    glFogf(GL_FOG_END, far);
    glFogfv(GL_FOG_COLOR, fogColor);
  }
  else
  {
    glDisable(GL_FOG);
    glClearColor(0.0, 0.0, 0.0, 1.0);
  }

  if (lineAAEnabled)
    glEnable(GL_BLEND);
  else
    glDisable(GL_BLEND);

  if (lineAAEnabled)
  {
    glEnable(GL_LINE_SMOOTH);
    glBlendFunc(GL_SRC_ALPHA, GL_ONE_MINUS_SRC_ALPHA);
  }
  else
    glDisable(GL_LINE_SMOOTH);

  if (depthEnabled)
    glEnable(GL_DEPTH_TEST);
  else
    glDisable(GL_DEPTH_TEST);

    glMatrixMode(GL_PROJECTION);
    glLoadIdentity();

  if(perspectiveXform)
  {
    glFrustum(-1.25, 1.25, -1.25, 1.25, near, far);
    viewxform_z = -5.0;
  }
  else
  {
    glOrtho(-2.0, 2.0, -2.0, 2.0, near, far);
    viewxform_z = -5.0;
  }
  glMatrixMode(GL_MODELVIEW);
}

/*------------------------*/
/* draw the cube */
```

```
GLfloat vertices[][3] = {{-1.0, -1.0, -1.0},
  {1.0, -1.0, -1.0}, {1.0, 1.0, -1.0}, {-1.0, 1.0, -1.0},
  {-1.0, -1.0, 1.0}, {1.0, -1.0, 1.0}, {1.0, 1.0, 1.0},
  {-1.0, 1.0, 1.0}};

GLfloat normals[][3] = {{-1.0, -1.0, -1.0}, {1.0, -1.0, -1.0},
  {1.0, 1.0, -1.0}, {-1.0, 1.0, -1.0},
  {-1.0, -1.0, 1.0}, {1.0, -1.0, 1.0},
  {1.0, 1.0, 1.0}, {-1.0, 1.0, 1.0}};

GLfloat fnormals[][3] = {{0.0, 0.0, -1.0},
  {0.0, 1.0, 0.0}, {-1.0, 0.0, 0.0},
  {1.0, 0.0, 0.0}, {0.0, 0.0, 1.0}, {0.0, -1.0, 0.0}};

GLfloat colors[][3] = {{0.0, 0.0, 0.0},{1.0, 0.0, 0.0},
  {1.0, 1.0, 0.0}, {0.0, 1.0, 0.0},
  {0.0, 0.0, 1.0}, {1.0, 0.0, 1.0},
  {1.0, 1.0, 1.0}, {0.0, 1.0, 1.0}};

void polygon(int a, int b, int c , int d, int face)
{

  /* draw a polygon via a list of vertices */

  if(drawLines)
  {
    glColor3f(1.0, 1.0, 1.0);
    glBegin(GL_LINE_LOOP);
      glVertex3fv(vertices[a]);
      glVertex3fv(vertices[b]);
      glVertex3fv(vertices[c]);
      glVertex3fv(vertices[d]);
    glEnd();
  }
  else
  {
    glNormal3fv(fnormals[face]);
    glBegin(GL_POLYGON);
      glColor3fv(colors[a]);
      glTexCoord2f(0.0, 0.0);
      glVertex3fv(vertices[a]);
      glColor3fv(colors[b]);
      glTexCoord2f(0.0, 1.0);
      glVertex3fv(vertices[b]);
      glColor3fv(colors[c]);
      glTexCoord2f(1.0, 1.0);
      glVertex3fv(vertices[c]);
      glColor3fv(colors[d]);
      glTexCoord2f(1.0, 0.0);
```

```
        glVertex3fv(vertices[d]);
      glEnd();
    }
}

void colorcube(void)
{

/* map vertices to faces */

  polygon(1, 0, 3, 2, 0);
  polygon(3, 7, 6, 2, 1);
  polygon(7, 3, 0, 4, 2);
  polygon(2, 6, 5, 1, 3);
  polygon(4, 5, 6, 7, 4);
  polygon(5, 4, 0, 1, 5);
}

/*-------------------------*/
/* These functions implement a simple trackball-like motion
control */

float lastPos[3] = {0.0F, 0.0F, 0.0F};
int curx, cury;
int startX, startY;

void
trackball_ptov(int x, int y, int width, int height, float v[3])
{
  float d, a;

/* project x, y onto a hemisphere centered within width,
height */

  v[0] = (2.0F*x - width) / width;
  v[1] = (height - 2.0F*y) / height;
  d = (float) sqrt(v[0]*v[0] + v[1]*v[1]);
  v[2] = (float) cos((M_PI/2.0F) * ((d < 1.0F) ? d :
    1.0F));
  a = 1.0F / (float) sqrt(v[0]*v[0] + v[1]*v[1] +
    v[2]*v[2]);
  v[0] *= a;
  v[1] *= a;
  v[2] *= a;
}

void
mouseMotion(int x, int y)
{
  float curPos[3], dx, dy, dz;
```

```
      trackball_ptov(x, y, winWidth, winHeight, curPos);

    dx = curPos[0] - lastPos[0];
    dy = curPos[1] - lastPos[1];
    dz = curPos[2] - lastPos[2];

    if (dx || dy || dz)
    {
      angle = 90.0F * sqrt(dx*dx + dy*dy + dz*dz);

      axis[0] = lastPos[1]*curPos[2] -
        lastPos[2]*curPos[1];
      axis[1] = lastPos[2]*curPos[0] -
        lastPos[0]*curPos[2];
      axis[2] = lastPos[0]*curPos[1] -
        lastPos[1]*curPos[0];

      lastPos[0] = curPos[0];
      lastPos[1] = curPos[1];
      lastPos[2] = curPos[2];
    }

  glutPostRedisplay();
}

void
startMotion(long time, int button, int x, int y)
{
  if (!trackballEnabled) return;

  trackingMouse = true;
  redrawContinue = false;
  startX = x; startY = y;
  curx = x; cury = y;
  trackball_ptov(x, y, winWidth, winHeight, lastPos);
  trackballMove = true;
}

void
stopMotion(long time, int button, int x, int y)
{
  if (!trackballEnabled) return;

  trackingMouse = false;
  if (startX != x || startY != y)
    glutIdleFunc(spinCube);
  else
  {
    angle = 0.0F;
    glutIdleFunc(NULL);
    trackballMove = false;
```

```
  }
}
/*----------------------*/
void display(void)
{
  glClear(GL_COLOR_BUFFER_BIT | GL_DEPTH_BUFFER_BIT);

/* view transform */
  glLoadIdentity();
  glTranslatef(0.0, 0.0, viewxform_z);

  if (trackballMove)
  {
    glPushMatrix();
    glLoadIdentity();
    glRotatef(angle, axis[0], axis[1], axis[2]);
    glMultMatrixf((GLfloat *) trackballXform);
    glGetFloatv(GL_MODELVIEW_MATRIX, trackballXform);
    glPopMatrix();
  }
  glPushMatrix();
  glMultMatrixf((GLfloat*)lightXform);
  setLightPos();
  glPopMatrix();
  glPushMatrix();
  glMultMatrixf((GLfloat *) objectXform);
  colorcube();
  glPopMatrix();
  glutSwapBuffers();
}

/*----------------------*/
void mouseButton(int button, int state, int x, int y)
{
  switch (button)
  {
    case GLUT_LEFT_BUTTON:
      trackballXform = (GLfloat*)objectXform;
      break;
    case GLUT_MIDDLE_BUTTON:
      trackballXform = (GLfloat*)lightXform;
      break;
  }
  switch(state)
  {
    case GLUT_DOWN:
      startMotion(0, 1, x, y);
      break;
    case GLUT_UP:
```

```
            stopMotion(0, 1, x, y);
            break;
    }
}

void myReshape(int w, int h)
{
    glViewport(0, 0, w, h);
    winWidth = w;
    winHeight = h;
}

void spinCube()
{
    glutPostRedisplay();
}

void userEventAction(int key) {
    switch(key) {
    case '0':  /* wireframe/polygon */
        drawLines =! drawLines;
        break;
    case '1':
        smoothEnabled =! smoothEnabled;
        break;
    case '2':  /* lighting */
        lightingEnabled =! lightingEnabled;
        break;
    case '3':  /* texture */
        texEnabled =! texEnabled;
        break;
    case '4':  /* fog */
        fogEnabled =! fogEnabled;
        break;
    case '5':  /* HSR */
        depthEnabled =! depthEnabled;
        break;
    case '6':  /* line aa */
        lineAAEnabled =! lineAAEnabled;
        break;
    case '7':  /* perpective texture */
        fastTexture =! fastTexture;
        break;
    case 'b':
        currentMaterials = &brassMaterials;
        break;
    case 'c':
        currentMaterials = &colorCubeMaterials;
        break;
    case 'C':
```

```
      currentLighting = &colorCubeLighting;
      break;
    case 'i':
      idleSpin =! idleSpin;
      break;
    case 'm':  /* mipmapped texture */
      mipmapEnabled =! mipmapEnabled;
      break;
    case 'p':  /* perspective/ortho */
      perspectiveXform =! perspectiveXform;
      break;
    case 'r':
      currentMaterials = &redPlasticMaterials;
      break;
    case 'w':
      currentLighting = &whiteLighting;
      break;
    case 27:
      exit(0);
    default:
      break;
    }
    userSettings();
    glutPostRedisplay();
}

void keyboard(unsigned char key, int x, int y)
{
    userEventAction(key);
}

/*-----------------------*/

typedef struct menuEntryStruct {
    char *label;
    char key;
} menuEntryStruct;

static menuEntryStruct mainMenu[] = {
    "lines/polygons",       '0',
    "flat/smooth",          '1',
    "lighting",        '2',
    "texture",              '3',
    "fog",             '4',
    "HSR",             '5',
    "line smooth",          '6',
    "motion",               'i',
    "ortho/perspective",    'p',
    "quit",                 27,
};
```

```
int mainMenuEntries =
  sizeof(mainMenu)/sizeof(menuEntryStruct);

void selectMain(int choice)
{
  userEventAction(mainMenu[choice].key);
}

static menuEntryStruct materialsMenu[] = {
    "brass",              'b',
    "white",              'c',
    "red plastic",        'r',
};
int materialsMenuEntries =
  sizeof(materialsMenu)/sizeof(menuEntryStruct);

void selectMaterials(int choice)
{
  userEventAction(materialsMenu[choice].key);
}


static menuEntryStruct lightingMenu[] =
{
    "white",              'w',
    "color",              'C',
};
int lightingMenuEntries =
  sizeof(lightingMenu)/sizeof(menuEntryStruct);

void selectLighting(int choice)
{
  userEventAction(lightingMenu[choice].key);
}

void setMenuEntries(bool init)
{
  int i, sub1, sub2;

  if (init)
  {
    sub1 = glutCreateMenu(selectMaterials);
    for (i = 0; i < materialsMenuEntries; i++)
      glutAddMenuEntry(materialsMenu[i].label, i);
    sub2 = glutCreateMenu(selectLighting);
    for (i = 0; i < lightingMenuEntries; i++)
      glutAddMenuEntry(lightingMenu[i].label, i);
      glutCreateMenu(selectMain);
    for (i = 0; i < mainMenuEntries; i++)
      glutAddMenuEntry(mainMenu[i].label, i);
      glutAddSubMenu("materials", sub1);
```

```
            glutAddSubMenu("lighting", sub2);
            glutAttachMenu(GLUT_RIGHT_BUTTON);
    }
}

/*----------------------*/
void
main(int argc, char **argv)
{
    glutInit(&argc, argv);

    glutInitDisplayMode(GLUT_DOUBLE | GLUT_RGB | GLUT_DEPTH);
    glutInitWindowSize(500, 500);
    glutCreateWindow("colorcube");
    glutReshapeFunc(myReshape);
    glutDisplayFunc(display);
    glutIdleFunc(spinCube);
    glutMouseFunc(mouseButton);
    glutMotionFunc(mouseMotion);
    glutKeyboardFunc(keyboard);
    initSettings();
    userSettings();
    glutMainLoop();
}
```

10.2 Other OpenGL Features

Although we have not covered all OpenGL functions, we have covered most of them. Our major omissions are in covering some of the extra buffers available in OpenGL—which we will introduce in the next section—and in some of the more detailed functionality available through some of the extensions and GLU. Probably the most important are the use of the OpenGL tessellator and the use of NURBs. Both these facilities are supported through the GLU library.

With the tessellator, we can get around the restriction that OpenGL guarantees correctness only for convex polygons. The code in the tessellator will handle general polygons, even ones that are not simple. Unfortunately, there are many options and parameters that must be specified to tell the tessellator how we wish polygons to be handled. Not only are there options that determine how the polygon is to be displayed but also we have to give the tessellator explicit instructions on how to handle complex cases such as in Figure 10.4. Due to this complexity, we will not discuss tessellation further.

NURBS curves and surfaces provide far more flexibility than do the Bézier curves and surfaces. Consequently, they are very popular in the CAD and animation communities. However, like tessellators, the extra flexibility comes at the price of requiring the user to define many parameters and options. In addition, the use of NURBS requires more understanding of their mathematical underpinnings

Figure 10.4 Complex polygon that must be tesselated before rendering

than we can present here. The OpenGL Programming Guide covers both the GLU tessellator and the GLU NURBS functions.

10.3 Buffers

OpenGL supports a few other buffers, although not all of these buffers need be available on all implementations. These are the **accumulation** and **stencil buffers**. In addition, there may be extra color buffers (**auxiliary buffers**). All these buffers are initialized and cleared in the same manner as the color and depth buffers. Each has its own identifier (GL_ACCUM, GL_STENCIL, GL_AUX1, GL_AUX2) and can be opened and cleared as the other buffers, as in the code:

```
glutInitDisplayMode(GL_RGB | GL_DOUBLE | GL_STENCIL |
   GL_ACCUM);

glClear(GL_COLOR_BUFFER_BIT | GL_CLEAR_DEPTH_BUFFER_BIT
   | GL_ACCUM_BUFFER_BIT | GL_STENCIL_BUFFER_BIT);
```

The auxiliary buffers behave as do the front and back buffers but are never displayed. Hence, we can use them with the same functions we used for reading and writing in Chapter 7. Some potential uses of these buffers are for **multipass rendering**, where the same objects are rendering more than once. One typical application is for producing images for an immersive environment. Here we want to create images for the front, back, sides, and even the ceiling and floor of a physical room that has light projectors for each surface. We can write an OpenGL program that can produce these images using six virtual cameras and rendering into six color buffers.

10.3.1 The Accumulation Buffer

If you start working with images using OpenGL, at some point you will come up against the limited precision of color buffers. Consider the following compositing problem. Suppose that we have a set of images that we would like to merge into a single image. The obvious approach is to use the blending functions from Chapter 7. Suppose that we are working with a typical implementation that has eight bits for each of red, green, and blue in its physical color buffers. If we simply add corresponding RGB values for the images, we will probably exceed the 1.0 maximum for the color components. If we scale the color values to prevent exceeding this maximum, we reduce the precision of each color because although OpenGL uses floating point values in its calculations, the components are stored physically with the limited eight bits per component precision.

One solution to this type of problem is to create a buffer, the accumulation buffer, that has more bits per color component (usually 16 bits per component). We can add the contents of a color buffer into the accumulation buffer using a scale factor. Once we have accumulated all the images, we can read out a scaled version of the accumulation buffer back into a color buffer, thus maintaining the available color resolution and not overflowing a color buffer. We need only one function glAccum() to use the accumulation buffer, if one is available.

---

void glAccum(GLenum operation, GLfloat value)

defines the **operation** performed with the accumulation buffer (**GL_ACCUM, GL_LOAD, GL_RETURN, GL_ADD,** or **GL_MULT**) and the associated constant (**value**).

The operation GL_ADD allows us to add images in with the specified constant multiplier. The operation GL_RETURN returns the scaled contents of the accumulation buffer to the present drawing buffer.

The accumulation buffer provides some new and interesting capabilities for multipass rendering. For example, suppose that we render the same scene multiple times, each with the camera moved (or **jittered**) slightly, and accumulate these images in the accumulation buffer. Each of the images will have slightly different aliasing artifacts that will be averaged out in the accumulation buffer. Thus, we have performed antialiasing on the whole scene, rather than on a line-by-line or polygon-by-polygon basis.

10.3.2 The Stencil Buffer

Stencils are masks that we can use to determine where to draw. A typical use of the stencil buffer is to create windows of arbitrary shape within the rectangular drawing area of the viewport. For example, we can create a round porthole by forming a stencil buffer starting with all 1's and by putting 0's in a circular area. Then, as we draw in the color buffer, each pixel we form by rasterization is tested against the stencil buffer to see if it should be drawn in the color buffer. We can create more complex behaviors using the stencil buffer because we can modify its contents depending on the value of the pixel generated by the rasterizer.

10.3.3 Fragment Tests

Although we have referred to the pixels that are produced by the rasterizer, in OpenGL the rasterizer produces **fragments**, which contain all the information needed to update pixels in the frame buffer pixel. For example, if only a part of a pixel is occupied by a particular polygon, the rasterizer can produce a fragment whose color reflects the amount of the pixel that is covered by the polygon.

Fragments that are produced by the rasterizer go through a sequence of tests—scissor, alpha, stencil, depth—and operations—blending, dithering, logical—on their way to the color buffer. We have seen most of these tests and operations in previous chapters. For example, the depth test involves comparing the depth of the fragment with a depth in the depth buffer. Blending and logical operations determine how fragment's color is combined with the color value is already in the color buffer at the fragment's location.

Usually these tests and operations are performed routinely as part of the standard rendering process. However, we can also program these tests directly to accept or reject pixels. For example, with the **scissor test**, we can specify a rectangular area in which all fragments are accepted and all fragments outside of it are rejected. Such operations and tests are of particular importance in interactive applications.

10.4 Writing Portable, Efficient, Robust Code

We would all like to write programs that can be ported to other systems and will run without modification, regardless of the differences in hardware. We would also like our programs to run efficiently on all systems. And, of course, we would like them to be readable and easy to modify. It would be nice if we could say that every OpenGL program possessed all these features.

Although OpenGL programs tend to be clear and fairly portable, there can be problems. One is that once we start using advanced features, such as the accumulation and stencil buffers, we often lose portability, as these features are not supported on all implementations. Although we could check in our programs for the existence of the features, it is not clear what a program should do—other than report the missing features and exit—if the desired features are not present.

Differences in the properties of the display are easier to handle as we can use the inquiry functions, such as `glIntegerv()`, to obtain the properties of a particular display and adjust within the application.

Efficiency is a more difficult issue. First, with few exceptions, the underlying algorithms are hidden from the user. We do not know—nor do we usually need to know—how an OpenGL implementation fills polygons or interpolates textures. Second, different implementations have been optimized using different criteria. Hence, even if we buy a board with excellent triangle-rendering speeds, the board might not have the same relative performance for texture mapping. This situation is especially noticeable with commodity graphics cards, most of which have been optimized for the operations required in games. Thus, a particular card may not be quite as optimal for another application such as scientific visualization or CAD.

Finally, as the capabilities of graphics hardware continue to improve at a rapid pace, the limiting factor in many applications is not the time required for graphics operations but rather the time taken to move data. Fortunately, OpenGL provides sufficient functionality and is close enough to the hardware that it should be an important graphics API for years to come.

Looking to the Future

CHAPTER

11

OpenGL version 1.0 was released in 1992. It was designed to be an API for real-time graphics. OpenGL was designed to be stable so that code that was developed with it would not have to be rewritten for different hardware or changed because the core standard changed. When we look at the incredible changes in the cost and capabilities of graphics hardware, it is remarkable how well OpenGL has held up over the last 12 years. Nevertheless, OpenGL has and will continue to evolve. In this final chapter, we discuss this evolution and where OpenGL is heading.

11.1 Versions and Extensions

OpenGL has two mechanisms for change. The first is through new versions that are approved by the OpenGL Architectural Review Board (ARB). The latest version is OpenGL 1.5. All new versions are backward compatible so that code that was developed on an earlier version should run on any later version. The second mechanism is extensions. Unlike version changes that come as a whole and apply to all configurations, extensions may apply to only some systems, such as those of a select group of manufacturers, and may be supported on an extension-by-extension basis.

11.1.1 OpenGL Version 1.1

The first upgrade to OpenGL appeared in 1995. In many ways it was the most significant upgrade in that it was able to add many features that were lacking in version 1.0 but did not become apparent until users had some experience with the initial release. Version 1.1 is still the most widely used version and is the one that is default with Windows systems.

Perhaps the most significant addition provided by Version 1.1 was vertex arrays. As we saw in Chapter 4, vertex arrays can dramatically reduce the number of function calls to display geometric objects, especially with lighting and texture. They also provide a concise mechanism for representing meshes where vertices and edges are shared by more than one polygon.

The second major addition provided by Version 1.1 was better mechanisms for handling texture. About the time that OpenGL appeared, advances in graphics hardware made texture mapping a practical way to represent effects that were not easily modeled with shaded polygons. Applications needed fast access to more than a single texture. Version 1.1 provided texture objects, texture proxies, and texture copying from the frame buffer.

Version 1.1 also added logical operations for RGBA colors, which allowed techniques such as the rubberbanding through the logical drawing modes that we introduced in Chapter 7 and polygon offset in Chapter 2.

11.1.2 OpenGL Version 1.2

Version 1.2 was approved by the ARB in 1998. At that time, applications such as medical imaging were finding that volume visualization techniques using three-dimensional textures could provide real-time viewing of large data sets. OpenGL Version 1.2 provided the necessary support in the API by extending OpenGL texture mapping functionality to incorporate three-dimensional texturing.

The other major advance was the addition of the imaging subset that we introduced in Chapter 7. From the perspective of how the standard had been developed, the imaging subset was treated differently in that although it was part of OpenGL, the standard did not require it to be present in every implementation.

Historically, image processing and computer graphics were distinct areas. The latter was concerned with geometry and the former with manipulating pixels. As hardware evolved, the imaging subset arose because hardware had evolved to the point that graphics and imaging could be performed on the same hardware. OpenGL had anticipated some of this by the inclusion of a parallel pixel pipeline. However, because this pipeline was primarily used for texture mapping, many of the image-processing operations such as table lookups, histograms, and convolution could not take advantage of capabilities in the hardware. Although it was possible to do most standard image-processing operations by reading images back into processor memory and carrying out operations in software, the overhead was prohibitive and application programmers would prefer to use available hardware.

11.1.3 OpenGL Version 1.3

Version 1.3 was released in 2001. Most of the additions were aimed at providing better texture-handling capabilities. These additions include support for compressed textures, multiple-texture units, and cube map textures (used in environment maps).

Version 1.3 also included transpose matrix functions. This addition allows application programs to send matrices stored row by row as in C to be sent to

OpenGL rather than by the outdated Fortran-based column order that is the standard OpenGL method.

11.1.4 OpenGL Version 1.4

Version 1.4 appeared only one year later in 2002. Although it added some functionality to the core that had formerly been in extensions, such as automatic mipmap generation, its major contribution was an ARB extension for vertex programs. We shall discuss extensions in Section 11.2. Philosophically, this version demonstrated a major change shift in that it recognized that the fixed function pipeline upon which OpenGL is based was becoming dated. Hence, adding the vertex program extension paved the way for future changes to OpenGL that would allow the API to keep up with advances in hardware.

11.1.5 OpenGL Version 1.5

Version 1.5, released in 2003, continued the trend started with Version 1.4. There are only a few minor changes to the core, but the OpenGL shading language (see Section 11.5) was added as a major extension with the expectation that it would be the basis for a major future change to the standard.

11.2 OpenGL Extensions

Changes to OpenGL tend to reflect the consensus of the graphics community as to what is core to a graphics implementation. This consensus does not reflect what is available at the high end, nor does it allow for features that might be particular to a small group of manufacturers. To get around this difficulty, OpenGL provides an extension mechanism that allows certain features to be accessible via OpenGL, even though these features may not be available on all implementations.

Individual manufacturers can propose and implement extensions. If these are accepted, the names of the extensions then contain a substring identifying the source. Other extensions are proposed by groups of manufacturers, are approved by the ARB, and have ARB extensions. For example ARB_vertex_program and ARB_fragment_program are both ARB extensions.

As hardware evolves, high-end features that were only available as extensions become part of later versions of OpenGL. Examples include the imaging subset and vertex programs.

11.3 Going Beyond Real-Time Graphics

OpenGL is focused on real-time graphics. Even though OpenGL does not specify many aspects of the underlying architecture, in reality it has always been supported by a pipeline architecture. Although this architecture still is dominant in the real-time market, both in the commodity market and for high-end scientific work, there are needs that are not readily served by OpenGL. In this section, we examine some of the issues with respect to more sophisticated rendering than is possible with the standard pipeline, and in the next we will examine recent advances in programmable pipelines.

One problem with real-time systems is that we are limited as to the complexity of the rendering. Until recently the most complex shading that was implemented in hardware was based on the modified Phong model. The simplicity of this model was unacceptable for applications that required more physically realistic effects or more complex effects that are used, for example, in the animation industry. Consequently, many applications used off-line rendering, often involving large numbers of general-purpose processors. Although there are multiple alternatives to the pipeline model, including ray tracing, radiosity, and more ad hoc approaches that can combine multiple rendering styles, many of the software interfaces to such systems are based on Pixar's RenderMan interface.

Within RenderMan is a shading language that allows the application programmer to define shaders—the RenderMan Shading Language. We will examine this approach in more detail in the next section.

We have noted that OpenGL is not object oriented. For the most part, objects are defined in an application program, then passed through the pipeline. The only memory of these objects is their images in the frame buffer. In order to move the objects, such as in an animation, we have to regenerate them in the application program. The major exception to this mode, known as immediate-mode graphics, is through display lists. However, display lists are limited in their functionality. For example, we cannot edit OpenGL display lists.

A more general approach with an object-oriented flavor is through scene graphs. An image or scene can be thought of in terms of all the elements that we need to specify it: the geometric objects in the scene, the lights, one or more cameras, and attributes such as the material properties of the objects. In Chapter 5, we saw how we could describe a model with interrelated parts with a tree and we could code that tree in OpenGL in a mechanical manner. Suppose that we expand those concepts and consider the tree in Figure 11.1 that includes nodes that represent the light source, material properties, geometric objects, and camera. If we traverse this tree in the same order as we did in Chapter 5, then we translate it to OpenGL and produce an image something like that in Figure 11.2.

Figure 11.1 shows the same figure that we presented in Chapter 5. However, all the information about the image is in the tree of Figure 11.1. This tree is known as a **scene graph**. This graph is decidedly object oriented and provides a high-level method for describing both whole scenes and objects within a scene. Note that we could easily add additional nodes for additional geometric objects, for additional material properties, to add additional light sources, and even to add additional cameras.

We might conclude that OpenGL has little if anything to do with the scene description and is merely one way of rendering a scene graph. However, if we look at how scene graphs have evolved, we come to a somewhat different conclusion.

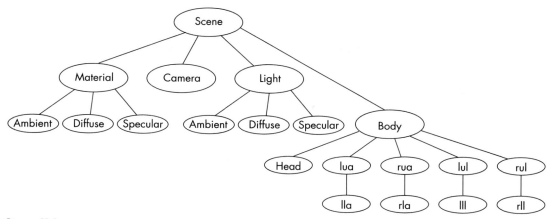

Figure 11.1 Simple scene graph

Figure 11.2 Image from scene
graph in Figure 11.1

Suppose that we want to develop a scene graph language. One of the first problems we would confront is what kinds of geometric objects we would want as our building blocks. This question is essentially the same as was confronted by the developers of APIs such as OpenGL. The answer today should be a set of atomic primitives that can take advantage of the existing hardware and APIs. This answer is essentially the one that all developers of existing scene graph APIs—Open Inventor, Java 3D, VRML, Open Scene Graph—agreed upon. Consequently, these standard scene graph APIs almost always rely on OpenGL for rendering.

Because scene graphs are at a higher level than OpenGL, an application programmer who wants to use scene graphs can often avoid writing a program using the scene graph API by specifying the scene through a text file that provides an alternate method of describing the tree. This method of describing graphs allows scene graphs to bring in information from disparate settings and allows scene graphs to be used in a distributed Web-based environment.

11.4 Programmable Pipelines

As we have seen, virtually all commodity graphics cards are based on a geometric pipeline. For many years, this pipeline was somewhat fixed and comprised stages for transformations, clipping, projection, and shading. Performance improvements were measured in terms of how many shaded triangles could be rendered per second. When the support for texture mapping became common, performance was then measured in terms of texture-mapped shaded triangles per second. Recently, we have seen a major advance in the capabilities of commodity graphics cards that is revolutionizing our concepts of what is possible with real-time graphics. Graphics processors have become programmable; that is, the functionality of some of the major units in the pipeline can be altered by user programs. There are two blocks that presently can be programmed. The first is the block that processes vertices. In terms of the fixed-function pipeline, this block was responsible for computing vertex colors using either specified colors or by computing colors using the modified Phong model. A program that can be loaded into the programmable version of this block is called a **vertex shader**. The second block that can be altered is the one that processes fragments after rasterization. Fragments (see Section 10.3.3) are produced by the rasterization process and contain the information to update pixel colors. Fragment processing must deal with both texture and opacity. Programs that can alter the processing of fragments are called **fragment shaders**. The programmable pipeline has a structure illustrated in Figure 11.3.

11.4.1 Vertex Shaders

The vertex processor can be looked at as a stream processor. It takes in a stream of vertices and outputs another stream of vertices. Each vertex has not only a position but also other properties such as a normal, texture coordinates, and one or

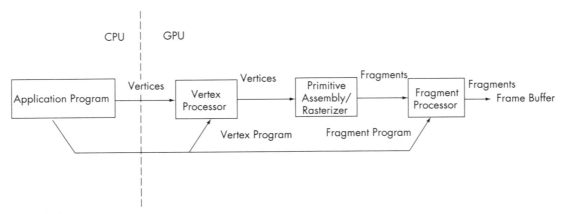

Figure 11.3 Geometric pipeline with programmable shaders

more colors. In the fixed-function standard pipeline, these values are set initially by the application program but are modified by the pipeline. For example, vertex positions are changed by the model-view matrix while vertex colors are computed by the modified Phong model.

Now suppose that we can program the computations in the processor. We could use a lighting model other than the Phong model to compute colors for each vertex. Such models could be physically more realistic but would need only the same information that is used by the Phong model. We could also create special effects as are used in animations. For example, we might have a geometric entity change its colors as the program is executed. Because these vertex programs are executed within the graphics processor, once the shader has been loaded into the processor, the vertex processing runs in parallel with the OpenGL program running in processor memory. Consequently, even though some of these effects could be done in the application program, the vertex program avoids costly state changes in OpenGL, offloads vertex processing from the CPU, and avoids bottlenecks of transferring data between processor memory and graphics memory.

11.4.2 Fragment Shaders

The fragment processor comes into play after the vertices have been assembled into geometric primitives—line segments, polygons, quads—and rasterized. Thus, each primitive produces a set of fragments that define its interior. Fragment processing assigns colors to these fragments. In the fixed-function pipeline, the fragment colors are determined by a combination of interpolating vertex colors and texture values.

The programmable fragment processor allows the application programmer to write a fragment shader that alters these colors. The fragment processor works on a stream of fragments and in a manner similar to the vertex processor has access to various data that are attributes of each fragment. In particular, the fragment shader can access one or more texture coordinates, light properties, normals, and camera properties. Thus, shading can be computed on a per-fragment basis rather than on a per-vertex basis as with the fixed function pipeline or vertex shaders. Techniques such as bump mapping that perturb the normal across an object can now be done in real time, something that was not possible previously.

11.5 Shading Languages

From a programming perspective, the vertex and fragment processors are special-purpose computers that have their own low-level instruction sets with which we can write shaders. In many ways, writing low-level shaders has much in common with writing assembly language code. The application programmer must know the architecture and write many detailed instructions. In a manner similar to the development of standard high-level programming languages, we prefer to have a higher-level interface that shields us from many of the details of the hardware and provides higher-level constructs such as control structures with which we can write short, powerful programs. Recently, there have been multiple efforts to develop high-level interfaces to programmable GPUs. Most of these efforts owe much to Pixar's RenderMan Interface,[1] which was developed in the 1980s.

11.5.1 RenderMan Shading Language

The animation industry requires high-resolution images as final output. Both the required resolution and the special effects in these images make it impossible today to produce these images with real-time renderers. Rather than a single pipeline that handles the entire computer-generated imaging (CGI) process, we can separate it into two phases: modeling and rendering. Most of the effort in modeling deals with building geometric objects and animating them. High-resolution output is not required at this phase, nor is high-quality rendering. This part of the process can be carried out on standard workstations with commodity graphics cards.

The second phase of the process, rendering, is usually done off-line and need not be done in real time. In fact, a single frame that contains many objects and complex rendering effects can require minutes or even hours to render. This part of the process is usually done on a cluster of general-purpose processors.

The hardware and software for the modeling and rendering phases are different. The only tie that need exist between them is an interface that could be in the form of a file that is the output of the modeler and the input to the renderer. Such a file will contain the description of the objects and their motions, attributes such as surface properties, light source descriptions, and specifications for effects and data such as textures that might exist only on the renderer. Pixar specified such a file format that has become standard and also the basis for other interfaces.

Of particular interest to us is the RenderMan Shading Language that gives application programmers the flexibility to design sophisticated shaders. We can understand the elements of this language by starting with the standard Phong shader. It has three components—diffuse, specular, and ambient—each of which can be computed independently using material properties, light source attributes, the position of the vertex, and the four vectors that we discussed in Chapter 6. We can write algebraic expressions for the Phong shader that use the normal arithmetic operations and standard vector operations such as the dot product. As most programmers know, a standard algebraic expression can be written as a tree data structure. Once we realize that the Phong shader can be written as a tree data structure, it is fairly simple to extend this concept to other shaders by adding

---

1. See Upstill, S., *The RenderMan Companion: A Programmer's Guide to Realistic Computer Graphics*, Addison-Wesley, 1989.

nodes to the tree and altering the contents of its nodes. This concept of a **shading tree** is fundamental to much recent work on shading languages.

In addition to a shading tree, RenderMan contains an additional concept crucial to shading languages: environmental variables. The programmer can assume that certain variables required for the shading calculation, such as normals, texture coordinates, and light source information, are in the environment and are available to the shader. Although when RenderMan was developed, its capabilities could only be used with off-line rendering, programmable pipelines can process many expressions in languages similar to the RenderMan Shading Language in real time. Hence, as OpenGL has evolved, many of the ideas in recent extensions are inspired by RenderMan.

11.5.2 The OpenGL Shading Language

The OpenGL Shading Language was adopted as an ARB extension in 2003. The main goal of the language is to provide a high-level interface to programmable pipelines and thus avoid the difficulties with assembly-like code. The language is based on C and can be used to produce both vertex and fragment shaders. Imbedded in the specification are descriptions of what a vertex shader and a fragment shader can do. In addition the programs have access to the OpenGL state so that OpenGL state information are available to the programmer.

The OpenGL Shading Language contains the standard C data types and adds others that are useful for graphics applications including two-, three-, and four-dimensional matrices and vectors. Consequently, we can write expressions such as

```
vec3 u, v, w;
mat3 a, b, c;
w = u * v; /* dot product */
c = a * b; /* matrix matrix product */
w = a*u;   /* matrix vector product */
```

The vertex and fragment shaders each have built-in variables. For example, a vertex shader writes the variable

```
vec4 gl_Position;
```

as its output while the shader can use standard OpenGL attributes such as

```
attribute vec4 gl_Color;
attribute vec3 gl_Normal;
attribute vec4 gl_Vertex;
```

in the calculation. In addition, most of the OpenGL state is also available. For example, the model-view matrix is available as

```
uniform mat4 gl_ModelViewMatrix;
```

11.5.3 Cg

Programmable pipelines are a major advance to graphics hardware and as such are of interest to more than the OpenGL community. In particular, there is a large community of developers in the Windows world who work with Direct3D rather than OpenGL. Rather than have separate APIs for accessing programmable hardware for OpenGL and Direct3D, NVIDIA and Microsoft developed the Cg (C for graphics) language.[2] Cg is virtually identical to Microsoft's High Level Shading Language (HLSL). Although Cg lacks the direct tie to OpenGL state variables, in reality Cg and the OpenGL Shading Language are very similar and provide access to the same facilities to the application programmer.

Both the OpenGL Shading Language and Cg are evolving, as is the hardware. Consequently, only a few high-end commodity cards can implement the shaders that can be written by application programmers. Unlike most other OpenGL functionality, where we can be sure that an application program will run on virtually all hardware, vertex and fragment shaders are extensions and thus may run on only certain hardware. An additional problem is that even if the implementation supports programmable shaders, the complexity of a shader will affect whether it will compile and run. Many of these difficulties are transitory, and we should expect to see advances in the future that will make programmable pipelines both more powerful and more easily accessible.

---

2. See Fernando, R., and M. J. Kilgard, *The Cg Tutorial*, Addison-Wesley, 2003.

Function Index

Subject Index